GREEN ALL OVER

Peter Aves

Capital Transport

GREEN ALL OVER

Country Buses 1955–1969

Peter Aves

Capital Transport

Previous page RF 550 comes up the narrow lane approaching Abinger village on a journey to Holmbury St Mary, and perfectly illustrates the nature of the more rural Surrey Hills routes. The 412 blind display was unique in the Country area, the final destination at Sutton being shown as a qualifying point to Holmbury St Mary since London Transport did not wish to confuse intending passengers that the bus was heading for the 'other' Sutton. The driver is Percy Archer – known to everyone as 'Curly' – one of the three drivers who lived in Holmbury St Mary, and one of Dorking's longest serving drivers. He retired at the end of 1971 at the age of 70 having begun his career with East Surrey in the 1920s. (London Transport Museum)

Opposite In 1956 and 1957, the service on the 410 and 411 was augmented on Saturday afternoon with two extra journeys per hour between Reigate and Bletchingley. They ran to provide additional capacity for shopping in Reigate and Redhill and are discussed in chapter two. Two extra buses were rostered for these, and because they interworked between journeys to Bromley, they were part of the 410 schedule and operated with RLHs although there was no need for lowbridge buses on these journeys. RLH 39 has arrived at Bletchingley and waits opposite the White Hart hotel before performing a U-turn across the A25 to return to Reigate. It was one of eight new RLHs from the second batch which went to Godstone in October 1952 and spent its entire working life there before being replaced with RTs in November 1964, after which it was soon sold and exported to America. (Norman Rayfield, 2RT2 Group)

First published 2018

Published by Capital Transport Publishing Ltd
www.capitaltransport.com

Printed in the EU

Contents

Introduction and Acknowledgements

This book covers the period which began in the early 1950s when London Transport's great fleet replacement programme was coming to an end, and passenger numbers had reached their peak. It finishes at the end of 1969 by which time the entire Country area was losing heavily.

The mid-1950s were perhaps the Country area's 'Golden Era'. Even the smallest villages had a good service into the nearest town. People could go there in the evenings to the cinema or bingo, there were several journeys for Saturday shopping, and relatives could be visited on Sundays with timetables which ran until late evening for the return. Whempstead in Hertfordshire was probably one of the smallest hamlets served with a population of fewer than 100 in the early 1950s. Yet in 1955, the 384 route ran eight journeys from there into Hertford and seven to Stevenage during the week with the last journey leaving Hertford as late as 10.00pm on Saturdays. Even on Sundays there were four journeys until 8.00pm in the evening. Larger villages such as Ide Hill had an hourly service into Sevenoaks every day including Sundays, and where routes like the 425 between Dorking and Guildford benefited from weekend leisure passengers as well as a sizeable town at each end, then the villages along the way had a frequent service all day well into the evening seven days a week. Mechanisation in farming, and the aspirations of a younger generation however served to reduce rural populations, the result of which was that passenger numbers on rural routes began to fall away. It was however the exponential increase in the ownership of cars and televisions that would have the most damaging effect on passenger numbers.

RF 663 has just turned round the island in the centre of Ide Hill village on its way to Scollops Road, a remote road junction at the bottom of Ide Hill itself and about a mile from the village. Journeys from Sevenoaks to Scollops Road ran directly, but the return trips ran back through the village to Sundridge hospital before returning to Sevenoaks – never a convenient arrangement for the few passengers who used them. Only three or four journeys a day ran beyond Scollops Road to Four Elms, and the route is covered in some detail in chapter five at the time when it was finally abandoned not long after this picture was taken. There is just a solitary passenger for the last leg down the hill to Scollops Road.

By the time of my first Green Rover in 1962, the Country area's best years had passed, but there were plenty of passengers. On that first Green Rover I went from West Croydon to Westerham and from there on a 485 to Edenbridge. This was my first ride on a GS, which that June day was GS 1, and I could not have known then that almost 40 years later I would drive that same bus into Oxted on one of our running days. We went on into East Grinstead, and by the time the 434 arrived there, the bus had a standing load. From there we caught a 424 to Reigate and a 414 back to Croydon. A few weeks later I repeated part of this and on GS 3 from Westerham to Edenbridge, I did not know that a few weeks later, all the GSs from Chelsham would be replaced with RFs. We went on to East Grinstead, Reigate and Dorking where we rode on GS 39 on a 433 up to Coldharbour. I mentioned in 'Green No More' the lasting impression which the 433 made on me, and I count myself fortunate that I have had the opportunity to have driven GSs over the route several times. Readers may feel that there are perhaps too many references to GSs and their routes in the book, but I make no apology for the fact that – like many other people – they were undoubtedly a particular favourite of mine, and I was fortunate to travel on many of them while they were still in normal service. They were an important if small part of the rural route network which suffered most of the cuts once the peak passenger numbers had passed. Indeed, many of them had a short life with London Transport for no other reason than the routes on which they ran which were either abandoned completely or drastically cut back.

If it were not for a bridge having a weight restriction on the 327, 2RTs would not have been deployed in the Country Bus area on normal service. They weighed 5cwt (a quarter of a ton) less than the standard post war RT and were used to replace some of the last STLs as a temporary measure until the bridge was strengthened. RT 128 was one of the seven RT2s repainted for use at Hertford. They were all replaced at the end of August 1957 when the bridge was strengthened, then stored at Potters Bar garage, later seeing use as trainers in the Central area. (Norman Rayfield, 2RT2 Group)

Over the rest of the 1960s I travelled over almost every route, but the main interest was the very rural nature of the routes and villages they served so close to London. I travelled on GSs from Hertford to Chapmore End and Knebworth, along the single track lane to Tewin and Welwyn, and on a Thursday journey from Bishops Stortford to Standon through the tiny hamlet of Wellpond Green. In September 1965, I travelled on GS 13 on an afternoon Tuesday market day 386 journey from Hitchin, The lane between Ardeley and Cottered is the narrowest road anywhere in the Country area, with low banks on either side between fields and there the bus met a man on a bike coming the other way. The road was so narrow that the man had to get off his bike and clamber up the bank to allow the bus to pass! It is also worth recalling that we had left Hitchin with standing passengers, all with bags and shopping and even after Ardeley still had about 10 passengers on board for Cottered and Buntingford. Other GS trips included the 309 and 336A routes at Rickmansworth, and to Ewhurst on the 448 a few weeks before Tillingbourne took over the whole route. RFs took me to Four Elms; Holmbury St Mary; Weston; the Chesham routes; on the 352 from Berkhamsted to Dunstable; on one of the few 317A journeys through Nettleden; Hertford to Bishop's Stortford; Dorking to Guildford; Luton to Hitchin; St Albans to Whitwell, and Hertford to Stevenage many of which traversed miles of narrow winding lanes. In the end I rode on almost every RF operated route. RLHs took me from Westerham to Reigate and Guildford to Staines. The overriding memory is the good loads on so many journeys. One Saturday afternoon in 1967, I left Dorking around 4.00pm on a 414 towards Reigate, the conductor having directed the last few passengers boarding at the White Horse upstairs as the lower deck was full. But within a few short years passenger loads like that would become a passing memory

In 'Green No More' I made mention of how much I have learned from the many like-minded people l have been fortunate to meet. There are too many to name, but above all, my colleagues at Country Bus Rallies, Alan Charman, John Huxford and Colin Rivers have been the source of memories which have helped to make these books more than a simple record of London Transport's Country Buses. I am particularly grateful to Alan Charman who supplied the Dartford tunnel memorabilia, LT's schedule of one man conversions and other items from his own collection.

Thanks also to Sid Huxford, John's father, who was a Leatherhead driver for many years, and whose recollections of driving the 408 and 470 have added to the story. Les Bland and Norman Osborn, both former conductors, passed on their reminiscences which have been included. Laurie Akehurst has once again been particularly helpful in checking the text, correcting some errors and adding some insights which add to the narrative. He also supplied copies of Country area allocation books which were missing from my collection,

In sourcing the photographs for this volume, I particularly wanted to find as many as possible which had not previously been published. Hugh Taylor kindly allowed the use of a number of the late Peter Mitchell's collection, and Laurie Akehurst generously made many of his available. My thanks go to Jim Whiting at Capital Transport for his assistance in arranging access to these and for many from his own collection.

In researching this volume, I was fortunate in being allowed access to the TfL archives which yielded much valuable information and I must thank Stephanie Rousseau at TfL for her help and patience in locating the information I requested.

The 301 and 302 were the first routes to receive new RTs in July and August 1948. Twenty-three went to Hemel Hempstead and seven to Tring – all with RT3 roofbox bodies – a maximum of 24 being required for the many additional shopping and works journeys described in chapter two. Hemel Hempstead's RT 619 stands in Buckingham Street terminus in Aylesbury waiting to set off for Watford Junction alongside an Eastern National lowbridge Bristol K5G on the trunk route to Luton which shared the same road as the 301 as far as Tring. The 1933 Act placed restrictions on local journeys between Aston Clinton and Aylesbury on the 301 and Green Rovers were never valid over this section. The K type has the white steering wheel to remind the driver that the bus is 8 feet wide, and the difference in height between the RT and the K is very apparent. (Norman Rayfield, 2RT2 Group)

I first began the idea of these books more than 10 years ago and have learnt a great deal more about the Country area whilst writing them. It was Laurie Akehurst who first suggested I contact Jim Whiting, and the encouragement of both of them has been a significant factor is completing what has been a most enjoyable project. The original idea was for a single volume, but this would have been simply too large for one book. The book was therefore split into two, the obvious break between them being January 1970 when London Country took over. This split allowed space to add more detail and photographs to both books.

Last of all, as I did in 'Green No More' I must again mention my wife Christine with grateful thanks for her endless patience in having a lifelong bus enthusiast for a husband.

Although I missed the 'Golden Age' by a few years, I was still able to cover the Country area before the worst of the decline took effect. But the 1960s were the end of an era which would never return. As I write this, it is now 56 years ago since I caught that 403 from Croydon to Westerham and began what would be more than 20 years of exploring London Transport's Country Bus routes. I am very glad I had the opportunity when I did.

Peter Aves
September 2018

1   Introduction

New RTs replaced STLs on the 405 and 414 in March and April 1950. It would be a further three years before the last pre-war STLs were withdrawn from Country area all day service, although a few remained until 1954 rostered for peak services and duplicates until the last RTs had been delivered. This fine period photograph shows STL 2263 on a 405 to Crawley (LT Museum)

At the end of the Second World War, the majority of London Transport's fleet was beyond its normal service life with significant numbers of vehicles being in poor condition. In 1945, London Transport identified around 2,800 double deckers which would be at least 15 years old by 1950, plus a further 1,870 which would be 12 years old. With 1,100 trams also needing replacement, around 5,700 new double deckers were required in less than five years. The single deck bus fleet was in need of equally urgent replacement and it included 450 buses which would all have been replaced by 1945 had it not been for the war years. Only the Green Line fleet was slightly less pressing, although even this would require replacement from about 1950 or 1951. If this was not a sufficiently daunting challenge, passenger numbers increased almost exponentially as men and women were demobbed and returned to their pre-war occupations, and by 1948 passenger levels had risen by some 40% above immediate pre-war levels.

By the time the fleet renewal had been completed in 1954, around 8,000 new buses had been built and delivered in less than eight years in a feat of engineering and production which would never be repeated. There had been many difficulties to overcome and at times older buses that were beyond economic repair were having to be scrapped at a faster rate than new buses were being delivered.

London Transport's forecasts for the total number of new buses required for the Country Bus area were based principally on the anticipated population growth around the Home Counties, the major factor of which was the New Towns Act of 1946. Six existing small towns or villages within the Country area were designated under the Act as 'New Towns' at Crawley, Harlow, Hemel Hempstead, Stevenage, Hatfield and Welwyn Garden City. Land at Chessington had been considered for development, but Crawley was chosen instead since it offered much greater scope for future expansion. The choice of Crawley was also influenced by proposals to expand what was then a small airfield at Gatwick into a second airport for London. Concurrent with their development, the London County Council (LCC) purchased large areas of land in the outer London suburbs and Home Counties for what became known as 'LCC Overspill Estates'. In the Country area the largest were at Aveley in Essex, one part of which became Belhus Estate, at Sheerwater and Merstham in Surrey, Oxhey near Watford, and at Britwell in Berkshire adjacent to Slough. Between them these were forecast to grow to a total population of approaching 50,000 by the early 1960s. Two further Overspill Estates were at Debden and Harold Hill just inside the Central area plus some of the land at Chessington which became the Copt Gilders estate. There was also Borehamwood on the boundary between Central and Country areas. In addition to the Overspill Estates, almost every town in the Country area embarked on council house building programmes encouraged by a Government that recognised the pressing need to replace war damaged and sub-standard housing, much of which was little better than slums.

The fleet of new Green Line RFs were all in service by the time the 725 was introduced in July 1953, although insufficient spare RFs were available to operate the route. By this time, the number of former 10T10 coaches still in service was reducing rapidly, almost all of them having been relegated to bus routes as an interim measure before the RF buses were delivered. Their use on the 725 however was a necessity for a short period and this fine shot of T 647 on the forecourt of Staines garage would have been taken towards the end of its life. (LT Museum)

The acute shortage of buses during the late 1940s was exacerbated by the need for additional buses to cover new route developments. Between 1946 and 1954, around 30 Country Bus routes which could be described as 'town services' were extended or diverted as new housing areas were built. Completely new routes in Stevenage, Harlow and Crawley were started together with new routes serving the growing LCC Estates. A further 15 completely new, largely rural routes were begun, seven more extended to previously unserved places, and six specifically for hospital visitors. Whilst most of the rural routes had been introduced to satisfy a rapidly increasing demand at the time, many would prove to be at best marginal, and some completely unsustainable as increased private car ownership took their passengers. Several of these minor routes would be withdrawn in the aftermath of the 1958 strike, a few more in the mid-1960s, and the skeleton time-tables on those routes which remained when London Country took over were almost all abandoned in the early 1970s.

Green Line routes were also adjusted to take advantage of new business. Part of the 723 was diverted to run through Belhus estate and the 716 similarly diverted near Woking to serve Sheerwater estate. A completely new route started in July 1953 between Gravesend, Dartford and Windsor. Numbered 725 it ran through the outer suburbs to the south of London – linking important centres at Bromley, Croydon and Kingston – and was an immediate success.

London Transport was able to start new routes and extend others without the formality of applications through the Traffic Courts which operators everywhere else were required to do. The 1933 Transport Act set up the London Passenger Transport Area (LPTA) within which London Transport was given the authority to provide and co-ordinate services. London Transport was permitted to operate anywhere within the LPTA, and up to ten miles outside the boundary provided agreement could be reached with other operators already running services along the same roads. There were also specific roads outside the LPTA where London Transport could operate without agreement from other operators. There were

RT 979 was one of 19 new RTs allocated to Hertford in September and October 1948, initially for route 310/310A. Its original RT3 body was replaced on overhaul in 1956, and a few years later, in Green Line livery, it was sent back to Hertford in 1962. A Ford Anglia overtakes it as it works a 327 to Nazeingwood Common with very few passengers. The 327 was an early omo conversion in 1964. (Alan Cross)

however restrictions on carrying local traffic within some towns on the borders of the LPTA – Luton being the main example where Luton Corporation and United Counties ran all the town services. The LPTA boundary was a line drawn between what were mainly the outermost points served by the route network which existed at the time, with the exception of Aylesbury, West Wycombe and Forest Row to which routes continued beyond the boundary as 'unrestricted outward workings'. More importantly perhaps, the Act also drew a second boundary line to enclose what was termed 'The Special Area'. Within this, London Transport had absolute autonomy to run services without a licence from the Traffic Commissioners, whilst other operators (which London Transport rather disparagingly referred to as 'Foreign Operators') had to apply for an annual permit to run a service, the granting of which was entirely at London Transport's discretion. In many places the boundary of the LPTA and the Special Area were one and the same, but there were parts of west Surrey, north Sussex, Bedfordshire, Buckinghamshire and north Hertfordshire where the Special Area boundary was some distance inside that of the LPTA. The LPTA had the effect of creating an artificial boundary which in practice could not be crossed by either London Transport or adjoining operators, and which led over time to an inefficient and inconvenient route pattern in many towns along the boundary, Crawley, Guildford, Gravesend and High Wycombe being examples. London Transport also guarded its area with a generally inflexible approach, so that 37 years after it was created little had changed when London Country assumed control in 1970.

The Transport Act of 1947 had created the British Transport Commission (BTC) which set up a number of 'Transport Executives' – London Transport becoming one of them. LTE approached BTC to discuss boundary changes and to be allowed

The 352 was one of the more rural routes and ran between Berkhamsted and Dunstable on the north western edge of the Country area. Tring garage operated the timetable on Saturday and Sunday, but the Sunday service was a victim of early service cuts as passenger numbers fell away. The Saturday service continued to be crew operated until November 1964, using a 15T13 bus until replaced with an RF in 1962. T 790 stands at the terminus at Dunstable Square waiting to return to Berkhamsted while the driver chats to a passenger in the background. This was also the terminus of the 343 and 337 routes and the 713 Green Line, and the old split bus and Green Line stop flag with the 'fare stage' sign and the original box timetable frame are all redolent of the time. (Peter Jones)

The 361 was one of the minor crew operated routes converted to omo with GSs in 1954. It ran roughly every hour from Rickmansworth to Chorleywood, and was later combined with the 309 to form one route linking Rickmansworth to both Chorleywood and Harefield. GS 76 was one of Gerston's initial allocation and had a very short life with London Transport being withdrawn at the end of 1962 after the major reductions in GS allocations of October that year. It is now preserved and has run in service on several of Country Bus Rallies running days. (Alan Cross)

to operate more services outside the strict limits of the LPTA. Even before the War, the former London Passenger Transport Board had sought to obtain such powers, but in 1949, LTE submitted formal proposals. These were, to say the least, ambitious and geographically far reaching. They proposed extending the LPTA boundary to include the whole area then operated by Aldershot & District and Thames Valley, as far east as Basildon (another 'New Town'), and over much of Southdown and Maidstone & District's territory, almost to the South Coast. There were further proposals that the LPTA might even extend eastwards beyond Basildon to Southend. Even at the time, such an expansionist plan must have been seen as unworkable. How London Transport could possibly have been able to manage such an area, never mind the obvious hostility from those operators who would be subsumed into this vast empire is difficult to comprehend. Operational sense prevailed however, the only major change being the transfer of Eastern National's operations from Grays in 1951. Some cross-town working with Thames Valley in Slough, and with Southdown at Crawley was also agreed later. To the south, any agreement with Southdown and Maidstone & District was impractical since both companies were part of the British Electric Traction (BET) group which had not been nationalised and was not therefore controlled by BTC. In the end, apart from these changes, the LPTA boundary remained as it was.

But despite all the forecasts of growth, the peak number of passengers had been reached around 1949, and as the 1950s began bus usage was beginning to decline. 1950 was a poor year financially for London Transport as a whole. The decline in passengers combined with increased wage costs conspired to halve the operating surplus achieved in 1949, and worse still was around £4 million less than in the peak year of 1948. Country buses experienced a drop in passengers of over 2%, but on Green Line it was almost 7% as weekend and off-peak traffic fell away. There were some exceptions and the very successful programme of Country bus excursions in 1949 was repeated in 1950 with equal success, but the overall downward trend was beginning to become evident. The results for 1951 proved to be the worst since the end of the war and the first time that the overall surplus from fares fell short of meeting total interest and capital expenditure criteria set by BTC.

Given the huge – almost overwhelming – passenger numbers in 1947 and 1948, these reductions were nevertheless small and Country buses and Green Line coaches continued to carry large numbers of passengers all day. Despite these first signs of declining traffic however, the industry as a whole was generally slow to recognise the longer term consequences and the need to reduce operating costs. In London Transport's case just over 60% of the Country bus fleet was not capable of being one man operated, and with the whole RF fleet being worked with two man crews, only the GSs were one-man operated. Although most of the bus RFs would eventually become omo it would be the end of the 1950s before this was achieved, by which time the levels of crew operation had become a serious financial burden, just as they would across the whole of Britain's rural bus networks. On the single deck Green Line routes it would be the late 1960s before any conductors were removed.

With the delivery of the last RTs in 1954, the fleet replacement was complete. Even then, London Transport found itself with a surplus of new buses for which there was no immediate work. No fewer than 81 Country RTs were surplus and had to be stored – mostly at Loughton garage – on chocks minus wheels collecting dust, where most of them remained until they were used to replace older buses in 1958. There were also a number of GSs for which there was no immediate use.

While the forecasts for growth had seemed valid in the late 1940s, they proved in time to be considerably over-optimistic. London Transport, like all other operators, would soon find themselves being squeezed between rising costs and falling revenues, a situation which would prove irreversible. Over the following 15 years there would be continuing reductions in timetables and London Transport would never fully overcome its difficulties.

The 719 was started in July 1956 and took advantage of the expansion of Hemel Hempstead and new estates at Abbots Langley. The route ran to an hourly headway and proved very successful. RF 271 waits on the stand in Hemel Hempstead bus station while one of Rover Bus's Bedford SBs is on the stand opposite working the route to Chesham which was operated jointly with route 316. (Alan Cross)

2   After the Peak: the mid-1950s

The new estate at Temple Hill in Dartford had its first bus service when the 481 began in 1949, being replaced in May 1950 by journeys on the 477 extended from the town centre. In October 1953, these were in turn replaced with a new route 499 which was extended further into the estate using one bus to run a half hourly headway on the 10 minute journey. In Bow Arrow Lane in 1957, RT 4032 has stopped at a set of traffic lights which still used the old distinctive black and white post. (Peter Mitchell)

By 1955, the six new towns and the overspill estates were becoming well established. By the end of the 1950s, the new towns alone would add around 117,000 to the Home Counties population, about double the total of the former towns and villages on which they were founded. In addition to the new towns, Hertfordshire alone saw an increase of over 170,000 in its population during the 1950s; Surrey almost as many, and this enormous rise in potential passenger traffic was for a time instrumental in providing the Country area with some of the increased volume it had predicted when ordering its new fleet. The Green Line network in particular benefited from this growth at first, the services in the new towns providing valuable additional revenue, at least for a few years until private car ownership began to hold back and then reduce passenger numbers. The expansion of the new towns and resultant population explosion would prove over time however to be a far greater threat than benefit to the Country Bus department, for with all the extra people and employment came affluence and the ability to buy a car and a television, ownership of both rising rapidly from the mid-1950s. Across the country as a whole, average earnings rose by about one third over the last half of the decade, and car ownership increased nationally by around 250% in the ten years from 1951.

The last RT deliveries in 1954 had included 21 in Green Line livery which went to Grays for the 723/723A from Tilbury to Aldgate, serving the rapidly expanding Belhus Estate at Aveley, and passing the vast Ford works at Dagenham. These RTs replaced new RFs which by then were only two years old, but the need for greater seating capacity took precedence over the better comfort of the RFs, although it is worth noting that economies were achieved in the conversion as 24 scheduled RFs were replaced by only 18 RTs. The RFs made spare at Grays were then allocated around the fleet to provide additional capacity for duplicates for the 1954 summer schedules. In 1953 there had also been a proposal to extend the 722 Green Line route from Hornchurch to Aveley, given the traffic potential this huge estate might offer by providing a link to Romford. In a first indication of falling traffic however the 722 was already losing money outside peak periods; indeed the peak hour timetable itself had already been reduced. In a memo from the Operating Manager (Country Buses) dated 12th January 1954, he considered that the extension would not be worthwhile, and as we shall see, the 722 suffered a long, slow decline over the next decade.

In April 1952, the growing Belhus estate at Aveley had its first bus service with routes 328/328A, followed seven months later by the 328C to provide a link to Rainham. Bus routes to the estate would be altered frequently as new houses were built and in May 1953 the 332 replaced the 328A. RT 1058 was one of 23 new RTs sent to Grays in 1948, and has reversed into the original terminus at Eskley Gardens. The estate was referred to as 'Aveley Estate' until 1955 when part of it became known as 'Belhus'. The incomplete roads and new building works illustrate the expanding housing. (Peter Mitchell)

In the 1950s the demand for travel at Christmas remained very high, and on Christmas Eve 1955, a full normal day's service operated on all routes right up until the last departures. On Boxing Day and the following day, a full Sunday service was run everywhere including on such minor rural routes as the 386. On Christmas Day itself, no fewer than 123 buses were rostered (all crew operated), services running from around 9.00am with the last buses back in their garages by 3.00pm. On some routes a frequent service was run, the 403 operating to a 20-minute headway between Chelsham and Croydon, the 346 every 15 minutes to Oxhey, and the 480 every 15 minutes between Denton and Dartford. The 321 provided a 30-minute service all the way from Rickmansworth to St Albans (and hourly on to Luton). There were also a few very early works journeys with Grays running the 5.09am and 6.59am to Coryton Oil Refinery for the morning shift with a lunchtime return bus. Northfleet ran two buses out at 5.10am to Denton and Kings Farm for workers to get to Rosherville and Swanscombe, and Dartford ran an early 477 journey for staff to get to Joyce Green Hospital. A few garages ran out only a single bus, but Northfleet, Leatherhead and Grays each required twelve, Watford fifteen, and Windsor nine. In addition to the bus routes, 171 Green Line coaches were required, a service being run on every route. Whilst only four garages (Hitchin, Dunton Green, East Grinstead and Amersham) had no bus operations on Christmas Day, every garage running Green Line routes put out coaches. The late morning departures from the 'home' garage left insufficient time for the coach to make the return trip and be back by 3.00pm so many coaches made a one-way single trip with crews meeting at a convenient point en-route to change over and return to their home garage.

Coryton Oil Refinery was the easternmost point of the Country Bus area, and was linked to Grays by works service 349, which replaced Eastern National's service 35 taken over in the changes at Grays in 1952. RT 3502 is at Coryton terminus while the conductor returns to the bus, perhaps waiting for workers going home after their shift. (NS Service)

Whilst this was an intense level of service for Christmas Day, it had however been significantly reduced from the beginning of the decade. On Christmas Day 1950, 208 buses had been scheduled, with services running much later – until 5.00pm. Hourly frequencies had been run over the full length of several cross country routes such as 335, 353, 339, 410, 424 and 462, and rural routes such as the 331, 350 and 425 had a service. Even the 402 and 455 did, which ran parallel with Green Line routes that ran to their usual 30-minute headway. By 1955 however, of all of these had ceased. Although Green Line services also finished by 5.00pm in 1950, frequencies were in most cases the same as normal, with a run out of 187 coaches. This level of Christmas Day service could not be sustained, and the reductions by 1955 were followed year on year by a steady pruning back as private car ownership became the means by which people travelled to friends and relatives.

But the peak had passed. The total number of buses for the new fleet had been based on London Transport's forecasts of passenger growth in the expansion of the new towns and estates together with the demand for new routes which, while they seemed valid in the late 1940s, proved in time to be considerably over optimistic. The completion of the replacement programme in 1954 threw up a large number of spare buses for which there was no immediate work. In addition to the surplus RTs referred to in chapter one, there was no immediate use for some 15 GSs. The original order for 69 had been intended to replace the 58 Cubs scheduled in May 1953 but had been increased to 84 to allow the conversion of some rural crew routes to GS omo. In the event, the number of GSs actually used for these conversions was small, and they remained the most under-employed buses on the fleet for their entire service life.

To the north of Slough, areas of new housing were built on land at Wexham Court Farm, and the estate's first bus service began in April 1956 using the number 457B. Initially it ran to an hourly headway which increased to half hourly during Saturday shopping hours, and there were six journeys on Sunday afternoon. RT 4771 was one of those stored from new before going to Windsor in May 1959 and is nearing the terminus in Slough town centre. The 457B was replaced a few months later by the 400. (Alan Cross)

The 396A was Harlow's first town service. It began in February 1952 and ran between the 'Green Man' pub in what was still Harlow village to First Avenue, at a place called simply 'Road E', since the new roads were still being laid out and hadn't been named. The journey time was only seven minutes, and required one RT running to a 20 or 30 minute headway. By the time this picture was taken in the early 1960s, the route had been extended a short distance from the town centre to Hare Street in one of the expanding estates. Frequency had been increased to every 12 minutes, with journeys serving the railway station at Harlow Mill on the line to Liverpool Street. RT 1071 is nearing the terminus at Hare Street. (Peter Mitchell)

Whilst the new fleet provided more than enough capacity, staff shortages had become a constant issue. Full employment in construction and manufacturing brought about by increased demand for new housing and consumer goods had led to wide choice for workers in the job market. The wages paid to bus staff had dropped back in comparison to other industries since about 1950, and factory work offered regular hours in contrast to the shift work over a seven-day week which was a necessity in a job 'on the buses'. There were disputes over rest day working and overtime during the autumn of 1954, which had the effect of worsening the already poor staffing levels. For a time, in late 1954, the whole of the 710, 720A and the London to Windsor section of the 705 Green Line routes had to be temporarily withdrawn, and in the end the 1954 winter schedules could not be introduced on the planned date due to the general shortage of crews. The network was badly affected again during 1955 by a further series of strikes and working to rule as crews reacted to the severe cuts in services which they saw as threatening jobs. Given that there was already a shortage of drivers and conductors, and that some of the service cuts were designed to reduce the effects of these shortages rather than cut staffing numbers, then the Union's response by striking and working to rule was very much counter-productive, but indicative of Union intransigence which so blighted labour relations throughout the 1950s and 1960s.

Despite these first signs of decline however, the Country area remained busy with consistently high loads. Weekend traffic was falling away at a faster rate, but there was still the need for much duplication at peak times and to cater for additional numbers of shoppers particularly on Saturdays. It is worth looking at some areas of the network in more detail to understand the high levels of service which were commonplace before cuts began to become necessary as passenger numbers declined.

HEMEL HEMPSTEAD TO WATFORD

Hemel Hempstead and Tring garages operated the frequent 301 and 302 trunk routes into Watford requiring much duplication, and had one of the most intense levels of service anywhere on the network. These ran along the A41 which even in the early 1950s, before the expansion of Hemel Hempstead itself, was quite urban in character. There were factories along the Grand Union Canal including the large paper mills at Apsley, and it was only beyond Boxmoor that the route began to run into open country through the small towns of Berkhamsted and Tring before Aylesbury was reached. The main 301 route ran the whole length of the road from Watford to Aylesbury running parallel with the 302 as far as Two Waters before that route turned off the A41 into Hemel Hempstead. The 706 and 707 Green Line routes paralleled the 301 all the way to Aylesbury on a joint timetable with the 708 which, like the 302, ran into Hemel Hempstead. In 1955, the 301 and 302 ran to a ten-minute headway between Two Waters and Watford, supplemented by a 15-minute headway on the Green Line routes, providing a total of ten journeys an hour. On Saturdays after mid-morning, a supplementary timetable gave a further four journeys per hour between Watford and Two Waters, two each per hour running into Hemel Hempstead as route 302, the other two running on to Berkhamsted on route 301. The 1955 timetable also included two late Saturday afternoon journeys from Tring garage to Aylesbury and back. These were timed to leave Aylesbury for the return journey, just three minutes in front of the main departures for Watford to provide extra capacity for the large number of people returning from an afternoon shopping in Aylesbury. Even the Sunday 301 and 302 headway was 15 minutes, increasing to ten minutes after lunchtime,

The 301 and 302 were the first routes to receive new RTs in 1948, Tring and Hemel Hempstead receiving a total of 30 RTs between them to run these busy routes. RTs would run the route for the next 27 years, the longest period of continuous operation on any Country Bus route. RT 1010 was transferred to Hemel Hempstead in May 1960 and after 18 months went to St Albans until withdrawn in January 1964. It was one of the last RT3 roofbox bodied buses in service. On a fine sunny day it is about to turn out of Clarendon Road into Watford High Street at the start of the run to Aylesbury. (Alan Cross)

and as the Green Line routes ran to the same timetable seven days a week, there were therefore eight journeys every hour between Watford and Two Waters on Sunday morning, increasing to ten in the afternoon. This level was maintained right up until the last bus left Watford at 10.52pm. In fact the timetable provided for the last 301 and 302 to leave Watford at the same time on Sunday night, both buses running back together as far as Two Waters garage before they went their separate ways. Even beyond Boxmoor where the route became more rural, the 301, 706 and 707 between them provided no fewer than six or seven journeys per hour all day, seven days a week. A feature of the 301/302 schedules was the number of works journeys run to and from Apsley Mills. There was a particularly intensive service at lunchtimes in an era when many workers lived relatively close by, the timetable providing for them to go home for lunch. The lunchtime buses left Two Waters garage at 12.24, 12.25 and 12.26 for the short run to Apsley, and a timetable note over the 12.25 departure states *'five buses will run'*. Of the total of seven buses, four then worked journeys on the 377 or 378 to areas north of the town centre, while the other three worked into the town itself. The return trips were timed to give workers about 35 or 40 minutes for lunch, and the 1.16pm 302 departure back from Hemel Hempstead town centre noted that *'three buses will run'*. Tring and Two Waters between them put out 15 RTs seven days a week to work the basic 301 and 302 timetable plus another eight for duplicates and the supplementary works journeys, and the three Green Line routes shared by East Grinstead and Chelsham at their southern ends needed a total of 29 RFs excluding peak hour and weekend duplicates, of which there could be several. During the week therefore, a total of 52 buses was required to work along the busiest part of these routes.

RURAL ESSEX

The Country area covered only a small part of rural Essex to the north west of the county where it bounded Hertfordshire. Like that county, there were some very remote areas, Bishops Stortford and Epping being the only towns of any size in this part of Essex, both being on the boundary of the LPTA, and Epping also being on the edge of the "Special Area". Services to the east and north were the preserve of Eastern National from their depots at Chelmsford and Bishops Stortford which ran some infrequent and indirect routes to Harlow and Ongar. The area to the south of Epping ran into some affluent outer suburbs of London which in the 1950s saw much new development, not least some less affluent estates at Debden.

The 396 took a direct route north up the main A11 to Bishops Stortford passing through the small village of Harlow, and the larger settlement at Sawbridgeworth. During the week, it ran to a 30 minute headway, increasing to 20 minutes from mid-afternoon, whilst on Saturdays, the 20 minute headway began mid-morning, increasing to 15 minutes after lunch. Sundays enjoyed a 30 minute headway from mid-morning, requiring ten RTs which included runnings on the 396A/396B. These were short routes which linked Harlow village and the station (Harlow Mill today) to the New Town centre which, by 1955, had been laid out and housing developments were well under way. During the week, these routes ran separately from the 396 for much of the day, but on Sunday afternoons, they ran from Epping to provide a 15 minute headway as far as Harlow, the 396A/B then running every half hour into the New Town. The 396A had been Harlow's first town service, introduced in February 1952, simply as 396 at first, the "A" suffix being added in January 1953 to distinguish it from the main route. It had been run with just one bus running a short distance from Harlow village to a point known then as "The Dashes" just short of what would become the town centre. By 1955, the route had been extended, a 396B variant had been added and a 30 minute headway ran all day Sunday, on which day an additional 30 minute service ran on the 396 from Epping into the New Town centre at Fourth Avenue. The main purpose of this was to provide a facility for the many people who travelled up from east London to visit friends and relatives who had moved out to Harlow New Town, and who could easily reach Epping by Underground on the Central Line.

The service along the A11 was enhanced further by a 30 minute headway on the 720 Green Line route from London, thus providing between four and eight journeys per hour all the way to Bishops Stortford. A feature of the 720 schedules was that because there was a long run out from Epping in the morning, all five coaches ran to Bishops Stortford as 396 before returning as a 720 to London, although in the late evening all the coaches ran back to Epping as 720. A direct route into Harlow New Town had begun in July 1954 when the 720A was introduced, followed two years later by an extension of the 718 from Epping. These provided three journeys per hour seven days a week, and as more people moved from east London into the New Town, weekend visitor numbers increased markedly to the extent that, for several years, almost every Green Line departure from Harlow New Town on Sunday evenings was duplicated to cater for all these passengers. This was in addition to the very large numbers of day trippers who had travelled out to Epping Forest, which required much duplication from late afternoon. For summer 1955, Epping had ten rostered Green Line duplicates, but these were often insufficient, and Epping's weekend duplicate schedules were among the most numerous of any garage.

The text refers to the 339 which, although providing important links to Epping, Ongar and Brentwood, served some less populated areas along the way. The transfer of Epping garage's routes to Harlow in May 1963 is discussed later in the book, and the 339 was extended from Epping to Harlow as part of the many changes. RT 1084 runs through the deserted High Street in Brentwood near the end of its journey to the station. The intermediate blind includes Potter Street, so this picture was taken after the extension to Harlow. The bus is one of Epping's allocation transferred to Harlow, and stayed there until August 1965. (Peter Mitchell)

Epping's other route along this boundary was the 339 through Ongar to Brentwood and a short distance further to Warley. Although Warley was on both the LPTA and "Special Area" boundary, the 339 and Central area 247 were London Transport's only routes there, frequent services being run by Eastern National. The 339 had an auxiliary service, completely remote from Epping, running between Warley and Coxtie Green, a small village just to the west of the road north from Brentwood. In order to accommodate these journeys, the 339 timetable was arranged oddly. The basic service was half hourly from Epping to Ongar, three buses per hour from Pilgrim's Hatch to Warley, and hourly to Coxtie Green. An hourly through service ran from Epping to Warley, but there were few through journeys in the opposite direction, the majority running hourly only as far as Ongar where buses ran to Shelley at the north end of the town. From there, they ran back on a short five minute journey to the "Two Brewers" pub at the south end of Ongar before turning and running back to Epping. This required five RTs, and for crews who worked Coxtie Green journeys and some peak hour shorts from Brentwood, the timetable was arranged such that they took their meal relief in Brentwood at the Eastern National depot.

The expansion of Harlow New Town would, over the next few years, lead to many alterations to the service pattern of the 339 and 396, and the opening of Harlow garage in 1963 would result in fundamental changes which are described in Chapter Four. Other than its extension from Epping to Harlow, the basic level of service on the 339 suffered some reductions, although much less than the steep decline on the 396, and electrification of the main line railway which paralleled the 396 and 720 to Bishops Stortford would prove to be a major factor in a more rapid decline during the 1960s.

In the immediate post war years, Epping's rural operations were limited to just one route. The 399 ran from Coopersale just outside the town, through Tylers Cross, Roydon and Stanstead Abbotts to the station at St Margarets on the line to Liverpool Street. It ran to roughly an hourly headway with alternate journeys extended on to Ware and Hertford. The 399 schedules were complex with journeys interworked with the 308 and 384, one bus even coming from Hitchin which ran a bus into Hertford on the 384 each day and whose roster included a return to Coopersale during the day. Six journeys each way ran on Sundays, and the route was crew operated until the comprehensive changes to the east-west route pattern through Hertford described later in the book. Two other routes had been added as the network began to expand after the war. The 393 began in June 1949 to provide a new link from Harlow to Broxbourne and Hoddesdon and crossed the 399 at Tylers Cross.

The 393 required two buses running to an irregular timetable, buses running out to Tylers Cross on the 399 to take up service. The Sunday service was very limited, only three journeys being run by one bus from mid-afternoon until early evening. From Harlow village, the 393 passed through Nettleswell, Hare Street and Great Parndon which even by 1955 had not been overcome by the development of the New Town. Hare Street was one of the first of the main housing areas to be developed, and Nettleswell Cross would become part of Harlow Town Park near the New Town centre. The roads followed by the 393 in the early 1950s would be unrecognisable today, Harlow eventually swallowing Great Parndon and extending almost to Tylers Cross. In the early 1950s, Hoddesdon and Broxbourne were relatively small towns on the main A10, but both began to see much new housing and development so that the 393 gradually became a more important link. New GSs replaced the Cubs in 1954, and by the late 1950s some duplication was required on Saturdays as numbers of shoppers grew rapidly. To increase capacity, omo RFs replaced GSs in October 1956 and the timetable settled down to a regular hourly headway seven days a week, Epping continuing to roster an additional bus for duplicates on Saturdays. As part of the complex changes to the east-west routes across Hertford, it was extended to Welwyn Garden City in October 1958. Expansion of Harlow, Hoddesdon, and Welwyn Garden City had, by the start of the 1960s, transformed the 393 from a minor rural service to one of the more important single deck routes in the northern Country area.

The same could not be said of the 381. From its inception in 1950, it had never been intended as more than a minor service, almost solely for people who wished to go shopping in Epping. A trip into central London was possible by travelling on the Central Line, but it would have been necessary to return to Epping no later than 4.00pm before the last bus left for Toothill. There were never more than five journeys a day, and the bus used was very much underemployed. The first reduction on the 381 did not come until 1966, however, when the Saturday timetable was reduced from five to four journeys; these ran until the summer schedules of 1969 after which only two Saturday journeys remained. The Monday to Friday service was virtually unchanged, but London Country abandoned the entire route in 1971. Epping and Hertford's allocations evolved to include complex cross working whereby Epping's buses at various times included runnings on the 308, 308A and 331 as well as the 381 and 393. Epping contributed five buses to this pool which included the 381 journeys. Other than a short period in 1959, GSs remained on the 381 until the major changes in 1962 which are described later.

THE THAMES ESTUARY

The River Thames was characterised along much of its length from Southend towards London by industry along both banks. Tilbury and Gravesend were opposite each other and linked by a frequent passenger ferry service operated by British Railways. London Transport derived much revenue from its routes serving factories, cement works, docks and fuel refineries in the area as well as significant new housebuilding which accelerated rapidly from about 1950. After Eastern National's Grays area routes were taken over in 1951, they continued to operate routes from Chelmsford and Southend into Grays and Tilbury including the four hour long 51/53 routes all the way from Harwich, Clacton and Colchester, but London Transport operated all the local routes in the area. The furthest east point served was the Shell Haven oil refinery at Coryton where the 349 ran a works service from Grays. Other routes run solely as works services were the 367 and 368 from Grays and Tilbury to the large Bata Shoe factory, on which only workers in possession of special weekly tickets were permitted to travel. Two other purely works services were the 357 and 379 to Tilbury Docks which were part of a roster of ten RTs which worked across all these routes as well as most of the 323/A/B which were cross town services from Purfleet through Grays to the estates north of the town. The main trunk route was the 370 from Tilbury Ferry through Grays to Romford, and formed the Country area's main link to the Central area. The 370A ran some short journeys mostly at peak times from

In the dreary urban surroundings that typified many of the routes in the Grays area, RT 4187 has arrived at Chadwell St Mary. The 379 was one of Grays's numerous works services and consisted of just one single trip each way to and from Tilbury Docks, a journey time of only 11 minutes. It was withdrawn in October 1965, the journey thereafter being covered by an additional facility on route 367.
(Peter Mitchell)

The 367 was one of two works services to the Bata shoe factory at East Tilbury. The 368 ran from Grays itself, while the 367 linked the factory to Tilbury Ferry. A total of seven buses arrived just after 7.00am each morning and five more before 9.00am for the office staff, with similar numbers in the afternoon after the factory shift and the office staff finished work, Grays also rostering additional RTs for duplicates. RT 4187 turns in front of the Bata Hotel which was provided as a staff hostel and was the afternoon departure point – the morning journeys running a few yards further to turn in front of the factory itself. (Peter Mitchell)

Workers could purchase specially printed weekly tickets and conductors punched a hole on the relevant day for each journey to and from work. The date of this is uncertain, but at 1/11d, for the week, the return journey each day from Chadwell St Mary cost just over 4½d. (Capital Transport Collection)

RT 1100 turns from Clarence Road by the Queens Hotel to terminate at Grays Memorial on short local route 374 from Uplands Estate. Paines department store and the lady with the large pram show Grays as it was half a century ago. (Peter Mitchell)

Tilbury Ferry to Purfleet. This was an important busy route running to a 12-minute headway during the week, ten minutes on Saturday, and 15 minutes Sunday, and with an end to end running time of one hour 16 minutes, a maximum of 19 RTs were rostered. The 371/371A/371B ran to a 10 or 15 minute headway from Tilbury through Grays to Purfleet or Aveley, and half hourly on to Rainham where connections were made with Central area routes from east London and Romford. These routes ran though West Thurrock where the link road from the Dartford Tunnel would eventually connect with the main A13. The only other link to the Central area was a limited Saturday shopping service between Aveley and Upminster numbered 328C. The large LCC overspill Aveley Estate to the west of Grays has already been referred to and its continued expansion gave rise to many alterations to routes and schedules. It had been sited there initially for workers at a new tile factory which had been built after the war, but as the area expanded elsewhere, it became ever more important as its population increased and people moved from areas of east London which had high proportions of poor housing, much of it war damaged. In 1955, Grays rostered 60 RTs which included two for the unadvertised service from Aveley to the Bata factory which used weekly tickets and were noted in the allocations as "guaranteed journeys". Other than a very few journeys to the then small village of Bulphan, Gray's routes ran through almost no open countryside anywhere. A further works service, remote from Grays, was the 375 which linked Rainham and its railway station to a factory on Rainham Marshes at a point where there had once been a ferry across the Thames to near Erith in Kent. It ran every few minutes in peak hours and was crew operated by four 15T13 single deckers, but was never completely viable. Page 106 describes London Transport's failed attempt to convert the 375 to omo in 1959, after which the route came to an abrupt end.

The 328 was part of the complex pattern of routes which crossed Grays and went through a number of alterations over the years. RT 3189 is working a short journey between Grays and Stifford Clays but shows the intermediate blind for the whole route. (Norman Rayfield, 2RT2 Group)

Along the south bank of the Thames, services were equally intense, and large new estates were developed in Gravesend and Dartford. In May 1955, Northfleet garage rostered 47 RTs, with a further 24 from Dartford, the majority of which ran busy town services. Gravesend remained a border town following the 1933 Act which had resulted in Maidstone and District's former operations from Dartford being transferred to London Transport, following which the strict demarcation of the LPTA prevented both London Transport and Maidstone and District from crossing the boundary at Gravesend. London Transport served the estates at Kings Farm and Christianfields south of the town, the boundary line being the road from the town to the latter. Maidstone and District's 21 and 23 ran out of Gravesend along the same roads at LT's town services, but such were the restrictions imposed by the 1933 Act that they were not allowed to carry local passengers between the town centre and the limit of LT's routes, the same restriction applying to the 27 and 46 over the short distance to Denton, which was the terminus of the 480. This situation was still in force when London Country took over, and it was not until rationalisation resulted in London Country taking over Maidstone and District's town services much later that the restrictions came to an end and a more efficient network would come about.

The principal route was the 480 running from Denton just east of Gravesend to Dartford, Crayford and Erith. The section to Dartford ran every five or six minutes all day, reducing to every 15 or 20 minutes on to Erith, the whole of the route being run by Northfleet garage and requiring a peak run out of 24 RTs – half of its total allocation. The remainder were all rostered to the 487/488/495/496 town services between the estates mentioned above and Northfleet and Swanscombe. In the days when every town had an early closing day, when shops closed at lunchtime, the schedules of these routes were unusual in requiring four fewer RTs on Wednesday afternoon. There were factories at Rosherville on the

The 467 and 491 worked a joint schedule, most buses changing from one route to the other at Horton Kirby. The 467 rain into the Central area to terminate at Sidcup and the 491 ran to Belvedere, both routes being almost entirely suburban in nature. RT 4050, obviously in need of a thorough clean, picks up in Dartford on a wet day in dreary surroundings typical of the route. (Denis Battams)

bank of the river just west of the town, and Northfleet ran some works services linking Denton and the housing estates to Rosherville. These were operated as part of supplementary schedules from the main town service allocation, but an unusual working ran on the 480A from Rosherville to Denton, rostered for a bus from the rural 451/490 allocation and which was run with a C class Cub before replacement with a GS in 1954. Dartford ran a number of town services, and its scheduling included seven RTs rostered solely to Supplementary Schedules plus two more as 'Special Duplicates' for its many journeys to factories and local hospitals. The 475 and 486 ran works journeys to factories on Crayford Ness, an area of marshland on the Thames including the Thames Ammunition Works which closed at the end of 1963 followed by the withdrawal of the 475 and 486 journeys. Many other works journeys were run to the large electricity generating station at Belvedere, Littlebrook power station, the Wells firework factory, and large hospitals at Joyce Green, Mabledon and Bow Arrow Lane, all of which were close to Dartford. Frequent shuttle services were also run to all the hospitals during visiting hours on several routes. One of Dartford's main operations was on the 467 and 491 which ran from Horton Kirby south of Dartford, through the town to Crayford, Bexleyheath where the routes separated, the 467 running to Sidcup and the 491 to Belvedere. Much of these routes ran into the Central area and were in reality no different from the Central suburban routes in character.

Dartford had a minority share of two other routes with Swanley garage. The 423 ran from Longfield through Watchgate into Dartford and on to Swanley, its timetable including a number of suffix numbered workings for the works and hospital journeys. Dartford rostered only two RTs to the 423 and its variant, but on Sunday afternoons, five more were added for Hospital journeys plus a further two "*to instructions*" for duplicates to cover the large numbers of visitors to all the local hospitals, many of whom travelled to Dartford by train. The 401 was one of many longer routes which linked urban areas to the countryside, and ran south of Dartford through the Darenth valley to Sevenoaks. The route started from Belvedere through Bexleyheath and Crayford to Dartford with a 30 minute headway, increasing to 15 minutes on Saturdays, with journeys extended to Eynsford. South of there, the route ran through attractive open country below the North Downs, and was never better than hourly on to Sevenoaks. In 1955, Dartford had an allocation to the 401 on Saturdays only, when five additional RTs were required to operate the frequent service to Belvedere, but duplicates might be run as far as Sevenoaks on Sundays to carry the many people who wanted to travel out into the countryside. For many years, the 401 timetable was transformed on Bank Holiday Sundays and Mondays when a 15 minutes headway operated right through to Sevenoaks all day until the last bus since the area remained very popular with day trippers.

The other important route operating into Dartford was the 477/477A through Wilmington and Swanley to Orpington and Chelsfield, and although including some sections of "country lane", was a suburban service roughly on part of the boundary between the Country and Central areas. There was a general 30 minute headway to Orpington, with additional journeys between Crockenhill and Dartford, increasing to every ten minutes over this section on Saturdays, and although Dartford ran some local works and hospital journeys on the 477, the whole route was operated by Swanley garage. The 479 was a very minor route running via an indirect route from Farningham through Horton Kirby and Darenth into Dartford. Swanley ran the route with just one GS (replacing a Cub in 1954) which operated back and forth all day to an irregular timetable, which in the days when private car ownership had yet to grow included a Sunday service from mid-afternoon to late evening. The small village of Darenth was the only place on the 479 not served by other routes, Horton Kirby, Farningham and Sutton At Hone all having frequent services into Dartford. The 479 was therefore virtually pointless, and it was one of the minor routes abandoned in the cuts following the 1958 strike

The 423C consisted of just one return journey from Watchgate to Downs School on schooldays only and was worked as part of Dartford's supplementary schedules. The morning journey from Watchgate was run by the bus which first worked a schools journey from Littlebrook on the 423B, and RT 3185 displays the intermediate blind for this route. It is quite likely that the conductor will not change it for such a short trip, having only wound on the correct route number.
(Capital Transport)

Northfleet garage ran some rural mileage to the south with services going via three different routes to Longfield. South of there, the 451 and 490 ran up the hill to Hartley before turning off by the war memorial along a residential road to terminate at Hartley Court at a point where the road narrowed to single track, buses reversing round the small island at a road junction. The 490 ran via Southfleet and New Barn, the 451 via Betsham and Westwood, although there were only a very few journeys this way, run solely as a shopping facility into Gravesend or as positioning journeys for the 490. During the week, there were gaps of two hours between journeys during the day, but on Saturdays the frequency was hourly with additional journeys on Saturday afternoon as far as Longfield. The 489 and 489A ran via the same route as the 490 to Southfleet, then via Westwood to Longfield. Here the 489 ran south to the village of Ash where buses reversed into a side road by the "White Swan" pub to turn. During the 1960s, a new "village" at New Ash Green was developed about two miles south of Longfield, and the additional traffic from here was an important factor in preventing a reduction in the 489 timetable. From Longfield, the 489A ran through the hamlet of Longfield Hill and down to Meopham, just outside the LPTA boundary. The hourly direct route from there into Gravesend was provided by the long 122 route from Brighton operated jointly by Maidstone and District and Southdown, whose buses were operated by crews from either company in the complex scheduling of the route. During the week, an hourly frequency ran to Longfield, alternate buses running on to Ash or Meopham, but on Saturdays the service was doubled to half hourly and every hour beyond Longfield. As a link to Gravesend, the 489A served no purpose whatsoever, and the road between Meopham and Longfield provided minimal passengers, its only real use being a link to the railway at Longfield station, which although in Longfield itself remained as "Fawkham" for many years. This link to the railway provided all these routes with significant additional passengers from the large numbers of commuters who travelled into London. Several short journeys were run to link to the station, and duplicate buses were run on the 490 from Gravesend in order to provide an extra bus to run some of these to and from Longfield. The combined service on the 489, 489A and 490 provided three journeys every hour on Saturday morning between Southfleet and Gravesend increasing to four in the afternoon, and during the week there were frequent departures during peak times and for school journeys.

GS 79 was one of those without work when delivered, a situation discussed in the text. After eight months in store at Garston, it went to Reigate briefly before being allocated to Northfleet in November 1954. It then spent its whole life there before being withdrawn in November 1962 as a further casualty of the cuts that year. It would have run on the 490 on most days and has stopped at Longfield station on a return journey to Gravesend. Although busy at times, the 490 was not authorised for buses larger than GSs due to the short section of single track lane at Southfleet, a restriction that was later relaxed as odd journeys were rostered for RFs. (Lyndon Rowe)

The 450 traversed some very narrow lanes to the south of the main Gravesend – Dartford road to link Betsham, High Cross, and Bean to both towns, running every two hours seven days a week, although the Sunday service would be reduced to just one return journey by 1963 and withdrawn the following year. Until the late 1960s, the road from Bean village down to the main road at Greenhithe was a narrow country lane, passing part of the huge chalk quarry that would one day become the site for the Bluewater shopping centre, the lane itself disappearing beneath a busy dual carriageway linking the M2. The most infrequent route was the 492 from Gravesend to Longfield after which it ran down the valley through Fawkham to West Kingsdown on the main A20. It had been introduced in May 1949 purely as a shopping facility to Gravesend and ran just three journeys during the week, although the Wednesday service had been withdrawn in September 1955, there being no need for a service that day as it was early closing day in Gravesend. It was at best only marginal from its introduction, and did not survive the drastic cuts following the 1958 strike. West Kingsdown had a two hourly link to Dartford through Fawkham and Longfield at weekends, although the need for a Sunday service can never have been great. The 452 timetable was arranged to provide a regular hourly headway with the 450 from Dartford through Bean as far as High Cross where the two routes split, the 452 running down to Westwood where it followed the same road as the 451, 489 and 489A to Longfield. Dartford had no single deck allocation (other than the RFs for the 725), so that the 452 was run by Northfleet. On Saturday morning, the bus ran to Dartford as a 480, a note in the allocation book stating that the bus for the 450 and 452 should carry a 480 fare table. On Sunday the bus ran light from Northfleet, but at the end of the day, on arriving back in Dartford, it ran the last bus back as a 450.

All these rural routes were covered by three RFs and eight GSs, one of which was rostered for the Monday to Friday duplicates and additional Saturday afternoon 490 journeys. The 489 and 489A were completely crew operated with the RFs, the exception being a couple of the evening peak journeys from Longfield which were worked by a GS from the 451/490. At various times, there was also one crew worked RF journey on the 490 on schooldays. RFs replaced GSs on the 452 in 1959, and the Sunday service was abandoned in October 1965. There were few other changes to these routes and it was the mid-1960s before the timetables were cut back to any extent, Sunday services being greatly reduced as they were everywhere else. Despite many narrow lanes, all the routes were approved for RF operation except for the lane between Betsham and Westwood on the 451 and 492 which was restricted to GSs and was perhaps the narrowest of all. Indeed, London Country had to retain a narrow BN for the remaining journeys down this road until the beginning of 1981 when it was finally approved for Leyland Nationals. Having driven a GS along this lane myself, there is almost no point at which a Leyland National could pass any other vehicle, but operation along here was short lived as these odd journeys were withdrawn.

Green Line routes from Tilbury and Gravesend were, in the mid-1950s, an important link to London, enhanced further by the introduction of the 725 in 1953 which served many important places across south London. The 723 ran from Tilbury via Chadwell St Mary to Grays, then followed the main A13 Southend road all the way through east London to Aldgate. In July 1951, the 723A was added to serve the Aveley estate, and the 723B in July 1954 to run direct into Grays via the Dock Road. By 1956, the total combined service increased to every 15 minutes all day, increasing further to every ten minutes after late morning

RF 106 was one of 20 new RFs allocated to Grays in January 1952, followed by six more in April. The local population was increasing rapidly, a situation accelerated by the building of the large estate at Aveley discussed in the text. The capacity of the RFs soon proved inadequate, and their tenure was shortlived when they were replaced with the second batch of Green Line liveried RTs in July 1954. The original Green Line blinds were not as clear as those which replaced them as RF 106 shows as it heads to Tilbury. (J.G.S. Smith)

Saturday. At peak times, some journeys ran within two minutes of each other, some turning at either East Ham or Blackwall Tunnel to relieve the coaches coming from Aldgate which might already be full. The relentless decline of these routes to a basic 30 minute headway by 1969 is covered at many points later in the book. On the opposite side of the Thames, the routes fared slightly better in terms of any gradual reduction. Northfleet and Staines ran the 701 and 702 to a combined 30 minute headway which remained little changed until the late 1960s, and the 725 was still running to its 30 minute headway at the beginning of 1970 when London Country took over, although the number of weekend and peak duplicates had been greatly cut back.

The final section of the 702 Green Line route to Sunningdale ran beyond the LPTA boundary at Virginia Water. Aldershot and District's express coach service from Aldershot to London covered much the same roads as the 702 into London, and this last leg of the 702 never carried large numbers of passengers and its gradual decline is discussed later in the book. RF 151 was one six new RFs sent to Staines in February 1952 to replace 10T10s, and stands in the yard at Sunningdale station ready for the long journey to Gravesend. (J.H. Aston)

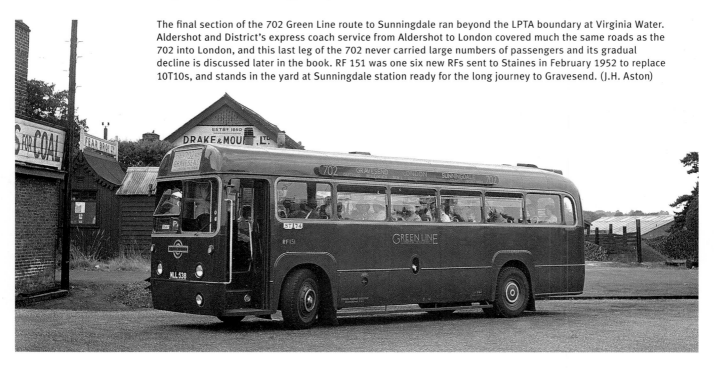

The 483 was Crawley's first 'new town' route. Started in May 1953, it ran a short distance from 'The George' in the town centre to Northgate with a journey time of just six minutes, requiring one RT to run a 30 minute service. It was withdrawn in January 1958 as part of an agreement reached with Southdown who extended their route 23/23A to Northgate where their garage was located, thus avoiding empty running to and from the town centre. RT 1042 has reversed at Northgate terminus and the unfinished estate road still has open fields in the distance.
(Peter Mitchell)

THE CROYDON TRUNK ROUTES

Without doubt, the most intense services of all were the trunk routes radiating out from Croydon across the whole of the southern area. No fewer than nine different garages supplied the buses for the Croydon routes, all of which were entirely crew operated with RTs, and the scale of operations was intense throughout the day. The May 1955 schedules required a combined allocation of 93 RTs Monday to Friday, 87 Saturdays, and no fewer than 80 on Sundays. The greatest contributions came from Chelsham (23), Godstone (20), Reigate (18) and Leatherhead (17), while the garages at Dunton Green, East Grinstead, Dorking, Crawley and Guildford were all further out from Croydon and contributed smaller numbers. Three of Dunton Green's allocation to the 403 did not in fact reach Croydon since they were allocated to the Westerham–Sevenoaks–Tonbridge section which had an increased frequency and was duplicated during peak hours. In the course of a whole day, more than 700 different platform staff operated into and through Croydon on these routes, and the total of 93 RTs on Monday to Friday was around one seventh of the total RT allocation for the entire Country area network.

The routes combined over common sections for some distance into Croydon, the joint headways giving a very frequent service, shown by the following table:

COMMON SECTION		FREQUENCY (MINUTES)		
		Mon–Fri	Saturday	Sunday
408/470	Leatherhead–West Croydon	15am / 10pm	10	15
405/414	Redhill–West Croydon	15	10	15
409/411	Godstone–West Croydon	15 till 2.30pm 7/8 after 2.30pm	7/8	20 am 15 pm
403/A/B/408/470	Wallington–Croydon–Chelsham	5/10	5/10	15

The 403 and 409 in particular had several additional journeys at peak hours, and during the day the combined service from Croydon along the Brighton road through Purley on the 405, 409, 411 and 414 had between eight and 12 buses an hour all day. In 1955, during Monday to Friday peak hours there were 63 arrivals at West Croydon between 7.30am and 9.00am, and 41 departures between 5.00 and 6.00pm in the evening peak plus four others from South Croydon on the 409. Demand was such that some journeys were also duplicated and the 4.51pm 409 departure was duplicated for its entire length to East Grinstead. Some 403 departures from Croydon left within a couple of minutes of each other and to cater for shopping demand into Croydon in the morning, the 9.51am and 10.21am 408 journeys from Warlingham Park Hospital to Guildford were duplicated from Chelsham as far as Croydon by buses operating as 403. There were also a number of scheduled duplicates which did not appear in the public timetable but which were run on a regular daily basis. Even this level of service was augmented further when additional 'Express' journeys were added to the 403 in December 1955. These operated only in Monday to Friday peak hours between Croydon and Warlingham and cut seven minutes from the normal journey time. When the service began, there were nine journeys in to Croydon in the morning and 15 back in the evening, a timetable which had been little reduced 15 years later when London Country took over.

It was only at their outer ends that the Croydon services could really be described as 'country' routes. The whole section of the 408 and 470 from Chelsham all the way to Epsom (which the 403, 403A and 403B paralleled as far as Wallington) was in reality a high frequency suburban route, and the others were equally suburban for most of the way as far as Caterham or Redhill. After Leatherhead the 408 onwards to Guildford, although running through some open country, served several villages along the main road, and still carried substantial numbers of passengers. A 30-minute headway was maintained all day during the week until the evening, increasing to twenty minutes on Saturdays. Only on Sundays was it reduced to every hour, but even then additional short journeys as far as Effingham ran all afternoon and into the evening. Trips to the cinema were still an important part of social life, and on Sunday evening, an extra journey left

On 1st October 1962, RT 2516 has arrived at Warlingham Green at the end of the two hour 14 minute run from Guildford. The text refers to the hard work the 408 and 470 entailed for the crews – the 470 and they have just seven minutes layover before the return journey. The complete 'rounder' duty referred to was often repeated twice in the same day. (Tony Wild)

Epsom for Leatherhead at 10.30pm only four minutes before the through journey from Chelsham to cater for the extra demand as the cinema performance finished. With fewer stops and some faster running after Leatherhead, the 408 was one of the Country area's classic long distance trunk routes, and with an end to end running time of 2hrs 16mins, was one of the longest. The 470, which was combined with the 408 as far as Leatherhead, then ran to Dorking, turning off the main A24 to run up through Mickleham village and down the hill to Burford Bridge. This was the main stop for Boxhill, where huge queues could build up on Sunday afternoons as passengers waited for their bus home. The Dorking leg had the same frequencies as the 408 to Guildford, except that to cater for Boxhill traffic, the Sunday frequency was half hourly from late morning for the rest of the day.

The 408 and 470 were hard work for the crews. Leatherhead crews referred to a duty on the 408/470 as 'up the hill' due to the long climb from Croydon to the top of Sanderstead Hill where there was a watering point if the radiator needed topping up. The descent of Sanderstead Hill was designated a 'third gear hill' and a request stop at the bottom needed careful judgement by the driver with any sort of load on board. Between Leatherhead garage and Warlingham Green there was a total of 90 stops, and exactly 90 minutes were allowed in the timetable regardless of time of day or day of the week. With a majority of short distance passengers and frequent stops, the conductor had to be very alert and quick on the bell all the way. At really busy times, the bus would stop at most of the stops along the route, and even a few seconds delay by the conductor at each stop could result in losing three or four minutes along the route. The drivers had to be equally quick. Sid Huxford, a Leatherhead driver for many years, recalls pulling up at stops with first or second gear already selected before the bus came to rest, holding the bus on the footbrake and looking in the nearside mirror. If people were boarding, then as soon as the last passenger had their foot on the platform, the right foot came off the brake and over the accelerator anticipating the bell from the conductor. There was often no time for changing up 'by the book', it was a matter of stabbing the operating pedal down and up rapidly, with the accelerator pressed down as the left foot came up. Running to time was essential on a high frequency route, and if a crew were a few minutes late, they would have to pick up passengers who would have caught the next bus behind. Worse still, late running would cut into their layover time. At Warlingham Green, only seven minutes were allowed and, although through journeys to Chelsham had 13 minutes, this was barely long enough to visit the toilet and get a cup of tea in the canteen. When a duty often involved taking over at Leatherhead, then running all the way from Warlingham back to Guildford, the layover was essential.

The 403 and its variants to Farleigh and Warlingham Park Hospital were in reality no different from a suburban Central area route, at least as far as Chelsham. After Chelsham garage the 403 ran into open countryside with the long gradual climb on to the North Downs at Botley Hill where the route turned left for the long descent to Westerham. After the intense service up from Croydon, the section to Westerham was never better than hourly, mainly because the 706 Green Line route ran over the same road, and with the 707 coming up from Oxted, combined with the 403 to give three journeys an hour all day into Croydon from Botley Hill. At Westerham, the 403 crossed the long 410 Bromley to Reigate trunk route, and the famous 'Westerham connections' between the two routes lasted into London Country days 20 years later. After Westerham, there was a busy section along the main A25 into Sevenoaks carrying heavy loads all day, and with

The 403 provided important links all the way from Croydon to Tonbridge. It received new RTs in February 1950 and they ran the route continuously for the next 28 years, although the section south of Chelsham was converted to omo in 1971. Although RT 2267 carries a CM garage code it was never officially allocated to Chelsham, but spent 10 years at Dunton Green where the 403 schedules involved swapping buses at the end of each day. It has just pulled out of Sevenoaks bus station. (Peter Mitchell)

The basic service to Warlingham Park Hospital was hourly seven days a week, but on Wednesday and Sunday afternoon there were many additional journeys for hospital visitors. RT 2503 waits in the layby at the terminus by the Hospital with the large shelter to cater for the extra passengers on visiting days. The driver is immaculate in full uniform. Chelsham first received 26 new RTs during 1950, but this bus was one of ten more sent to Chelsham in August and September 1953 to replace the last of its STLs which had been rostered to many of the 403 workings. RT 2503 had been allocated to Dunton Green when new in 1950, and spent eight years at Chelsham. (Peter Mitchell)

the parallel 705 Green Line, there were four journeys every hour between Westerham and Sevenoaks. In the evening peak, two departures from Sevenoaks were duplicated as far as Brasted and Westerham. The run on from Sevenoaks down River Hill to Hildenborough and Tonbridge was equally busy and combined with the 402, 704 Green Line and the 454 which took the 'country' way via Weald before Hildenborough, there were five or six journeys an hour between Sevenoaks and Tonbridge. The 403 was a consistently busy route and operated over some very hilly roads, and the long steep climb up River Hill with a good load was a test for any bus as was that from Westerham up to Botley Hill.

The section between Chelsham and Westerham on the 403 was the least busy and often traversed with few stops which could lead to some early running. On the way to Westerham, this did not matter since a minute or two waiting time was allowed there to ensure the connections with the 410, so that arriving there a little early was no problem as the crew simply waited for time before going on. In the other direction though, arrival at Chelsham too early might incur the displeasure of the inspector if he was outside the garage, although crews due to change at Chelsham would be happy to arrive a bit early. Many of the Dunton Green rosters involved the crew working through to Croydon or Wallington, to come off at Chelsham on the way back. With a five-minute headway from Chelsham into Croydon, some of the Dunton Green crews would wait at a request stop a short way before the garage, then run down late so they could run up behind a Chelsham bus into Croydon. Norman Osbourn, a young Dunton Green conductor

Two routes served Smallfield Hospital near Horley, both routes running just one return journey on Sunday afternoons for hospital visitors. The 482 from Caterham started in March 1953, and an additional journey on Thursday was soon added. On a quiet Sunday afternoon, RT 3153 has just left Caterham Station while an unidentified RT in the background is on a 409 to West Croydon. (Peter Mitchell)

The 851 linked the London to Brighton main line at Three Bridges to Smallfield Hospital and began in May 1954. RT 4731 has arrived at the Hospital from Three Bridges with what appears to be a good load. The 424 timetable also provided some added shuttle journeys between Horley Station and the Hospital on Thursday and Sunday afternoons. (Peter Mitchell)

in the early 1960s, recalls doing this often, though understandably it was not popular with Chelsham crews! The 403A and 403B ran from Chelsham to Farleigh Village and Warlingham Park Hospital respectively and were generally hourly, but the intense service on the 403B for hospital visitors was a measure of demand in the mid-1950s. On Sunday afternoons between 1.45 and 4.30 there were no fewer than 17 journeys, with three buses leaving within the space of five minutes at 4pm to take visitors back to Croydon. On Wednesday afternoon, ten extra journeys were run up to the hospital.

Although the 409 and 411 had a high frequency, the routes had a more rural feel to them. The climb up to Old Coulsdon and across the Common to Caterham was more pleasant, and beyond Godstone the 409 was a fast running route with few stops, which, apart from odd extra peak hour journeys, was never more than hourly since the 708 Green Line provided the faster link to Caterham and Croydon every half hour. Between Godstone and Reigate the 411 shared the road with the 410 route, and benefited from constant heavy demand for travel into Redhill and Reigate with a combined 15-minute headway all day right up until the end of service. The demand for shoppers returning home on Saturday lunchtimes was such that in 1955 and 1956, four additional journeys were scheduled back to Godstone running between the regular 15-minute headway. Redhill and Reigate were growing and, as demand along the corridor to Godstone increased, on

Saturday afternoons from October 1957 two additional journeys an hour as far as Bletchingley were added to meet this. This gave a capacity of 330 seats per hour into Redhill and gives an idea of just how busy these routes could be. At the outer end of the 409, the section beyond East Grinstead to Forest Row was outside the 'Special Area', its operation being permitted as an *'unrestricted outward working'*. Maidstone & District and Southdown shared a garage in East Grinstead, and the road to Forest Row was also covered by the M&D 91 to Tunbridge Wells and Southdown's 89 to Eastbourne, so with the 409 there were three buses an hour to Forest Row, although the timetables were never co-ordinated to give an even headway. At Forest Row, the 409 originally terminated by simply performing a U-turn across the main A22 at the top of the High Street, but by 1961 this had become hazardous so that buses ran a short distance off the main road to reverse into the road leading down to the railway station. Even this became difficult so a little later buses ran down to the station itself to turn round, but were not permitted to carry passengers after setting down at 'The Swan' on the High Street since this was the limit of the permitted outward working under the 1933 Act. A sensible terminus would always have been at the station where the occasional passenger might have been able to change between bus and train, but by the time this was finally permitted in 1968, the branch line had shut and the station closed!

The terminal arrangements on the 409 at Forest Row are described in the text and from 1961, buses ran light from the main road to the station where they reversed to stand in front of the station building to wait for the return journey. RT 3131 was transferred to Godstone in October 1961 and waits at the station. The branch line passenger service remained for another few years, but the 409 was never allowed to carry passengers to and from the station until the line had been closed. (Tony Wild)

With such intense levels of service, there was some rivalry between 409/411 and 405/414 crews over the common section from Purley into Croydon. This was often stop-start in heavy traffic, and the trick was to run right behind the bus in front to avoid having to pick up anybody on the way into Croydon terminus. There was a stop on the 409 and 411 at the bottom of Stoat's Nest Road just before the route turned out on to the main A23. It was common practice for the Godstone conductors to jump off at the stop and walk the few yards to the junction to see if a 405 or 414 was coming up from Coulsdon. If so, the crew would wait a few seconds until the bus had passed the end of Stoat's Nest Road, then pull out and run up behind it. There then followed a game of 'cat and mouse' all the way into Croydon. For years, the 405 and 414 crews had only four minutes layover at Croydon, so they did not always appreciate being tailed if it meant they had to pick up a few extra passengers. If nobody wanted to get off however, it was not unknown for the 405 and 414 drivers to sail past a few stops and leave the passengers to the 409 or 411 behind them! With the Central Bus routes also covering this road, there was a bus every minute or two, so there was much overtaking by the Country Bus crews in an effort to preserve their short layover at Croydon.

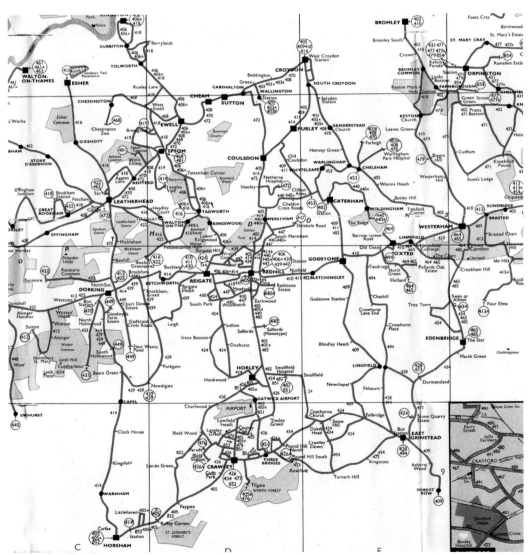

The 405 and 414 were largely suburban most of the way to Redhill, and south of there the 405 continued as a suburban route almost all the way to Crawley, passing Gatwick Airport and the ever expanding industrial area between there and Crawley itself. Passenger numbers between Redhill and Horley justified many extra journeys over this section all day, with even more running on Saturdays when three extra RTs were required to augment the service to Horley. After Reigate, the 414 however became a true Country Bus route. Turning off the main A25 at Buckland, it went down a narrow lane into Betchworth village with overhanging trees brushing the sides and roof, before returning to the main road into Dorking, after which the route served a succession of villages strung out along the A24 all the way to Horsham. Late running at Dorking was not unknown, and the 44 minutes allowed in the timetable on to Horsham did not allow drivers to take it easily. With frequent stops along the way, this could be an exhilarating ride if the driver was trying to catch up time, and was one of the best sections of all Country area RT trunk routes. The 414 and 470 both served Dorking, but Dorking garage only ever ran a minority share of the 414 and never had an allocation on the 470. It had three RTs allocated to the 414 which despite the gradual reductions in the timetable, survived for 20 years into the 1970s before its allocation finally began to be cut back. The route required eight or nine RTs, and for a brief period up to 1958 it needed 14 on Saturday, when Dorking had four allocated, and no fewer than 17 on Sundays when Dorking sent out five RTs to provide the duplicates for the heavy loads of day trippers.

Country area double deck routes required frequent trimming of trees on many roads. 969J had been converted from STL 1503 which dated from 1936 and was one of five pre-war STLs converted for use as tree loppers across the Country area. They were all withdrawn in 1963 to be replaced by five purpose built vehicles on Thames trader chassis, four of which survived to be transferred to London Country in 1970. The drop down platform with its wire supports and makeshift handrail would certainly not comply with modern safety standards. (Alan Cross)

THE SURREY HILLS

While the Croydon trunk routes provided the main link to Surrey from the London suburbs, there were a number of rural routes which linked the villages in the area to the main towns, principally Reigate, Dorking, Leatherhead and Guildford. The link between Dorking and Guildford had always carried good loadings. With a succession of villages all the way along the route, an important country town at each end, and high demand from weekend day trippers, the 425 route was one of the most successful single-deck routes run by the Country Area. The route had originally been shared with Aldershot & District's 25 from Aldershot to Dorking but after the changes which followed the 1933 Act, it fell wholly inside the LPTA, Aldershot & District's share being transferred to London Transport.

The 425 remained consistently busy, and the 1955 summer schedules required a Monday to Friday allocation of eight RFs, four each from Dorking and Guildford. Although only five buses were needed to run the basic 30-minute headway, there were extra peak journeys, with one bus allocated to work the short journeys from Dorking to Westcott which ran all day to provide a 10- or 15-minute combined headway to Westcott. On Monday to Friday after 3.00pm, the half-hourly headway was increased with a third through journey every hour. On Saturdays, to reflect the higher demand, the headway was increased to every 15 minutes, and with the additional short workings ten buses were needed to work the route. In 1955, there were as many as 94 departures from Dorking to Westcott on Saturdays between the first bus at 6.45am and the last at 10.22pm, and the high level of passengers justified the route's crew operation. A note in the allocation book for 18th May 1955 relating to Sunday working on the 425 illustrates how many additional day trippers could be carried on a fine Sunday. Five buses were needed for the all-day half-hourly headway, but additional unscheduled journeys were run in fine weather, with a 15-minute headway in the afternoon. Guildford and Dorking both had an additional RF allocated *'to operate to instructions'* which were used to run duplicates, while a further note stated *'alternate journeys liable to be withdrawn between Westcott and Albury during inclement weather'.* Even in bad weather this still left a 30-minute headway all day on Sundays, but the additional short journeys were still operated between Guildford and Albury at one end and between Dorking and Westcott at the other, even if the weather was bad.

On a fine summer day in 1956, the conductor of RF 672 leans out of the rear door to change the blind and provide a lookout for the driver before reversing at Gomshall on a 425 short working from Dorking. The running number DS 201 indicates one of the many duplicate journeys operated on this route, particularly at weekends, although the necessity for them would rapidly decline in the 1960s. (Alan Cross)

The more rural 412 ran in parallel with the 425 as far as Wotton, then turned off the main A25 at Manor Farm to run up to Abinger, Holmbury St Mary and Sutton. Once off the main road, the 412 climbed a narrow lane between high banks and overhanging trees to reach the tiny village green at Abinger. Just beyond there at Parkhurst Corner, the route turned right and climbed steadily up through ancient woods before dropping steeply down a narrow twisting lane to Holmbury St Mary, a picturesque village

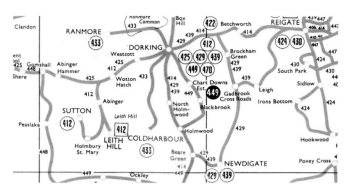

This extract from the 1956 map shows the short section of the 412 which terminated at Leith Hill (Leylands Road). The square box around the 412 route number at the terminus indicated that the route operated on weekdays only. This issue was the last map to show the Leith Hill working which was withdrawn that year. (Author's collection)

little changed today with its triangular village green and the Royal Oak pub. After Holmbury, there was a short five-minute run along the valley to Sutton where buses reversed round in front of the Volunteer pub before the run back to Dorking. An outstation had first been established at Holmbury St Mary in 1927, the bus being parked up every night in the yard of the Royal Oak, its regular crews living in the village. This bus ran the main service into Dorking every day, and from pre-war days until the London Country era, the basic two-hourly timetable during the week remained almost unchanged. There were also additional hourly journeys every afternoon as far as Parkhurst Corner, running originally seven days a week, although the Sunday journeys were all withdrawn in 1954. Although these additional journeys left Dorking between the main service to provide an even headway, the returns from Parkhurst Corner were timed to depart back to Dorking only seven minutes behind the through service from Sutton and Holmbury, thus ensuring they almost always ran empty. In an early example of cuts to rural timetables, although the Saturday journeys to Parkhurst Corner were retained, the summer 1956 schedules saw the withdrawal of the Sunday journeys, and the Monday to Friday service cur back to just three in the afternoon.

The oddest part of the 412 however was the strange leg which, at Parkhurst Corner on the main route, continued on up the hill for another mile to terminate at Leylands Road which was no more than a narrow side lane. Although this terminus was rather grandly known as 'Leith Hill', and there was a path to the summit nearby, it was some way from the top of Leith Hill itself. There was no habitation beyond Parkhurst Corner, and Leylands Road terminus was 'in the middle of nowhere'. The Leith Hill section had been added in 1947 in response to the increase in post-war passengers, but the necessity is unclear, although a few cottages on the edge of the hamlet of Friday Street were about half a mile down Leylands Road from the terminus. Even odder was the timetable of the journeys there. Departures from Leylands Road were at 7.56am, 12.40pm, 7.06pm and 10.36pm, having left Dorking at 7.23am, 12.07pm, 6.33pm, and 10.03pm. Initially, these ran every weekday, but by summer 1955, the last journey at night had been abandoned so that the 10.03pm from Dorking was worked by the outstation bus and ran instead down to Holmbury St Mary. Given the attraction of Leith Hill for weekend leisure trips, it is strange that there was never a Sunday service on this section, and it is difficult to see the purpose of the timetable since it was not convenient for either commuting or shopping trips into Dorking. The Leith Hill service probably carried almost no-one, and it is perhaps no surprise that it was one of the earliest casualties of service reductions, being abandoned completely after October 1955.

This delightful period picture appeared in the August 1961 issue of the London Transport Magazine, which included an article featuring operations from Dorking garage. This bus shelter at Westcott – which remains to this day – was the only thatched-roof one in the whole of the Country area. The women and children in their summer clothes are very typical of the era. The inspector just visible in the shelter is Albert Shirlock who was one of two 'squad' inspectors based at Dorking and had a long career with London Transport. (London Transport Museum)

The villages of Shere and Gomshall had a second link to Guildford by way of the 448 route, although this went by a different routeing from the 425, running over the Downs via Merrow and Newlands Corner, and was operated jointly with Tillingbourne Valley Motor Services. Between Silent Pool (near Shere) and Ewhurst, the route was inside the LPTA but outside the 'Special Area', and so London Transport had no powers to compulsorily purchase Tillingbourne, nor had ever challenged their operations on the route, so that joint operation had continued unchanged. The narrow section of road from Gomshall up to Burrows Cross on the way to Peaslake meant that the route was not approved for operation by RFs and the Leyland Cubs had been replaced by new GSs early in 1954. Peaslake was a large village, and combined with consistent traffic volumes from Shere and Gomshall, the route carried good loads. The limited seating capacity of the smaller buses meant that the route needed a higher frequency to meet demand, and a half-hourly headway, seven days a week had been operating since the mid-1930s to the extent that the 1955 timetable was virtually identical to the prewar one. The main service worked only as far as Peaslake, requiring three buses which were always split between two from London Transport and one from Tillingbourne. Beyond Peaslake, the service was very sparse, with only five journeys a day on to Ewhurst and which were only ever operated by London Transport. This ran along narrow lanes before the long drop down Pitch Hill into Ewhurst itself, and other than Coverwood School and a few large houses there was negligible traffic potential. The principal link from Ewhurst to Guildford was run by Aldershot & District's service 23 with double deckers on an hourly frequency. This ran via Cranleigh, and the need for a link from Ewhurst north via Peaslake must always have been tenuous, but the 448 timetable nevertheless continued unchanged. Indeed, despite the sparse traffic over the Ewhurst section, the Sunday service was run to exactly the same times as the rest of the week, the only difference being the early morning journey which did not run on Sunday.

This original timetable of the 852/852A was included somewhat strangely in the Leatherhead and District area booklet dated 1st April 1955 and was the only time it was published. Note the long gap in the afternoon service to Ewhurst on Thursdays to account for Horsham early closing day. London Transport met stiff opposition from local independent operators to their operation of the Ewhurst service, and Brown Motor Services took over that part of the route after only three months in 1955. (Author's collection)

EWHURST - HORSHAM - IFIELD - CRAWLEY - THREE BRIDGES — Bus 852 (WEEKDAYS ONLY, TT.4017)

[Timetable as shown]

D—Operates direct. (Route 852A).
P—From Faygate Rusper Road at 7 4 a.m.
R—Time at Faygate Rusper Road.
10—Thursday only.
X—Thursday excepted.
Z—Thursday and Saturday excepted.
§—Saturday only.

71

Although London Transport needed two GSs to work the main service, two more were required to cover the Ewhurst journeys and the 448A Guildford town service which had been introduced in August 1950 to serve some new housing at Pewley Way. The 448A ran seven journeys Monday to Friday and ten Saturdays to an irregular timetable, mostly worked by buses between trips on the 448. For many years, the 7.58am from Guildford to Peaslake ran back as a duplicate to the 8.28am up from Ewhurst so that two buses ran together all the way from Peaslake back to Guildford. These were timed to run only eight minutes behind the previous departure from Peaslake, and Tillingboure ran another journey twenty minutes before that. Until 1955, there were two duplicates so that three GSs were scheduled to work the 8.41am from Peaslake to Guildford in order to cater for the large number of morning shoppers, and is an indication of just how many passengers might be carried at the time. Moreover, two Saturday daytime journeys and a mid-afternoon Monday to Friday journey were also duplicated all the way from Guildford to Peaslake and back. Together with the 425, this meant that Gomshall and Shere had a minimum of four buses an hour almost all day seven days a week into Guildford, rising to six an hour during the day on Saturdays. With duplicates and additional peak journeys, this was one of the best levels of service anywhere on the Country Area's rural part of the network, and despite minor reductions, ran largely unaltered well into the 1960s.

There were two other independent routes from Guildford which augmented the 425 through Chilworth and Albury: Tillingbourne ran a route as far as Albury, after which it which climbed up the narrow lanes to Farley Green every hour, and Brown Motor Services ran a route every two hours seven days a week along the 425 route as far as Abinger Hammer where it turned south through Sutton and Holmbury St Mary and on to Forest Green where they were based. Some of Brown Motor's journeys from either Guildford or Horsham connected at Forest Green, so that most of the Guildford to Horsham route via Forest Green was run as a

GS 35 was one of five new GSs allocated to Guildford and entered service in December 1953, replacing Cubs on the 448 and 448A. It is alongside the garage in Guildford with the blind set for a short 448A journey of 11 minutes from the bus station to Pewley Way. The blind is the early version with the larger route number. The 448 and 448A were the only routes into Guildford which showed Onslow Street Bus Station as the qualifying point on the blinds – an anomaly which lasted until London Transport's share of the 448 was transferred to Tillingbourne in 1964. (Vectis Transport Publications)

The text refers to the takeover of the Hants & Sussex route between Crawley and Ewhurst after that company went into liquidation. This provided work for two more GSs which had otherwise stood idle since delivery, and GS81, 82, and 83 were taken from store and sent to Crawley. The section from Horsham to Ewhurst was shortlived and during the three months of L T operation, GS 82 passes through the hamlet of Wallis Wood on its way to Ewhurst. The 'Bull's Head' qualifying point on the blind was not used on the 448 or 449 blinds, but included only because Hants & Sussex had used it and LT felt the need to replicate it.
(Peter Mitchell)

through service. Although these routes were inside the LPTA, they were mostly outside the 'Special Area' in this part of Surrey, and London Transport had come to an agreement in 1935 for their continued operation, an almost unique situation given London Transport's powers. Most unusually, because Brown Motor's route paralleled London Transport's 412 between Sutton and Holmbury St Mary, LT's licence prevented them from carrying local traffic between Sutton terminus and the village forge on the road to Holmbury St Mary. Theoretically, this had the effect of anyone wanting to travel this short distance having to wait for Brown Motors' bus, but whether this was actually observed in practice is doubtful, particularly as the LT crews who lived in the village knew all their regular passengers.

A new route which came about by chance was the 852 to Ewhurst following the unexpected collapse of Hants & Sussex three days before Christmas 1954. They had run four routes from Horsham: the 31 to Loxwood and Plaistow, the local 32/32A to Roffey and Littlehaven, the 33/33A to Crawley via Faygate and Lambs Green, and the 34 to Ewhurst. Following Hants & Sussex's sudden failure, the route to Plaistow was taken over by Aldershot & District who numbered it 50A as it ran over some common roads with their existing route 50 to Plaistow and Haslemere. London Transport stepped in at short notice to replace the other services. The 32 and 32A Horsham town services were simply absorbed into the existing 434, and the 33 to Crawley and 34 to Ewhurst were combined into one route which London Transport numbered 852. The Hants & Sussex route into Crawley had run across the town to Three Bridges and Langley Green, but apart from a peak hour journey to Three Bridges station, London Transport curtailed the new 852 to terminate in Crawley. Having combined the two former Hants & Sussex services, the route was actually quite long and with a through journey time of just over 90 minutes, needed two buses all day.

It was not until October 1957 that the 405 replaced the 434 between Crawley and Horsham. Prior to that, in addition to the main 434 timetable, a shuttle service was operated to Littlehaven and Roffey Corner on the edge of Horsham, rostered mostly for double deck operation to cater for the heavy loads to and from the town. During the summer of 1956, RT 319 waits at Roffey Corner for the return to Horsham. The main A264 towards Horsham bears round to the left and buses simply performed a U-turn at the junction. The road layout at this point today is very different, with traffic lights and a very busy junction. (Alan Cross)

The entire route was very rural indeed with limited passenger traffic, and since there were a number of new GSs spare, three were allocated to Crawley to operate it. Hants & Sussex had run a two-hourly service to Crawley during the week, and although the 852 timetable was different, the same overall number of journeys was maintained. The timetable to Ewhurst was less regular, but again London Transport initially matched the previous service level, the exception being that Hants & Sussex's former Sunday service, which had amounted to two journeys on the Crawley section and no fewer than five on the route to Ewhurst, was abandoned. Indeed, it was probably the cost of the pointless Sunday operation of their routes which had contributed to Hants & Sussex's collapse.

In taking over the route to Ewhurst, London Transport immediately found themselves embroiled in controversy with other local independent operators. Ewhurst and Horsham were on the LPTA boundary but the whole of the route between the two was outside the 'Special Area'. The independent operators therefore contended that London Transport did not have an absolute right to run the route, which strictly speaking was true, and so in March 1955, after only three months, LT surrendered the Horsham to Ewhurst section to Brown Motor Services based at Forest Green. This was not a bad outcome for LT since this section was extremely uneconomic to operate. The route ran through a succession of small hamlets, and only served to take shoppers into Horsham and back. This meant that the first two journeys beyond Horsham in the morning ran virtually empty all the way to Ewhurst as did the last at 6.35pm and 8.05pm back from Ewhurst in the evening. The remaining Crawley to Horsham section however was almost pointless from the moment London Transport had taken it over. From Horsham, it followed the main road half way to Crawley where it turned off into Faygate village, beyond which Lambs Green had a pub and a few houses. After these the route ran on through Ifield Wood passing virtually no habitation until the Crawley to Charlwood road was reached, where the 426 route already gave a good service into Crawley. It soon became apparent that the nine journeys run after taking over the route were far too optimistic, and the timetable was soon cut back.

GS 29 is on a journey towards the Chart Downs Estate along a section of Chart Lane which would be unrecognisable from this picture. By 1956, the capacity of the small GS was becoming inadequate as the estate expanded, so that it was replaced with an RT for most of the timetable. GS operation was then confined to just four journeys during the week worked between trips to Ewhurst. The three Ewhurst journeys were abandoned in October 1958. (Peter Mitchell)

Ewhurst had a third route – the 449 from Dorking – which had been introduced in March 1950, its main purpose being a town service in Dorking to what was then a new housing estate at Chart Downs on the edge of the town. Three journeys a day however continued on across Holmwood Common to rejoin the main A24 at Holmwood, on to Capel then via Ockley and Forest Green to Ewhurst. These were designed for shopping in Dorking and efforts were made to promote the route as a way of exploring the Surrey countryside. After Chart Downs, apart from the Plough Inn and a few cottages at Blackbrook, there were almost no houses at all until the main road was reached at Holmwood, and after Capel the route all the way to Ewhurst yielded few passengers. Forest Green benefited from Brown Motors' link to Guildford and Horsham mentioned earlier, and Ewhurst had frequent links to Cranleigh and Guildford, so that Ockley was the only village served solely by the 449, and the value of its links to Dorking therefore was always tenuous. Such was the demand for postwar leisure outings that two Sunday journeys were also run when the route started, but they proved to be very short lived, being withdrawn at the end of the 1954 summer season for lack of passengers. In reality the three Ewhurst journeys during the week were never profitable, and they were one of the many casualties of the October 1958 post-strike cuts.

GS 45 spent its first year at Northfleet before being transferred to Dorking in 1955. Increasing traffic in Dorking High Street is evident as the bus waits in the queue on its way to Dorking North Station. It has come either from the bus station to run a journey up to Coldharbour or has just come down from Coldharbour and will run back to the bus station before its next journey. Apart from the first morning journey up to Ranmore which was run with an RF, the whole of the 433 timetable was run with one bus, running number DS 11 being used right up until the route was withdrawn in October 1968.
(Alan Cross)

Dorking's short 433 route was a rural service typical of many all over Britain running a short way out from a market town to serve small hamlets nearby. The journey time up to Ranmore one way was 20 minutes, and the other leg up to Coldharbour 15 minutes, requiring long steep climbs out of Dorking in both directions. The route up to Ranmore although not particularly narrow, was a long steady climb until the route emerged on to Ranmore Common high on the Downs with fine views southwards across the valley to Leith Hill. The final five-minute run along the Downs from Ranmore Common to Ranmore though, was probably one of the most pointless sections on any Country area route. Ranmore Common had a village shop and post office (although that closed in the 1960s), but beyond there, there were virtually no houses at all, and the terminus at Dog Kennel Lane where the buses reversed into a narrow side lane was one of the network's most isolated turning points. At the other end of the route, Coldharbour is a small village high on the Downs below the summit of Leith Hill. The route ran along a narrow lane for a couple of miles out of Dorking, followed by the ascent of Boar Hill where the road climbed 700 feet in the next mile or so.

Boar Hill is narrow between steep banks, with several places where a bus cannot pass another vehicle, and the gradient could sometimes mean the driver having to drop right down to first gear if he had any sort of load. On reaching the top, the lane ran on through woodland until a short drop down a single track lane to Coldharbour itself, where the bus reversed round an island into a track opposite the Plough Inn. This track led uphill past some cottages and the village cricket ground, then on through woods to the summit of Leith Hill itself, which was one of the attractions of the route for weekend visitors. The ascent of Boar Hill was perhaps one of the steepest climbs in the whole Country area and, before the more powerful GSs took over the route in 1953, the timetable had allowed the Leyland Cubs 18 minutes up to Coldharbour but only 15 minutes for the descent to allow for the fact that the climb was so long and steep. After the GSs took over, the timetable settled down to a basic format which, in the end, was little changed until the route was finally withdrawn in October 1968. There had been a half-hourly Sunday service to Coldharbour in the summer, but from summer 1954, as the new GSs had a higher seating capacity than the Cubs they replaced, the timetable then required just one bus all day on Sunday. The allocation for 18th May 1955 however shows two buses rostered on Sunday, with a third allocated for 'unscheduled duplicates'. These were run *'to instructions'* and on fine days would wait for trains arriving at Dorking North to carry people up to Coldharbour, or pick up in Dorking itself where people had come by Green Line. Timing however was important for these extra journeys, because a bus could not attempt the ascent of Boar Hill without waiting for the previous one to come down, and even between Dorking and the bottom of Boar Hill there were several places where two buses could not easily pass. This level of service was not to last however. From 1956, only one additional bus was scheduled, and in the aftermath of the 1958 strike, the Sunday service was withdrawn altogether for the start of the winter schedules on 29th October that year. Thereafter, the Sunday service on the route was summer only, worked by one bus until the final season in 1965.

Dorking had two other rural routes which were crew worked with RTs. The 439 ran from Redhill over Wray Common into Reigate, then via an indirect rural route through Leigh, Gadbrook and Brockham into Dorking. From here it paralleled the 414 trunk route along the A24 as far as Beare Green where it turned off for the final leg to the village of Newdigate. The road from Reigate Heath down Flanchford Lane and on into Leigh was very narrow in places, and the narrow single track bridge over the river Mole by Flanchford Farm was a tight squeeze. The other was the 429 and was a completely circular route which paralleled the 439 for almost its entire length. It followed the 439 from Dorking out via Holmwood and Beare Green, and on reaching Newdigate continued through the hamlet of Parkgate, and a little further on at Gadbrook it rejoined the 439 via Brockham back into Dorking. While Newdigate was a reasonably large hamlet, Parkgate was small, and between there and Brockham there was open country with minimal passenger traffic. That these routes remained crew operated with RTs until June 1965 was an oddity since passenger levels even in the 1950s would perhaps have made them an early target for omo conversion. But although there was a surplus of RTs, there were shortages of omo RFs in the late 1950s, and this may have been a reason why these routes were not converted until 1965, quite apart from what would have been stern Union resistance to the loss of more conductors.

These routes ran to a regular two-hourly headway requiring just two RTs. A bus worked from Redhill via Leigh to Dorking then via Holmwood to Newdigate as a 439, then with a six-minute layover changed to a 429 where it continued via Brockham back to Dorking. In this way, the bus covered the section from Gadbrook to Dorking as a 439, then an hour later as a 429. From Dorking, the working was reversed, running via Brockham to Newdigate as a 429, then as a 439 back through Dorking and Brockham to Redhill. This round trip took three hours and 56 minutes, giving a four-minute layover at Redhill Station before repeating the sequence. Reigate contributed just one RT, but Dorking needed no fewer than five during the week since the section between Brockham and Holmwood through Dorking was augmented with many additional journeys throughout the day. For many years two RTs left Dorking at the same time on Sunday evenings at 10.06pm after the cinema performance finished. One bus worked a 429 round the Newdigate circle, and the other a 439 via Leigh to Reigate, both buses running together as far as Gadbrook Cross Roads before they went their separate ways.

For a relatively small garage, the high levels of passengers on the Surrey Hills routes provided Dorking with the majority of its work. In summer 1955, in addition

to its allocation for the 414, it rostered a maximum of 12 single deckers (including four GSs) on the 412, 425, 433 and 449, and five RTs for the 429 and 439 on the rural routes, the four GSs even being required on Sunday. Dorking itself and the attraction of Boxhill also provided a good proportion of passengers justifying the daily Green Line allocation of 16 RFs plus duplicates. It was this reliance which in the end would decimate Dorking's operations as passengers fell away.

The rural nature of the 429 and 439 is discussed in the text, crew operation of both routes continuing longer than others of a similar nature. Their conversion to RF omo in October 1965 is covered later in the book, and these two pictures illustrate operation while RTs remained.

Top RT 4536 has just run round the green by the houses at the Strood Green terminus in Brockham having worked one of the many 429 short journeys from Dorking. At certain times, there was a frequent service from Dorking to Strood Green but the off peak journeys carried fewer people as the 1950s progressed. Two people are waiting at the stop on the other side of the road for a 439 to Leigh and Reigate.
(Alan Cross)

Bottom Dorking ran the whole of the 429 and 439 with the exception of one bus from Reigate whose working is described in the text. RT 4501 went to Reigate in February 1965 so did not spend many days on the 439 before omo conversion. At that time, Reigate ran daily duplicates on the 711 to London, and had four Green Line liveried RTs allocated. RT 4501 was one of these, but was used on bus routes when necessary. It has stopped at Strood Green, Brockham on route to Redhill, and has perhaps picked up the passengers in the background of the picture above.
(Alan Cross)

THE WESTERN EDGE

In the same way as the 339 and 396 covered the eastern boundary of the network, the 441 ran along a considerable length of the western boundary. From Staines, it reached the boundary at Englefield Green and followed it through Windsor, Slough and Beaconsfield to High Wycombe. The "Special Area" boundary was drawn on the same line all the way until just west of Beaconsfield where it ran north west, leaving High Wycombe and nearby areas outside, although still inside the LPTA. The 441 was an important urban trunk route with some stretches of countryside and ran to a 30 minute headway seven days a week with an end to end running time of one hour 36 minutes. Other than the obvious attraction of Windsor, Beaconsfield was also very popular with weekend visitors, and with High Wycombe an important country town, the 441 enjoyed heavy loads along much of the route. The timetable included a number of short journeys around Slough and an additional service to Hedgerley Village just off the main line of route north of Slough. Windsor and Staines rostered a maximum of 24 RTs to run the 441 which included journeys on a number of other routes and the 441C/D to Englefield Green and Virginia Water. There were four journeys per hour between Staines and Hedgerley Corner on the main road during weekday afternoons, and five per hour for most of Saturday daytime. At Old Windsor, the route ran alongside the Thames, and served Old Windsor hospital, much duplication being required for hospital visitors and at weekends for the large numbers of visitors who spent their day by the river. Slough town services grew significantly throughout the 1950s as many new estates were built, and even as early as 1955, 29 RTs covered the 407/417/446/457B/484 and their many variants which ran to a high frequency all day. An extremely busy route was the 457/457A which ran from Windsor to Uxbridge via two slightly different routes on leaving Slough and at Iver Heath. The 20 minute headway increased to 15 on Saturday mornings and again to 12 in the afternoon, whilst on Sundays the 20 minute afternoon headway was often insufficient to carry large numbers of visitors to Windsor who had travelled to Uxbridge by Underground or on the long 607 trolleybus route through west

When Park Royal and Weymann were unable to build bodies at a fast enough rate, in 1947 120 bodies were ordered from Cravens of Sheffield to accelerate delivery of new RTs Although similar to the standard design, there were a number of differences, the main one being the five bay layout. They were not entirely successful and had a tendency to leak in heavy rain, many of them being returned to Cravens for alterations to the external mouldings. They were allocated only to Windsor and Watford High Street garages and had short lives, all being withdrawn in 1956. RT 1419 was one of 11 delivered to Windsor in April and May 1949, and spent seven years there before withdrawal. It is laying over at Staines Central station on a short 441 working to Farnham Common on the 441 at the point where the journeys to Hedgerley village turned off the main route. (John Aldridge)

In 1956 additional journeys on the 457 were started as an experiment at Easter, Whitsun and then every Sunday from mid-July until mid-October. The journeys ran non-stop every 20 minutes from Uxbridge to Windsor with only two fares of 1/5d to Windsor Castle or 1/6d to the bus station. On a Sunday in 1960, RT 4543 has arrived at Castle Hill in Windsor and unloads its passengers. These express journeys ran until 1962 after which falling passenger numbers rendered them unnecessary. (Alan Cross)

London. Duplication was essential on fine days, and a Sunday and Bank Holiday additional non-stop express service was added for a period. The famous Pinewood film studios were close to Uxbridge and works journeys numbered 457C and 457D ran there from the main route.

The 458 linked Windsor, Slough and Uxbridge but via a more indirect routeing through Langley and Iver before running in parallel with Central area routes from Cowley into Uxbridge. The Monday to Friday 30 minute headway increased to 20 minutes after lunch and to 15 minutes at peak times, but like most other routes ran more frequently on Saturdays: every 12 minutes until early evening reducing to 15 minutes until the end of service. It justified a 20 or 30 minute headway on Sundays and was busy all day. Were it not for the low bridge at Langley station, it would probably have been operated with double deckers, but its consistent passenger loads justified its crew operation with RFs. There were no plans to convert the route to omo, but Windsor suffered persistent staff shortages which worsened in the 1960s to the extent that journeys on a number of routes had to be withdrawn at various times. In 1964 there were simply in-sufficient conductors to continue crew operation on the 458, so that in the 1964 winter schedules it was converted to omo.

A pre-war Central area route had run to the small estate at Richings Park near Iver, but when reinstated after the war, the Country area ran it as 459. It never enjoyed great success, a GS replacing the RF for around six months from October 1958 when one of Windsor's GSs became spare following the withdrawal of the 442. The timetable soon began to be cut back and by 1955, it ran only a couple of morning peak journeys and an afternoon shopping service, although an hourly service remained all day Saturday.

Windsor operated two very minor routes, one of which did not survive the 1958 cuts after the strike. The 442 ran from Slough to Farnham Royal, the only part of the route not being served by others being Stoke Poges village which in any event was only a short distance from the main 353 route. An hourly headway ran all day as well as Sunday afternoon, and on weekdays in the summer alternate journeys had been extended to the very popular Burnham Beeches but this ceased in 1954, after which the timetable was drastically cut back. By 1956 it had been reduced to just five journeys during the week and two on Saturday afternoons. After the strike, its withdrawal became inevitable, as did the once busier weekend service to Burnham Beeches which had been numbered 474, but whose passengers had drastically reduced as people increasingly used their cars for such leisure trips. The 445 from Windsor to Datchet Common succeeded only in that it ran alongside the Thames through Datchet village and provided a link from Windsor itself, running mostly to an hourly headway all day but not until early afternoon on Sundays. Windsor rostered two GSs to these routes, and although the 442 was withdrawn early, the 445 timetable suffered few serious reductions, GSs remaining on the route until the end of 1966.

Other than the 441, Staines garage ran the two RTs and one crew RF on the 466 and 469, two local routes serving Stroude, Thorpe and Virginia Water. The 469 ran some journeys a short distance to Knowle Hill, while others on both routes ran into the centre of Virginia Water itself at the station. The initial two hourly service to Knowle Hill would later be increased to hourly and although not always busy, they carried good loads into Staines and remained little changed over the years. Although they were in the end converted to omo, some crew working remained, and Staines retained a crew RF on Saturdays for some years to balance the rosters. An hourly service to Slough ran on route 460 which required four RTs to account for the augmented service at peak hours and short journeys to Datchet from Slough. The 460 paralleled Central route 224 as far as Wraysbury and was quite rural in nature for most of the way until Slough was reached.

The LPTA boundary ran just to the west of Slough where the Farnham Road cross the A4 Great West Road. The 1933 Act permitted Thames Valley to continue running into Slough operating frequent services in from Maidenhead via a number of different routes. Manor Park estate was just to the east of Farnham road, while the large developments at Britwell and the vast Trading Estate were just to the west. Cross town links to these areas were essential, but any strict adherence to the LPTA boundary at this point would have prevented them, so that in an early example of cross border working agreements, both Thames Valley and London Transport provided routes into Slough. The 407 which had run between Windsor and the Trading Estate was withdrawn and but reintroduced later to run as a cross town service from Langley village to Cippenham, and Thames Valley later extended their 66 and 69 route to Langley in a joint timetable. London Transport continued to serve the Manor Park area, while Chalvey just south of the A4 was left to Thames Valley.

High Wycombe operated the 455 trunk route along the A40 to Uxbridge, running to a 30 minute headway in parallel with the 711 Green Line to provide four journeys an hour. Between Uxbridge and Gerrards Cross, more journeys ran on the 305 which then ran through the Chalfonts to Beaconsfield. After the 305 was extended to High Wycombe in 1960, with the 441 between Beaconsfield and High Wycombe there were six journeys an hour every day. Even towards the end of the 1950s, this level of service began to prove over-generous, and it was the 455 timetable which began to be cut back. By 1955, on weekdays, the half hourly headway was reduced to operating between High Wycombe and Beaconsfield and hourly on to Uxbridge, but the full service remained all day at weekends. In the 1956 winter schedules, the Sunday service was halved, but reinstated for the summer of 1957. Gradual reductions by 1960 had reduced the Sunday service to only every two hours, and hourly the rest of the week although some peak hour journeys remained. The 305 had been extended from Beaconsfield into High Wycombe which, combined with the 455, retained some of the earlier headway, but the circuitous routeing of the 305 through the Chalfonts added around 20 minutes to the journey time. During the 1960s, the 455 declined rapidly, being reduced to little more than a peak hour and Saturday shopping facility. One scheduling oddity at High Wycombe was the operation of the 455A which ran from West Wycombe to Wooburn Green in two separate sections from High Wycombe. The road out to West Wycombe was outside the LPTA and strictly the preserve of Thames Valley, but London Transport continued to run just two or three journeys in order to preserve their running rights along the road which had been permitted following the 1933 Act. Wooburn Green was also served by a frequent Thames Valley service, but three journeys continued to be run there, turning off the A40 at Holtspur, for the same reason. These journeys had been renumbered 305 in October 1962, but this completely pointless and wasteful operation continued until 1969 by which time the Wooburn Green journeys had been reduced to just two on Saturdays.

The gradual decline of the 455 route along the A40 from High Wycombe to Uxbridge is referred to in this book. RT 3120 went to High Wycombe in November 1961 and spent three years there before moving on, and is crossing the roundabout in the centre of Beaconsfield on the way to Uxbridge. The Saracens Head timing point is out of the picture on the left on the other side of the crossroads.
(Peter Mitchell)

RURAL HERTFORDSHIRE

If the Croydon trunk routes represented the most intense inter-urban part of the Country Bus area, then the network of rural routes across Hertfordshire was at the opposite extreme. The routes from Hertford itself radiated in all directions from the town serving many tiny villages and hamlets, linked by miles of often very narrow roads. In May 1955, Hertford had a large mixed allocation of 59 buses plus 12 RF coaches for the 715 Green Line route which then ran to a 20-minute headway seven days a week. No fewer than 33 buses were required to run the schedules for the bus routes, some of which, although rural in nature, provided important links and often carried heavy loadings. Of these 13 were RTs, ten of which were allocated to the 331, 350 and 350A which linked Ware and Hertford to a number of villages to the north and enjoyed good loads for much of the day.

With a 30-minute headway to Buntingford Monday to Friday afternoons and all day Saturday, the 331 required four RTs, plus a fifth to work additional shorts to Standon and Puckeridge. Such was the demand on Saturdays that after lunch an RT worked out to Standon to run back at 2.18pm as a duplicate to the main journey from Buntingford, a feature which lasted until the cuts of 1958. The 350 and 350A provided an important link between Hertford, Ware and Bishop's Stortford and in 1955 an hourly headway ran during the week until early afternoon increasing to half hourly until the evening. There were extra shorts to Widford or Much Hadham, and even the Sunday service was hourly all day. This required five RTs, and like all Hertford routes there was much interworking of buses between routes. The schedules at the time rostered one RT allocated to the 350 to run a morning trip on the 327 which – because of the weight restriction at Hoddesdon – had to be a 2RT2 'prewar' type. This bus was noted in the allocation books as *'HG51 to be RT2 type only'* and lasted until August 1957 when the bridge in Hoddesden was strengthened and the RT2s could be replaced on the 327.

The 395 and 395A ran through Hertford along the 390 route as far as Watton, but passenger levels reduced to the point where the 395/395A were cut back to Hertford in 1957, leaving the 390 timetable on a much reduced service during the week. RT 3633 pulls away from a stop in Cromwell Road having left the terminus on the way back to Hertford. It was withdrawn at the end of 1963. (Peter Mitchell)

The rural nature of the 327 beyond Hoddesden to Nazeing, is shown in this picture of RT 62 which runs across Nazeingwood Common on its way back to Hertford. The bus was one of seven pre-war RTs allocated to Hertford for the 327 after its last STLs were withdrawn, and operated the route until standard RTs could be used once the weak bridge in Hoddesden had been strengthened. The 327 was an early conversion to omo in November 1964.

It was the single-deck routes however which were the truly rural part of Hertford garage's network, and while there were frequent minor alterations to timetables throughout the 1950s, there remained a basic allocation of around 20 single deckers to run the routes. When the GSs were introduced to Hertford in April 1954, they were first used to convert routes 329, 329A, 386 and 389 to omo replacing the crew operated ex Green Line coaches which themselves had been replaced on front line Green Line duties by new RFs two years earlier. In 1955 and 1956 the number of GSs required for service was eight Monday, Wednesday and Friday, nine Tuesday and Thursday, ten Saturday, and no fewer than eight on Sundays, reflecting the demand for leisure journeys still taken by those without cars at the time. The total number of buses required varied each day of the week since the 386 ran only Tuesday, Thursday and Saturday, the 329 had no service Tuesday and a different timetable on Wednesday from other weekdays, and the 329A ran only on Tuesday and Saturday. The 372 needed an extra bus to run duplicates on Wednesday which was Hertford market day, and all routes had an enhanced timetable on Saturdays.

The 329, 329A, 386 and 386A were some of the most infrequent routes of the whole Country Area, serving isolated hamlets and running along miles of narrow lanes where in many places a bus could not pass another vehicle. The 329A and 386 served Hitchin market days on Tuesday and Saturday, the 386 also running Thursday and Saturday for Bishop's Stortford market day. The 386 covered the full length of the route – over two hours from end to end – only on Saturday, and ran Buntingford to Hitchin on Tuesday and Buntingford to Bishop's Stortford Thursday. Operation of the 386 was remote from Hertford and required long positioning journeys to get the buses out to their starting points. The 386A was used only for positioning journeys to either Standon or Buntingford on Thursday, Saturday and Sunday via an extremely indirect route, and was perhaps one of the more pointless operations anywhere, running by way of the 350 route as far as Hadham Ford which route had a very good level of service anyway.

The 329A timetable remained unaltered right up to its demise in October 1965, and was one of the most remote routes ever run by the Country Area. Its sole purpose was to provide a morning and afternoon shopping journey into Hitchin on Tuesdays and Saturdays, the only place it served exclusively being its southern terminus in the small village of Datchworth. It crossed the main A1 Great North Road at Knebworth where the 303 and 303A and 716 Green Line provided a minimum of three journeys every hour to Stevenage and Hitchin. The part of Old Knebworth out to Nup End was served by the 329 daily into Hertford, and a little way beyond Nup End, at Tower Lodge near Langley, the 329A turned on to the Welwyn to Hitchin main road which was served hourly by Birch Brothers' famous long distance 203 route from London to Bedford. A few miles further on at Chapelfoot, Birch Bros 204 route from Whitwell joined the main road, also running hourly on Tuesday and Saturday. The bus for the 329A ran out to Knebworth on the 329 in the morning, and during layover at Hitchin was also used to run short journeys to Great Wymondley on the 386. For the entire post-war period, this duty was HG64 and ran as follows:

9.10am	329	Hertford Bus Station to Knebworth Station Road
10.03am	329A	Knebworth Station Road to Datchworth
10.21am	329A	Datchworth to Hitchin
11.13am	386	Hitchin to Gt Wymondley
11.26am	386	Gt Wymondley to Hitchin
12.30pm	329A	Hitchin to Datchworth
1.21pm	329A	Datchworth to Hitchin
2.13pm	386	Hitchin to Gt Wymondley
2.26pm	386	Gt Wymondley to Hitchin
4.04pm	386	Hitchin to Gt Wymondley
4.17pm	386	Gt Wymondley to Hitchin
4.30pm	329A	Hitchin to Datchworth
5.21pm	329A	Datchworth to Nup End
5.45pm	329	Nup End to Hertford

On Saturdays, the bus also ran the evening journeys to Nup End, and on Tuesday morning ran a 333 to Bengeo and Chapmore End before the 9.10am departure to Knebworth. The two gaps in the schedule were the driver's meal breaks at Hitchin. The afternoon trip from Nup End back to Hertford was completely pointless on Tuesdays, and in time the 5.21pm from Datchworth to Nup End was abandoned on that day. Instead, on arriving at Datchworth, the bus ran light down the narrow lane to Datchworth Green – a distance of only half a mile – where even more pointlessly it then was timed to run in service as a 329 back to Hertford. Even on Saturdays, the 5.45pm from Nup End served no purpose since it ran only 20 minutes behind another journey on the main 329 route which had run out to Knebworth. The 329 linked Knebworth to Hertford via Datchworth Green, Bulls Green and the picturesque village of Bramfield. The section between Bulls Green and Bramfield ran along narrow lanes through dense woods with only a handful of large houses and few passengers, while Bulls Green consisted of only a pub and a few scattered cottages. At the outer end, the route ran through Knebworth, turning off the Great North Road to run up through Old Knebworth to turn at a road junction at Nup End. Even in 1955, only three journeys ran on

Monday, Thursday and Friday, but Wednesday (Hertford market day) saw a two-hourly service. There was no Tuesday service at all except for the positioning journeys for the bus working the 329A. On Saturdays, there was a two-hourly headway which ran all day until the late evening. A short journey also ran out from Hertford to Bulls Green on Saturday morning so that it could duplicate the 9.25am from Knebworth back into Hertford, and at lunchtime the return short to Bulls Green was timed to leave three minutes before the main Knebworth journey. This was an over provision, but while the morning duplicate in from Bulls Green was withdrawn in 1958, the lunchtime return ran until 1964.

The second Hitchin market day bus on Tuesdays left Hertford bus station at 8.43am and ran as a 331 via the main A10 to Buntingford. The departure from Buntingford on the 386 was at 9.35am, and this was the first of four round trips made during the day until the last departure back from Hitchin at 8.10pm. On arriving back in Buntingford in the evening, the bus then worked as a 331 back to Hertford garage to complete its day's work. This represented a long day for the driver in the days before stricter limits on hours, taking his breaks during layovers at Hitchin. How many passengers actually used the last 8.10pm journey back from Hitchin can only be guessed at now, but it can never have been worth running even in the busier times of the 1950s. Its operation, though, represented LT's unchanging approach, and this late journey persisted until 1965 long after it could be justified. Positioning the bus for the service on Thursday and Saturday was by way of the 386A route which followed the 350 from Hertford to Hadham Ford where the route turned up the narrow lane to Wellpond Green and into Standon via the normal 386 routeing. The section through the tiny hamlet of Wellpond Green had begun in May 1950 when the 386 had been diverted from the direct main road route to Standon. Journeys to Buntingford ran via the 331 through Braughing and Hare Street and there were three trips between Bishop's Stortford and Buntingford with two more as far as Standon.

In 1955, the routes west to Welwyn (388) and east to Sawbridgeworth (389) were separate. The 388 was more frequent, and at its outer end had a few peak hour journeys extended a little way up the Great North Road from Welwyn village to Mardley Hill to provide a link for commuters to London from Welwyn North Station which the route passed. Otherwise the route terminated in Welwyn village at Prospect Place just off the A1 by some picturesque cottages. After leaving Hertford, past Sele Farm, there was no passenger traffic to be had all the way through woods along the single track winding lane into Tewin village. Tewin though was a large rambling village, and there was good traffic potential all the way along the rest of the route through Harmer Green into Welwyn itself. This justified the hourly headway that ran all day Monday to Saturday. Even on Sundays in the mid-1950s the 388 timetable had five journeys. On Saturday mornings the 9.00am to Welwyn and back was duplicated to account for extra passengers going shopping, and on weekdays, there were buses at 9.25am and 9.41am from Welwyn into Hertford. There were also two journeys within 20 minutes of each other after lunch on Saturday. The timetable though was compiled so that buses were not timed to pass each other along the half mile or so of single track lane into Tewin from the Hertford direction, but in reality there were a couple of timings over the years that meant buses needed to pass near Tewin. Having driven both GSs and RFs along this route several times myself, I can testify that passing another bus is impossible for much of the way, so how drivers actually overcame this situation is unclear!

The 389 from Hertford to Sawbridgeworth ran every two hours and linked many villages along the way. GS 72 was one of those sent to Hertford in April 1954 and stayed until August 1958 when it was one of the five GSs hired by Great Yarmouth. On its return apart from a brief spell at St Albans it saw no further use and was sold in 1963. The bus is seen in High Wych in 1956 and the rural nature of the route is evident.
(Peter Mitchell)

The 389 to Sawbridgeworth followed the main A414 which in those days went through St Margarets, Stanstead Abbots, Eastwick and Gilston. Half a century later all these villages have been by-passed by a fast dual carriageway, but then the A414 was a winding country road carrying little traffic. Harlow was only just being developed, so the 389 had no need to serve it and Sawbridgeworth was a large enough place to attract traffic on its own. The traffic potential was quite good all the way along the route, and it had a two-hourly headway seven days a week, supplemented by the 350A and 399 as far as Stanstead Abbots providing a good service to Ware and Hertford. After GSs had replaced former Green Line coaches on the 389, their lower seating capacity proved inadequate on many journeys, such that a morning and afternoon weekday journey were both duplicated on schooldays, while on Saturday afternoons the whole timetable was duplicated all the way to Sawbridgeworth and back. As part of the frequent re-organisation of Hertford's routes, the 388 and 389 were linked as one long route in October 1956, but the level of service over the combined route – including the duplication – remained unchanged.

The longest rural route from Hertford was the 384 which ran through miles of open country on a very indirect route to Stevenage, continuing further north along the Great North Road before running through Willian to terminate in Letchworth, the whole journey taking around 90 minutes. From Sacombe through Dane End to Whempstead, through Cutting Hill, and from Benington to Walkern, the roads were narrow all the way with many places where a bus could not pass another vehicle. Even in 1955 there were only seven journeys with a couple of extra peak hour journeys during the week between Benington, Stevenage and Letchworth. These operated via a slightly different route in Letchworth to serve the factories on the road linking the town to the Great North Road, and were run as 384B. On Saturday, there were some additional short journeys which ran from Stevenage just as far as Walkern to provide shopping facilities and a late evening return, and on Sundays there were five journeys with a sixth in the morning from Hertford to Dane End. Despite the sparse countryside and limited passenger potential, the route often carried good loads because of the links it provided to Ware, Hertford, Stevenage and Letchworth. Stevenage was still a small country town but attracted plenty of passengers, and by 1955 its expansion was well under way. The 384A was the infrequent service to the isolated village of Great Munden about three miles beyond Dane End along narrow, often single track lanes for much of the way. On reaching Great Munden, buses ran through the village for another half mile to an isolated cross roads by the school where they reversed, that being the first place where buses could turn. There were just two journeys in the afternoon during the week, and four Saturday afternoon and evening, all of which continued running long after they could be justified, and the decline is referred to later in chapter five. Like many routes, the Saturday timetable was greatly enhanced, and in the afternoon the 384/384A provided an hourly headway as far as Dane End until early evening. Hertford always operated most of the service but Hitchin ran one bus as part of an allocation which also included Epping and involved cross working on the 308, 308A, 384 and 399. Stevenage rostered an RT on a couple of Letchworth peak journeys, but otherwise RFs ran the whole timetable. The narrow lanes would have been ideally suited for GS operation but several journeys carried loads where the capacity of GSs would have been inadequate. GSs were never formally allocated to the 384/384A but were at times used as duplicates on the morning and afternoon schoolday journeys between Hertford and Dane End.

The 384A was one of the most infrequent rural routes, never running more than two journeys on weekdays and four on Saturdays. Great Munden is an isolated village reached along about three miles of largely single track lane from Dane End on the main 384 route, but although the timetable was eventually reduced to just two journeys on Saturday afternoons, it lasted until May 1976 before London Country finally abandoned it. The blind shows the qualifying point at the schools which were about half a mile beyond the village but the first point where buses could reverse at the cross roads. RF 604 is waiting in Hertford Bus Station for a driver to take the bus to Great Munden sometime in the late 1960s. (Simon Butler collection)

The 308 ran from Hertford to Newgate Street and was extended on to Cuffley in June 1951. After conversion to omo in July 1956, the route had a mixed allocation of RF and GS which remained the case until Hertford's last GSs were withdrawn in 1968. GS 33 was displaced from Amersham in October 1962 and spent 18 months at Hertford before being delicensed in 1964. After more than a year out of use, it went to Garston where it would become one of the last two in service in 1972. It is climbing up towards Bayford Green on a 308 to Cuffley. (Peter Mitchell)

Hertford ran two routes to the south to Cuffley (308) and Little Berkhampstead (308A). Brickenden and Bayford were reasonable sources of traffic, but there was little else to generate profitable passenger numbers, since Little Berkhampstead was a straggling, smallish community, and Newgate Street no bigger. The route down into Cuffley passed some large houses through an affluent area providing minimal traffic, having been extended there in June 1951, mainly to provide a link to the railway. Cuffley, typical of many such places on the outer fringes of London, had its rail link for commuters, but as a source of traffic it was not a major attraction for a route from Hertford since most passengers used the Central Area 242 route to either Cheshunt or Potters Bar. The Monday to Friday timetable was always sparse with eight journeys as far as Epping Green where the two routes split, four journeys each going on to either Cuffley or Little Berkhampstead. The actual timing of the journeys was also strange with the first bus out to Little Berkhampstead not leaving Hertford until 11.04am. On Saturdays though, the timetable was transformed with 14 departures from Hertford including the 2.34pm to Cuffley being duplicated as far as Newgate Street. The 1.49pm from Cuffley and the 2.01pm from Little Berkhampstead were timed to meet at Epping Green to run together back into Hertford to carry the extra afternoon shoppers, a process which was reversed later with two departures back at 4.34pm. In 1955 there were also five journeys on Sundays (three to Cuffley and two to Little Berkhampstead) but they became a victim of the 1958 cuts.

The other main east to west routes from Hertford had, in 1955, no real connections between them. The 393 ran from Harlow only as far as Hoddesden, the link over Hertford Heath from there into Hertford being run as part of the 342 route. The 393 was generally an hourly service worked with GSs from Epping and provided a link for Harlow village on the main A11. The villages of Nettleswell and Great Parndon, which were to be swallowed up by Harlow New Town, still appeared in the timetable, and this was very much a minor route until Harlow New Town began to expand. The 399 ran from Hertford to Epping and Coopersale, but although generally hourly, some journeys from Epping terminated at St Margarets since there were plenty of alternative buses beyond there to Ware and Hertford. To the west of Hertford, the 372 ran along the main A414 to Cole Green before turning off to run into Welwyn Garden City. It is difficult to believe now that there was no direct bus link between Hertford and Welwyn Garden City until the 372 was introduced in May 1948. The Hertford North to Welwyn Garden City branch line railway had provided a link, but even in the late 1940s this consisted of only a handful of trains each way, since Welwyn Garden was hardly developed and offered little in the way of worthwhile traffic. The 372 made use of a new road which had only been completed in 1948 to form a link from the A414 at Cole Green into the centre of Welwyn Garden City through the new housing areas then being developed. When first introduced, two small Leyland Cubs were used to run an hourly service, each bus working additional short town service journeys in Welwyn Garden between trips from Hertford. The route quickly became a success however. Displaced Green Line Ts replaced the Cubs, replaced in turn by crew-operated RFs in 1954 with additional peak hour and Saturday journeys including much duplication.

Before the 372 timetable was increased, buses arriving at Welwyn Garden City from Hertford ran short journeys across the town between Lemsford Lane and Great Gannet, to serve new housing areas then being expanded. These were numbered 372A, and RF 566 is at the turning circle at Great Gannet waiting to work back to Lemsford Lane. (Peter Mitchell)

Hitchin garage was the Country area's northern outpost. United Counties also had a depot in the town and ran the majority of services with main routes to Luton and Bedford, plus local routes to Letchworth and Baldock, the combined frequencies of which provided a ten-minute headway most of the day between Hitchin and Letchworth. United Counties also ran a couple of rural services into Hitchin together with Premier Travel, Smiths of Buntingford and Birch Brothers. Although best known for their long distance service from Kings Cross to Bedford and Rushden, which ran hourly and passed through Hitchin, less well known is Birch Brothers' network of rural routes that operated in the triangle roughly bordered by Hitchin, Luton and Welwyn Garden City. These, although inside the LPTA, were outside the 'Special Area' boundary and had thus continued unaltered after the 1933 Act. It was a very sparsely populated area providing only minimal passenger numbers. Birch's 204 service to Whitwell shared the route jointly with LT's 304 which ran on through Kimpton and Wheathampstead to St Albans. The Whitwell to Hitchin section was inside the LPTA but outside the 'Special Area' and LT's operations were limited to three journeys late afternoon and evening on Saturdays, and two on Sunday. These journeys had been retained to preserve LT's running rights over the route while the 'basic service' belonged to Birch. During the rest of the week, London Transport's 304 from St Albans terminated at Whitwell where connections were made with Birch 204 into Hitchin, which ran five or six journeys a day, with extra ones on Tuesday and Saturday for Hitchin market days. In 1955, Hitchin ran the 364 to Luton, 383 to Weston, and had one working on the 308/384/399. The 383 had been introduced in February 1948 to provide a daily link into Hitchin. The 383 also served a new housing estate at Walsworth on the edge of Hitchin which had a number of short journeys in addition to the two-hourly service to Weston. The route's introduction in 1948 however had met with fierce opposition from Smith's of Buntingford who already had an established route linking Weston to Hitchin, albeit only on market days. Smith's opposition was based on the fact that the route – although inside the LPTA – was outside the 'Special Area' and so London Transport did not have the right to operate over these roads without the required road service licence.

When delivered, the first 25 short RFs were used for tours and sightseeing. RF 16 went to Riverside garage when new in May 1951 and was one of ten repainted for use on Green Line routes in October 1956 to provide more capacity as the network expanded, although it was common practice for them to be used on bus routes. It served at six different Country area garages before being withdrawn from Luton at the end of the 1962 summer season. It spent only a short period as a spare coach at Stevenage at the end of 1959 and is working duty SV24, the 'spare bus' from the 383 allocation which ran additional peak and school journeys. It is on the stand at St Mary's Square in Hitchin waiting to work a short town service journey to Purwell Lane Estate. (S J Butler collection)

London Transport contended that the additional powers granted by the BTC referred to earlier gave them the right to introduce new routes such as the 383, albeit outside the 'Special Area'. Smith's, supported by the Passenger Vehicle Operators Association, took London Transport to court. Whatever the rights or wrongs, after protracted presentations, London Transport prevailed and the 383 became one of the first routes to receive new GSs in 1953. Although London Transport won the case, they received a great deal of criticism for what was widely seen as their high handed approach, and the 383 proved to be the only new route started in such a way. Indeed the handing over of the licence for the section of the 852 from Horsham to Ewhurst after only three months operation was an example of London Transport's more conciliatory approach following the criticism they had received in 1948.

United Counties' main trunk route from Hitchin to Luton was a busy double-deck service running every 20 or 30 minutes along the A505 through Great Offley and Stopsley, with a journey time of just half an hour, and was just north of the LPTA boundary. London Transport ran the rural 364 route to the south taking 56 minutes by a very indirect route, and was similar to the 384, traversing many sections of narrow winding lanes. Breachwood Green was the only reasonably sized village roughly half way between Hitchin and Luton and which had to be served by a double run off the line of the main route. The other villages along the way – Gosmore, Preston, Ley Green, Kings Walden, Cockernhoe and Tea Green – were all small hamlets, but since the route linked two important towns, then it justified an hourly headway most of the day, requiring two RFs from Hitchin. On Tuesday and Saturday, a couple of extra short journeys ran out to Preston and back, and Luton garage ran some peak hour journeys to Breachwood Green. On leaving Luton, the route passed the then huge Vauxhall motor works, and the entrance to what was then a very small Luton Airport. Just beyond there though, the road quickly became single track and went into open country – a very different scene from what it became as Luton Airport swallowed up acres of surrounding farmland towards Cockernhoe and Breachwoood Green over the next three decades.

Luton garage rostered RTs on a few 364/364A peak hour journeys to serve the large Vauxhall Motors factory near Luton Airport. On a wet day, RT 2516 waits outside the factory in the late 1960s to work one of these journeys on a 364 to Flamstead. The running number LS 9 on the bus was used for most of these journeys.

RURAL NORTH WEST ROUTES

To the north west of Hemel Hempstead were two largely rural routes providing an indirect link between Watford and Hemel Hempstead. Leaving Watford the routes shared the busy A414 to Croxley with several others after which they struck off the main road through the long straggling village of Sarratt, on to Chipperfield and Bovingdon. They then shared the road with the joint Rover Bus and LT 316 into Hemel Hempstead. During the week the section from Watford was every two hours with all journeys operating as 317, running on from Hemel Hempstead to Berkhamsted with a total through journey time of an hour and 50 minutes, but on Saturdays the 337 from Dunstable also ran through to Watford to give a joint hourly headway with the 317. The 318 shared the same road as far as Sarratt to provide more journeys, and on Saturday afternoons shopping traffic justified an hourly service to Sarratt which, with the 317 and 337, gave two buses an hour into Watford. There were even five 318 journeys during Sunday afternoon and evening as far as Sarratt to supplement the two-hourly 317 journeys. The 318A turned off the Sarratt road about three miles out of Croxley, into Chandlers Cross and a little way further to terminate at the small hamlet of Bucks Hill. This was less frequent but still ran ten journeys Monday to Friday, eight Saturday, and four Sunday afternoon and evening. Garston ran the 318/318A with RTs which had become necessary to cater for the higher loadings on the route through Watford to Abbots Langley, but in 1955 the 317 and 337 were operated by Hemel Hempstead with single deck 15T13s, which, with their 31 seats, had limited capacity on some journeys. These smaller buses though were adequate for the rural sections to Berkhamsted and Dunstable, so in July 1956 the imbalance was solved by withdrawing the 317 and 337 between Watford and Hemel Hempstead and extending the 318 on from Sarratt into Hemel Hempstead at roughly the same service levels, thus greatly increasing capacity. At the same time, the Ts were replaced with RFs on the 317 but continued to be allocated to the 337.

The 318/318A were busy routes through Watford linking the expanding estates at Abbots Langley through the town to Croxley, but beyond there the route ran through open countryside to the village of Sarratt, and was extended further to Hemel Hempstead in July 1956 to replace the single deck 317 and 337. The 318A served the isolated villages at Chandlers Cross and Bucks Hill on a limited timetable mentioned in the text. RT 4047 has stopped by the gasometers in north Watford to pick up on a journey to Bucks Hill. The wording on the building site hoarding would not be acceptable in today's more sensitive climate. (Alan Cross)

The 317, 317A and 337 shared a common route from Hemel Hempstead to Water End from where the 337 climbed up narrow lanes on to the downs through Gaddesden Row and Studham before running along the edge of Dunstable Downs to descend into Dunstable itself. The decision to continue running this with crew single deckers when the 317/317A were converted seems odd in hindsight as the 337 offered no more potential traffic than the route to Berkhamsted, but this had more to do with balancing remaining crew rosters and the number of converted RFs available than the actual passenger traffic carried at the time. The 337 was roughly every two hours Monday to Friday with a regular two-hourly headway Saturday, and in summer 1955 there were still six Sunday journeys. Hemel Hempstead's 337 schedules also ran the 352 short journeys from Dunstable to Dagnall during the week. This was one of the Country area's remotest routes which might have been profitable once, but carried few passengers after the peak had passed. For a short time there had been an additional service from Dunstable to Ashridge Isolation Hospital numbered 352A consisting of just a single journey on Wednesday and Sunday afternoon, but it had been an early post-war casualty. The full route ran from Dunstable to Berkhamsted, but since roughly half its length was shared with the 317 between Ringshall and Berkhamsted, the through service ran only at weekends. Between Ringshall and the main A41 at Northchurch, there was almost no passenger traffic as the route ran through open country past Ashridge Estate. During the week therefore, there was a limited service from Dunstable to the small village of Dagnall, running four journeys only on Wednesday and Friday with an extra journey on Wednesday evening, leaving Dunstable at 8.19pm. Why this late Wednesday journey was run at all can only be guessed at since the cinema (and bingo if there was any) would not have finished by then. When a 337 bus arrived at Dunstable it then worked the short 352 journey to Dagnall and back before returning to Hemel Hempstead. One bus was rostered to operate this but even with the minimum permitted layovers between each journey, the whole circuit took 2hrs 5mins giving an irregular

RLH 6 and T 775 lay over at Berkhamsted Station at the old stand on the offside of the road. This photo was taken in 1954 and Sundays were the only time when Amersham used RLHs on the 353, interworking them from the 305 allocation. The timetables for the 353 and 317 were such that buses were never timed to be on the stand at the same time, and there were no short 353 journeys to and from Amersham, so RLH 6 is working an unscheduled extra journey although the running number MA14 suggests it is part of the main service. T 775 has worked all the way from Watford on the 317, but the Watford to Hemel Hempstead section was transferred to the double deck 318 in July 1956 to provide increased capacity and the Ts on the 317 replaced with RFs. (Bus of Yesteryear)

Tring had a single T which they rostered to the 387 during the week. Passenger numbers rarely justified crew operation, which nevertheless continued even into London Country days to balance rosters on the 301/302 which became more unbalanced as peak and Sunday timetables were reduced. A rear nearside view of one of these buses is unusual, and T 790 stands on the forecourt of Tring garage waiting for the next journey.
(Travel Lens)

timing. Also because the return timings on the 337 from Dunstable needed to be the same every day, but the 352 Dagnall journeys only ran on Wednesday and Friday, the bus stood idle at Dunstable for 47 minutes between each journey on the other three days of the week to wait for departure time back to Hemel Hempstead. This arrangement, certainly one of the more wasteful of the Country area's workings, lasted right until 1972 when the 337 was withdrawn beyond Studham. Some further use was eventually made of the bus on Tuesday and Thursday by running four journeys to and from Kensworth on the 343A, but these ran for only a short period from 1967.

The Saturday and Sunday timetable over the full length of the 352 was run by Tring garage. The bus worked out from Tring in the morning in service as a 301 to Berkhamsted Station and the roster included the instruction that the bus must carry a 301 fare chart. There were five return journeys on Saturdays, the first leaving Berkhamsted at 10.53am, the last arriving back at Berkhamsted at 8.47pm when the bus then worked the 8.50pm 301 journey from Berkhamsted Station back to Tring garage. On Sundays the timetable was the same with the exception of the first round trip, giving four return journeys. Since the end to end running time was only 39 minutes with a headway of every two hours (although for some odd reason even this was not regular) the buses had a long layover in Dunstable of between 45 and 50 minutes. Tring ran this duty with a crew-operated 15T13 and must have been one of the easiest shifts. Crew operation was never justified, but apart from two omo duties on the local 387, Tring garage was entirely crew operated and had spare crews on Saturdays and Sundays when the 301 allocation was less than during the week.

The 352 was surely one of the least profitable routes, although one or two Saturday journeys did carry some shoppers into Dunstable. Perhaps more in hope than expectation, a Sunday service was operated on Easter Mondays until 1960, but the regular Sunday service to Berkhamsted was an early casualty being withdrawn in the 1957 winter schedules. Two Sunday afternoon Dagnall shorts were retained however, being worked off the 337 in the same way as the weekday journeys, but were short lived and did not survive the October 1958 cuts in the aftermath of the strike. Tring continued to operate the 352 on Saturdays, the bus being used on part of the 387 during the week. Crew operation of this bus to balance rosters from the 301/302 became increasingly unnecessary, but continued until November 1964 when the 352 became interworked with the 317 and 337 from Two Waters garage. Without having to work the 352 on Saturdays, the 337 ran to a regular two-hourly headway on that day with only a short layover at Dunstable, and this allowed just one bus to work the route between Boxmoor and Dunstable all day on a regular two-hourly headway.

The 317 and 317A were equally rural. After Water End, the 317 came to the cross roads at Great Gaddesden, where over the years odd journeys ran down into the village to turn at The Cock and Bottle pub. Beyond Great Gaddesden, the route traversed open farmland for some way before turning off the main road and up a steep narrow lane to Hudnall Common. Here it was joined again by the 317A which turned off at Water End to run through the hamlet of Nettleden along some very narrow lanes, and the two routes then ran together for another mile or so to Little Gaddesden. Here the 317A journeys turned in the car park of the Bridgewater Arms pub for the return to Hemel Hempstead, and the 317 carried on for about half a mile to Ringshall where it joined the 352 routeing to run across Ashridge Common to the main A41 at Northchurch. As referred to above this section of the route had minimal potential, but Berkhamsted and Hemel Hempstead did at least make a destination for shopping and commuting to work. In 1955, the 317 ran to a roughly two-hourly headway with eight journeys to Berkhamsted Monday to Friday and seven back to Hemel Hempstead. Two evening journeys which turned

Operation of the short journeys to Dagnall on the 352 is described in the text. There was virtually no passenger potential between Dunstable and Dagnall, the village itself being little more than a small hamlet. After the Saturday service from Berkhamsted was withdrawn, the Dagnall journeys continued with minimal passengers until London Country abandoned what was left in in February 1972. An empty RF 622 has reversed at Dagnall for the return to Dunstable as the driver fills in the waybill. (J.G.S. Smith)

at Ringshall during the week were extended on to Berkhamsted on Saturdays, and there were six Sunday journeys, later cut to five before all were abandoned after the 1958 strike. Before the 352 Sunday service was withdrawn from Berkhamsted, the common section between there and Ringshall had no fewer than ten Sunday journeys which was – even by 1956 – a wasteful over-provision on a route with so little potential. The first 317 into Berkhamsted each morning ran a short 301 back to Boxmoor Station direct along the A41 to provide an extra peak journey to the main 301 schedule, and from Boxmoor then worked the next 317 back via Gaddesden to Berkhamsted again. The 317A was always a very marginal operation with just four journeys through Nettleden during the week and only three on Saturdays. During the week, the last 317A from Hemel Hempstead left around 7pm, and on reaching Little Gaddesden the bus was timed to wait for a 317 from Berkhamsted, both buses then departing Little Gaddesden within a minute or two of each other, one via the 317, the other via the 317A back into Hemel Hempstead. The 317 from Berkhamsted might have had the odd passenger, but the 317A bus would have almost certainly run completely empty, and was another product of the wasteful and rigid operating practices which over time contributed to London Transport's worsening financial position.

Amersham garage was second only to Hertford in its network of rural routes. Its operations in the mid-1950s were interesting in that they ran the greatest number of the fleet's non-standard buses. The May 1955 allocation lists ten RLH, eleven GS, and five 15T13 which together represented about two thirds of its allocated bus fleet. The eleven GSs at the time represented the largest allocation of any garage although Hertford needed ten for its 1955 Saturday schedules when Amersham's GS run-out was reduced to nine. The majority of the single deckers worked routes based from Chesham out to Buckland Common and St Leonards on the 348, the 397 over the Chilterns through Cholesbury and Wigginton to Tring, and the 394 which was almost circular, running from Hyde Heath into Chesham and then via an indirect route to Great Missenden and passing very close to Hyde Heath again on the way. Chesham also had two town services to the council estates at Chesham Moor and Pond Park where route 348A had been introduced in October 1953 as that estate began to be developed. The 398 ran from Amersham to Beaconsfield (with two journeys run as 398A to Winchmore Hill), buses off the 398 being used to run the short 373 between Penn and Beaconsfield. Narrow sections of route on the 348, 397 and 398A meant that these routes were not then approved for RF operation, and because of extensive interworking between routes, it meant that the whole of the schedules for the 348, 348A, 373, 397, 398 and 398A were GS operated.

The total Monday to Friday morning run out for the 348, 348A and 397 was for five GSs with a sixth required on schooldays, this and one other running back to Amersham after the morning peak. Two of the remaining four buses ran light journeys to Amersham and back during the day for crew changes, but in the afternoon, all six were required again to accommodate extra school runs and evening peak journeys. On Saturdays, four GSs were required for the morning with a fifth leaving Amersham garage at 11.41am to augment services for the rest of the day. From Chesham Broadway, this bus ran a 348 short to Bellingdon followed by a 348A to Pond Park Estate, then running as duplicate bus to the 1.22pm 397 departure to Tring where two GSs were rostered to work right through to Tring and back together. On their return from Tring, they were timed at Cholesbury at 2.27pm only five minutes behind another short journey, thus

providing three GSs in the space of five minutes with a total capacity of 78 seats from Cholesbury into Chesham to cope with the volume of Saturday afternoon shoppers. This was despite the fact that Cholesbury and Hawridge were not particularly large and the road along the valley into Chesham had little other habitation, but shows once again just how popular Saturday afternoons were for shopping trips into nearby towns before many people had cars and when men still worked on Saturday mornings. The 348 was a short route which split at the outer end, terminating either at Buckland Common or the tiny hamlet of St Leonards, and although Buckland had been served before the War, the short extension to St Leonards had only been started in March 1947. Bellingdon, approximately half way along the route was larger, the timetable providing two buses every hour almost all day as far as there. There were extra peak hour and Saturday shopping journeys, and school buses were duplicated to bring children into Chesham. The service beyond Bellingdon was roughly every hour with Buckland Common having more journeys than St Leonards, and because the road as far as Bellingdon provided more passengers the large number of short journeys terminating there survived into the 1960s. Two GSs were rostered on Sunday afternoons, one running nine journeys on the 348 (six to Buckland Common and three to St Leonards) and the other seven journeys to Tring and back on the 397. The time-tables ran into late evening and it was after 11.00pm before the two buses returned to Amersham garage. Despite the large cuts to Sunday timetables on rural services in the late 1950s across the network – especially after the 1958 strike – the Sunday timetables of these routes remained unchanged right through until 1962 when the GSs were replaced with RFs.

The 397 timetable between Chesham and Tring was hourly with a few short journeys to Cholesbury and some duplication on Saturdays. On this journey however, GS 75 appears to be empty as it pauses by the end of a lane having just left Cholesbury with a Triumph Herald in the distance going the other way. The 397 was withdrawn in October 1962 to be replaced by an extension of the 348 when the GSs were replaced with RFs (Peter Mitchell)

RLHs 1–6 were delivered to Amersham in May 1950 where they were rostered to the 336. The 305 and 359 were officially rostered for RTs, but a temporary shortage of new RTs resulted in five more new RLHs from the second batch (RLH 46–50) being allocated in October 1952. These nine buses then covered almost all of the double deck workings on the three routes until more RTs could be made available. RLH 1 comes through Chalfont on a 305 to Beaconsfield. It was taken for overhaul in October 1956 and spent the rest of its life in the Central area until it was withdrawn from Hornchurch garage at the end of 1964.

The 394 was the other of Chesham's rural routes, and in 1955 was still crew worked with 15T13s, the sole exception at various times being a late evening short journey to Chartridge which was run with a GS off the 348/397. There were also a couple of GS operated morning schoolday duplicates to Chartridge. There were frequent short journeys all day to and from Chartridge, a straggling village only two miles from Chesham, the road there being largely inter-war 'ribbon development' which had come about with the Metropolitan Line service to Chesham, and provided plenty of passengers. The 394 ran through Chesham to Hyde End, the 394A to the estate at Chesham Moor, and a few journeys on the 394B to the Nashleigh Arms just north of the town centre. Passenger levels justified crew operation on these routes, but beyond Chartridge the route ran through more remote countryside on a roughly hourly headway to Great Missenden where it turned at the station. The other leg of the route out to Hyde Heath ran roughly every two hours with three journeys running on to Hyde End, which was only about half a mile from South Heath on the Great Missenden leg of the route, thus making an almost circular service. In 1955, four Ts were rostered to run the route on weekdays with a fifth to run additional school journeys. There was a small addition to the 394 when London Transport took over Lee & District's route to Kings Ash on 4th January 1956. This paralleled the 394 as far as Lee Common before running via the delightfully named Swan Bottom to terminate at Kings Ash where the bus reversed into a stone track at one of the most isolated turning points anywhere in the Home Counties. The Kings Ash and Swan Bottom journeys were numbered 394D and the rosters were adjusted without the need for additional buses, since the Kings Ash journeys were minimal with just two trips on Wednesday and Friday afternoons, three on Saturday afternoons and a fourth leaving Chesham Broadway at 8.22pm; this journey probably carried nobody beyond Chartridge. There were also some short journeys which went from Swan Bottom cross roads a few hundred yards to the Old Swan pub, including a late Saturday evening trip designed to pick up people after pub closing time which for a time doubtless enjoyed a good load. The timing of this allowed a 30-minute layover at the pub and one wonders whether the crew ever took advantage of the opportunity for a quick drink before returning to Chesham! The two Sunday afternoon journeys previously run by Lee & District were also retained but this represented a complete waste of resources. The Kings Ash leg was a failure from the start and was abandoned on 4th May 1958, having been run by London Transport for only a little over two years. The tiny hamlet of The Lee however retained a service since it was easily served by running round a loop from Lee Common via Swan Bottom so that the two Wednesday and Friday journeys continued to serve the village. On Saturdays though the service was increased considerably, even Sunday journeys being run round this way, lasting for several more years.

In 1955, Amersham garage rostered nine RLHs on weekdays and ten on Saturdays, and with the 336 and 359 both worked by them it was possible to complete the entire journey from Watford to Aylesbury by lowbridge double decker. The 359 at the time was also one of only three routes that the Country Area worked jointly with another operator, and ran to an hourly headway seven days a week with LT providing one bus from Amersham, and United Counties providing the other – usually a lowbridge Bristol K from Aylesbury depot. The 336 was a generally busy route, and combined with several others to provide a frequent service between Watford and Rickmansworth. It was paralleled by the 335 all the way from Watford to Chalfont providing a 30-minute headway before that route turned south for the long run to Windsor, and by the 703 Green Line which ran alongside the 336 between Rickmansworth and Amersham. On Saturdays, extra 336 short journeys between Watford and Chorleywood increased the frequency to 20 minutes, and there were a number of shorts between Chesham and Chalfont throughout the week. Linking Amersham, Chorleywood, Rickmansworth and Watford, passing Metropolitan line stations along the way, the 336 benefited from a good proportion of short distance passengers, helping to sustain the 1955 service levels longer than some lesser routes.

Despite Green Line weekend and leisure traffic beginning to decline, in 1955 passenger numbers reached a record 34½ million, having increased year on year from the 25 million carried in 1947. The success of the 725 begun in July 1953 was such that its initial hourly headway was increased to 30 minutes only nine months later, an improvement requiring six further RFs. In October 1955, the 717 from Woking to Welwyn Garden City was renumbered 716A and extended to Stevenage to augment the existing 716.

RF 17 was one of the 10 Private Hire RFs converted for Green Line service in 1956. It served at several garages as a relief coach, and its last summer was 1962 when it was allocated to Dunton Green. With a queue of traffic the other way, and with full Green Line roof boards in place, it climbs away from Riverhead on a 705 near the end of its long journey from Windsor. It was withdrawn in October 1962 and sold to a dealer the following year when several of these were disposed of. (Terry Cooper)

The 716 from Chertsey to Hitchin was reinstated in March 1946, followed two months later by the 717 from Woking to Welwyn Garden City. The two routes joined at Addlestone and then ran to a 30 minute headway all the way to Lemsford where the 716 continued on up the A1 Great North Road. The 717 was diverted through the growing LCC Overspill Estate at Sheerwater in December 1952, and renumbered 716A in October 1955 when the 717 number was used for a new additional service as described in the text. RF 150 picks up passengers in Kingston. (Capital Transport)

The 717 number was retained for a new service between London and Welwyn Garden City which diverted from the Great North Road to serve Welham Green, and six months later through the new estates at South Hatfield. These changes increased the service between London and Welwyn Garden City by 50% and doubled the service beyond there to Stevenage. The garage at Stevenage opened at the same time, and a further four RFs had to be found for its contribution to the new 716A. The success of the 725 led to the possibility of a similar route across the north London suburbs. Numbered 724, it would have run from Windsor through Hayes, Sudbury, Finchley, Tottenham and on to Romford perhaps even to Brentwood and would very likely have been as successful as the 725. Central area bus staff however – perhaps having seen the success of the southern 725 route – were very much opposed to the idea as they felt it would abstract traffic from their routes, and so the idea was never progressed. It was also an example of the obdurate thinking of the Union which would overshadow many attempts to improve the network.

Almost all garages that operated Green Line routes ran additional coaches to supplement the basic service, particularly at weekends. The daily run-out in the allocation book dated 18th May 1955 (excluding the east London RT-operated routes) required 204 RFs Monday to Saturday with just one fewer on Sunday to operate the standard timetable. The extent of duplication required can be appreciated from the revision to the allocations dated 13th July 1955 for the summer schedules. This listed a total of 248 RFs scheduled for Saturdays and no fewer than 271 on Sundays. In addition to these, 21 RTs were scheduled as duplicates on Saturdays, and 35 on Sundays. In total therefore 269 vehicles were scheduled on Saturday against a basic run-out of 204, and 306 on Sundays against a basic run-out of 203 – an increase of 50%. Some of the highest levels of duplication were on the 704 and 705 to cater for the large numbers of day trippers to Windsor as well as Westerham and Sevenoaks, both of which attracted many day trippers. With additional duplicates, Epping garage put out no fewer than 24 Green Line RFs on Sundays, to contend with large numbers of people from London's East End who would travel out to Epping Forest. Windsor ran an additional 11 RFs on Sundays, operations also including the 718 which served Kingston, Hampton Court and Staines along the River Thames – all popular leisure destinations – as well as Epping Forest at the northern end of the route. Dorking garage put out an extra eight RFs in addition to its daily schedule of 16 to run reliefs from London for passengers to Boxhill and Dorking itself. On Sundays and in school holidays, Romford garage ran the 726 through London to Whipsnade Zoo requiring six RTs for service. Even this number had two further duplicate RTs and fully loaded buses would leave Whipsnade in convoy in the late afternoon for the journey home.

RT 3248 was one of the large batch of 36 new RTs painted in Green Line livery and sent to Romford, where they replaced Daimlers on 1st August 1950. The 726 had been introduced in May 1946 to run only from London to Whipsnade, buses running light into London to take up service. It was altered to start from Romford in May 1954, and three years later served the large LCC Estate at Harold Hill. In the 1950s many duplicates were run on fine days and Bank Holidays, but the route would suffer a steep decline from about 1960. Passengers could board the return journey only at Whipsnade, and RT 3248 has stopped to set down at Baker Street on its way home.
(Alan Cross)

The 478 was a GS route with a few peak hour journeys worked with RTs from Swanley's 401 and 477 rosters, but GS operation was short lived. The route was extended in Swanley to St Mary's Estate and the last GS workings were replaced with RTs in October 1956. The 478 ran to a very limited timetable with only a few journeys running to West Kingsdown and Wrotham, and RT 1065 comes up an empty main road in Farningham village on a journey to West Kingsdown. It is difficult to believe that this road was on the main A20 London to Maidstone and Folkestone road until the by-pass was built before the War. (Peter Mitchell)

The 704 enjoyed frequent duplication on the southern section to cater for day trippers to Tunbridge Wells and Sevenoaks. RT 3149 is working a duplicate into south London as far as New Cross and has stopped opposite Clarks College in Bromley. The conductor is helping a passenger off the bus while the driver holds the bus on the handbrake and looks in the nearside mirror. On arriving at New Cross, it is likely that the crew will run back light to Dunton Green garage. (Alan Cross)

Even this was not always the full complement though. On particularly fine Sundays and Bank Holidays, even more buses would be on standby to provide further Green Line capacity and additional crews would be required to *'work to instructions'* to run ad hoc extra journeys over and above the scheduled duplicates. Dorking garage would post an inspector to control loading at Burford Bridge at the foot of Boxhill. With four Green Line coaches per hour, a 20-minute headway on the 470 and a 30-minute headway on the Central Area 93 (which was extended to Dorking on summer Sundays), plus scheduled Green Line duplicates, even this might not be enough in the late afternoon as queues of passengers built up for the homeward journey. The inspector would telephone Dorking garage, and an RT on standby *'to instructions'* would be called up to assist in moving the crowds.

Much more could be written about operations in other parts of the Country area. The frequent timetables and duplication described above were commonplace everywhere, but once the effects of falling passengers took hold, the process of constant cuts began in an effort to counter falling revenues. At first, only duplicates were withdrawn, but it quickly became necessary to begin stripping out some short journeys and additional shopping facilities. Ownership of televisions and private cars, which grew exponentially from the early 1950s, were the significant factors in rapid reductions of evening and weekend passengers, Sunday services on many bus routes quickly becoming an unsustainable financial burden. The aftermath of the strike in 1958 described in the next chapter was the catalyst for substantial cuts and an acceleration in service reductions which would continue unabated until the end of 1969.

For the first time, traffic congestion was beginning to disrupt running in central London, and some Green Line journeys began to suffer delays during peak hours as a result. Minor though these were – especially in comparison to what was to come – one of Green Line's main attractions was that its services were extremely reliable and ran on time. These delays represented the beginnings of a situation which would over time become one of the major factors in the slow death of the Green Line network described in *Green No More*. Outside the Central Bus area, however, private car traffic volumes had not yet begun to grow. The nature of the country towns and villages had changed little since pre-war days and was still very different from the traffic clogged urban sprawl which would overtake much of the Country area over the following 25 years.

The second half of the 1950s would see much unrest among the workforce and the process of endless cuts to services would begin to accelerate.

Britwell became one of the larger LCC Overspill Estates, built to the north of the main Bath Road just west of Slough. In December 1957, London Transport and Thames Valley began a joint service to areas of the new estate by extending their respective routes 484 and 64. In July 1959, route 400 replaced the 484 together with the 457B to Wexham Court Farm to form a new service linking these estates in one cross town service. RT 634 runs through some typical 1950s housing. (Peter Mitchell)

3 Strife and Cuts: the late 1950s

There was a further slight drop in passengers during 1956 including a 3% fall on Green Line routes. The poor summer of that year was a factor which contributed to this, but in the main numbers were still being underpinned by expansion of the New Towns, Overspill Estates, and new houses being built in most towns throughout the Country area. In fact the total Green Line mileage operated grew slightly in 1956 as a result of two new routes which were started that year. The 719 from Hemel Hempstead to London began in July, opening up a new route into London through Kingsbury and Kilburn, and between Hemel Hempstead and Watford, running via Abbots Langley which was then beginning to expand. A service via Hertford Heath numbered 715A to augment the existing 715 began in August and took a different route through north London to open up some further new links.

On the rural country routes, a tentative start had been made on converting routes to one-man operation. The experimental conversion of three RFs in 1954 have been well documented, but it is worth remembering how conservative all bus operators were at the time about introducing omo and dispensing with conductors on routes where passenger loads continued to justify two-man crews on all but the most infrequent rural services. Although pioneering types like the side-engined AEC Q had shown that an entrance forward of the front wheels was feasible, the underfloor-engined single decker with front entrance was still a relatively new concept in the early 1950s. The AEC Regal IV upon which the RF was based was one of the most influential buses in this development along with the Bristol LS (Light Saloon) which appeared in 1950 and proved to be as long lived and reliable as the AEC. But operators in general did not fully embrace the savings which omo could achieve, nor probably appreciated the necessity to move ahead with widespread conversion of less well used routes. The Tilling group companies for example, who had some of the most sparse rural operating areas in the country, were still buying the Bristol L type half cab rear entrance single decker into 1953, Wilts & Dorset even purchasing a final batch as late as 1954. Union agreements for one-man operation were also the subject of long and often difficult negotiations.

At least the Country area had agreements in place for conversions of routes to one-man operation. Although not directly part of this story, the Central area did not. The amount of omo operation on Central area routes had always been minimal, and the last routes had been converted to crew operation in 1949 as passenger numbers grew. London Transport simply allowed the omo agreement with the Union to lapse as it was thought there would be no likelihood of it being necessary in the future. Ten years later they would come to bitterly regret this when it became apparent that suburban RF routes needed to be converted to omo but it would take years of hard fought and often bitter negotiations to achieve agreement. Although Country area agreements were in place, the negotiations for the introduction of the large capacity Merlins on both Central and Country routes would result in long delays and great expense.

Apart from the GSs and the three experimental RF conversions, every single decker in the Country area fleet was still crew operated at the start of 1955, but other than the 30 half cab 15T13s, at least the Country Bus department had a fleet of single deckers that were all capable of being converted for omo. After the success of the experimental buses, the short 419 through Epsom was permanently converted to omo in May 1955, although five additional crew RFs remained rostered on Sunday afternoons for the additional journeys to Long Grove Hospital from Epsom. Seven months later the buses were transferred to the 316 which was converted from RT. These two routes constituted phase one of a process which would continue until December 1966 with the final phase ten. Phase one covering the 316 and 419 replaced ten crew duties with 12 omo duties and saved £3,016 in a full year (at 1955 prices). It is recorded that the conversion cost of each RF was £635, and later that year London Transport authorised the conversion of 60 more RFs, but it was not until May 1956 that the first 15 were ready, and a further year until the remaining 45 were converted by May 1957.

The 419 was the first route on which London Transport experimented with one man operation of larger buses in 1954, the success of which led to the conversion of the whole RF bus fleet. The route had been extended from Epsom to Long Grove Hospital and Brettgrave estate in May 1949. RF 546 runs into Epsom displaying the plastic PAYE sign which became standard from 1960. (Tony Wild)

Phase two of the conversion programme in July 1956 was more ambitious, covering the 308/308A/384/384A/384B/399 at Hertford and Epping, the 317/317A at Hemel Hempstead and the 394/394A/394D at Amersham. Garston also lost one crew peak hour duty when its working on the 319 was converted to GS. Across all the routes, 25 crew duties were replaced with 27 omo duties with a consequent saving of £10,972 per annum.

Initially, it was the crew operated Ts which became surplus, Hemel Hempstead and Amersham between them losing nine Ts. In May 1954, GSs had converted the 361 (Rickmansworth to Chorleywood) to omo, replacing Ts, and on the introduction of winter schedules on 17th October 1956, only nine of the original batch of 30 15T13s were still scheduled for service. Hemel Hempstead retained one of these, but it was used only on a works contract service for the de-Havilland factory in the town. Fine buses though the 15T13s were, they could only be crew operated and had quickly become surplus despite being only eight years old.

October 1956 saw the introduction of one of the most isolated rural routes of all. Numbered 807, it linked Stevenage to Letchworth via Weston and the remote hamlet of Friends Green. Weston already had a roughly two-hourly service on the 383 route into Hitchin, but the 807 was started in order to provide a link to Stevenage for factory workers and afternoon shopping, never providing any facility into Letchworth. The route out from Stevenage was along a mostly single track lane, and Friends Green was so small that it didn't even appear in the timetable, consisting as it did of a few cottages and 'The Anchor' pub which was the fare stage on the fare chart. There was a morning works journey into Stevenage during the week, and a return in the evening which was routed to serve the growing industrial area of Gunnels Wood. Other than that there was just an early afternoon run into Stevenage for shopping with a return trip back later on. The Saturday service consisted only of the afternoon shopping service, and even more of an oddity was that until 1962 there was a Saturday evening departure from Stevenage at 10.00pm. Hitchin garage ran the route when introduced with a GS, and the timetable meant that it was extremely inefficient to operate. For the morning works journey the bus ran empty from Hitchin to Letchworth, and on

The 361 was one of the minor crew worked rural routes converted to omo in 1954 with new GSs. Watford garage ran the route at the time, and on 31st May 1952, T 791 is at the car park terminus in Rickmansworth in the company of an RT, STL and former 10T10 Green Line coach which had been downgraded to bus work. (Alan Cross)

The 316A had nothing in common with the rural 316 to Chesham, and was a limited works service from Apsley Mills to the north of Hemel Hempstead. RT 3028 is about turn right onto St Albans Road back to the town and is running light back to the garage having completed the afternoon journey taking workers home from the Mills. The road sign with the A road number on top and the complete lack of traffic show the period in the early 1960s and illustrate just how different the area was 60 years ago. (Alan Cross)

arriving in Stevenage then had to run empty back to Hitchin since the bus was not needed again until the 2.37pm afternoon run from Letchworth. When this journey arrived in Stevenage, the bus stood idle for just over an hour until the return trip. When Hitchin garage closed in April 1959, the 807 was transferred to the new Stevenage garage. Although some dead mileage was eliminated by running some positioning journeys on the 384 to and from Letchworth, the timetable still meant it remained an inefficient service to run. Given the rapid decline in traffic experienced during the 1960s, it remains a mystery how this minor route survived. Even more bizarre was that the Stevenage rosters in LT years included a crew-operated RF which was used in peak hours for works 'supplementary schedule' and, in order to balance out the shift, there was a period when this bus also ran one of the afternoon shopping journeys on the 807.

RT 3495 was withdrawn at the end of 1963 and spent its last three years at Garston where it waits for a replacement crew while working one of the many short 321 journeys to Rickmansworth which were a feature of the timetable during busy shopping hours. The narrower destination blind on the RT3 roofbox bodies made it more difficult to read, and RT 3495 was one of the last in service.

An innovative new route was started in March 1956. Numbered 803, it was 28 miles long and operated as an express limited stop service from Uxbridge to Welwyn Garden City via Watford and St Albans and was intended to augment the 321 as far as St Albans and the 330 from there to Welwyn Garden City, in addition to providing links through St Albans. During the week, the off-peak service between Rickmansworth and St Albans was withdrawn after seven months, but on Saturdays it ran every half hour all day until early evening. Garston needed six RTs and the 803 ran to a fast timetable, the journey time between Uxbridge and St Albans being 21 minutes less than the parallel 321. When the Green Line network had been reinstated after the War, there had been an intention at one point to start a new route numbered 719 from Windsor to Luton via Uxbridge, Watford and St Albans, but this never materialised. The 803 therefore covered the most important part of this and was at first very successful. But within three years the Saturday service ceased completely as shopping traffic fell away. The Monday to Friday peak hour service however continued for many years and lasted well into London Country days, although it was cut back from Uxbridge, firstly to Maple Cross, then to Rickmansworth and later to Watford.

1957 proved to be a better year for the whole of London Transport's operations, producing a surplus for the first time since 1948. The Country area's net traffic receipts showed a large surplus, but the figure of £663,000 made on Green Line routes was reduced overall by the deficit of £192,000 from bus routes. Towards the end of the year, revenue had been artificially boosted however by the Suez crisis which led to short term fuel rationing and prevented a large proportion of private car usage. Although London Transport had to temporarily reduce fuel

The introduction of the new 803 Express route is described in the text, and was an immediate success. It soon became apparent however that the timetable was an over provision – the initial half hourly Saturday service being abandoned completely after only 18 months in October 1957. RT 4555 was transferred to Garston in May 1955 and soon after the route's introduction is seen at Uxbridge waiting to work to Welwyn Garden City. The Express routes used these attractive blue blinds to distinguish them from the normal routes.

consumption by 5%, 29 spare RTs were licensed for Country area service and some of the private hire RFs were drafted in as Green Line reliefs, and for a few short weeks passenger numbers increased significantly. For the year as a whole, the Country Bus area saw a small drop of just over 1% in passengers on the bus routes compared to 1956. But this was only a short term respite, and made no difference to the general trend of declining passengers. It was significant that London Transport's annual report for 1957 noted that fine weather could no longer be relied on to provide the levels of casual leisure traffic evident in previous years, and that evening traffic was dropping away, a principal reason being that around 45% of households by then owned a television. After the small drop in Green Line passengers in 1956, the network benefited from a large increase of 9.5% during 1957, a surprise given the evidence of a general decline. Although the total was boosted slightly by the effect of the Suez crisis, the year produced a new record of 36.7 million passengers, but it would prove to be the peak as numbers fell away steadily year by year although there was a short-term respite when passenger numbers reached 36 million in 1960. By late 1957, it was apparent that some service reductions were becoming necessary, and the winter schedules that year showed signs of how services were starting to be cut back.

On the Surrey Hills 425 the afternoon augmentation on Monday to Friday was reduced and the 15-minute Saturday headway reduced to 20 minutes, whilst the former 15-minute Sunday headway was by then hourly, with a half-hourly short between Dorking and Gomshall from around midday. The Sunday allocation was halved to four RFs, although Dorking though still retained one extra noted in the allocation book as, *'DS15 to operate to instructions'* for Sundays when fine weather

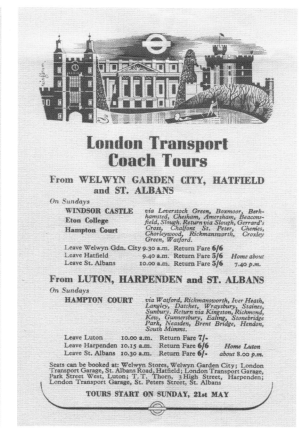

Tours at weekends were very popular and provided much additional revenue. Destinations such as Hampton Court, Windsor and Whipsnade could be guaranteed to attract a decent load of passengers and were run from many garages across the Country Bus area. In the South area, Boxhill and Knole Park at Sevenoaks were also popular. These two leaflets advertising were typical of many printed throughout the 1950s and 1960s, and the fares charged are of interest. (Capital Transport collection)

might still bring extra day trippers to Dorking by train or Green Line. Cuts in Hertford's rural routes saw its GS allocation reduced to five Monday and Friday, six Tuesday, Wednesday and Saturday, and seven Thursday which included one GS for 'Special Duplicates' on the 386 market day journeys to Bishop's Stortford. The reduction in the Saturday requirement came mainly from the conversion of the 386 from GS to RF on that day to provide more capacity. The biggest reduction though was in Hertford's Sunday GS allocation which had dropped from eight to five as the demand for Sunday services began its steep decline. Cuts were also becoming necessary on some of the frequent trunk routes. The 301 and 302 basic weekday frequency from Watford was retained, but there were quite large cuts to the rest of the timetable. The 302 retained its half-hourly Sunday headway, but the 301 was reduced to hourly from Watford to Aylesbury, requiring only three RTs instead of the nine just over two years earlier. Tring garage's share of this was just two RTs representing a big reduction from the previous five. With these cuts, Tring put out only three buses in total on a Sunday compared with seven just a year earlier, a disparity which gave rise to difficulties in balancing crew scheduling across the week. Many passenger journeys on Sundays were slightly longer, and these were therefore better accommodated on the Green Line route, which with the 301 still provided three journeys an hour out to Aylesbury. On Saturdays, the supplementary late morning and afternoon journeys in the 1955 timetable were greatly cut back. The former 27 extra journeys were cut back to just 11 with two others just running between Kings Langley and Watford, cutting three RTs from Hemel Hempstead's Saturday supplementary schedule. Tring also lost the two late Saturday afternoon 'shopping relief' journeys to Aylesbury and back. The only tiny improvement was the diversion of the 301C route off the main road between Northchurch and Berkhamsted via the new Durrants Farm Estate to give an hourly Saturday shopping service into Hemel Hempstead together with a few Sunday afternoon journeys.

The two rural routes from Rickmansworth (361 to Chorleywood and 309 to Harefield) had both run to an hourly Sunday headway with one GS rostered to each route, but from October 1957 the Sunday schedules were cut back so that just one bus could work both routes. The 361 was cut from seven to four journeys, and the 309 from hourly all day to just seven journeys on an irregular timetable which had gaps during which the 361 journeys were run. In Surrey, as part of phase three of the omo programme, the hourly 416 route from Leatherhead to Esher was extended over the whole of the 435 from Leatherhead to Tadworth where it connected with suburban Central area routes, the 406 to Redhill and Southern Region trains to London. The 435 had always been a single-deck operation which, with the 422, had provided two buses an hour from Leatherhead to Headley. Extending the 416 created one through route from Esher to Tadworth requiring two buses for its hourly headway, and the whole route was converted to omo as well as the 422 via Headley village at the same time. Leatherhead replaced five crew duties with four omo. Other than Headley Hospital and village along the way, there were limited passenger numbers towards Tadworth, and the road to Esher passed even then through some of the most affluent parts of Surrey. Passenger levels dropped away quickly on the 416 over a few years and successive timetable cuts would reduce the service substantially.

Not all of the 1957 service changes resulted in cuts however. The road between Crawley and Horsham was part of the single deck 434 and 473 routes from Edenbridge and East Grinstead. This itself was an important and busy route, but with the growth of Crawley New Town, passenger demand grew to the point where there was a need to convert the Horsham leg to double deckers. And so from the 23rd January 1957 the 434 and 473 were cut back to Crawley, and the 405 extended to Horsham as a simple solution to increase capacity which was also required to meet the expansion of Littlehaven where local journeys into Horsham saw increasing demand. The extended 405 route had a through running time of 1hr 55mins from Croydon, and with the need to roster buses efficiently, this meant only six minutes layover at Horsham and four minutes at Croydon, so that each bus could complete a round Croydon – Horsham trip every four hours. The basic 30-minute headway therefore required eight RTs, but a layover of even a minute or two longer at each end would have meant a ninth bus to maintain this. Late running could sometimes be a problem, and the increased passengers also added further demand, particularly in peak times and Saturday shopping hours. Demand on Saturday afternoon was such that to relieve the main service, additional buses were scheduled to leave Crawley for Horsham every half hour but just a minute or two in front of the through journeys from Croydon. The single deckers on the 434 and 473 retained conductors until October that year, although the extra RF allocated on Saturdays remained crew worked for some time, and the requirement for duplication out to Crawley Down became greater as Crawley continued to expand. After conversion to omo, East Grinstead's Monday to Friday allocation to the 434 and 473 was removed with their morning peak journeys to the growing Crawley industrial area being worked instead on the 424 or 438 routes. On Saturdays, East Grinstead retained one RF which remained crew operated, an arrangement that lasted for several more years into the early 1960s. Strangest of all perhaps, given the gradual decline in passengers, was that East Grinstead's RF allocated on Sundays remained crew operated until 1966. East Grinstead was one of a number of small garages the majority of whose operations were crew worked, and as Sunday services were cut back this led to rostering difficulties with little or no work for the crews on Sundays, so duties like the 434 remained to balance rosters. Another long lasting anomaly was the last journey every evening to Edenbridge which was run by East Grinstead and remained crew worked up to 1967, after which the Monday to Friday operation was taken over by a Crawley omo bus, although the Saturday evening journey continued to be crew operated into 1969.

The 476B was started in October 1956 to provide works journeys from Tilgate to the Manor Royal industrial area, and 18 months later extended to what was then the new railway station built to serve Gatwick Airport. In 1963, it was diverted away from Tilgate to Furnace Green and provided a 30 minute all day service to the town centre – a journey time of just five minutes. Development at Furnace Green had only just begun and RT 3636 has reversed at the end of the road with open fields behind. Within a few years, the 476B was replaced by the 476 when it was extended from Tilgate in a loop through Furnace Green as the development expanded. (Peter Mitchell)

The October 1957 omo conversions in phase three were extensive, covering 19 routes across eight garages, replacing a total of 53 crew duties with 57 omo duties and saving a total of £34,001 per annum. The changes also replaced five GSs with four RFs when the 333/333B at Hertford and 393 at Epping were changed over, a move influenced more by the need to increase capacity rather than remove GSs from operation. London Transport also calculated that with the completion of this phase 48.7% of the rostered single-deck fleet had been converted to omo.

Windsor remained as popular as ever, and for summer 1957 the 457 from Uxbridge had an additional express service which ran to a 20-minute headway non-stop between Uxbridge and Windsor to carry the heavy loads which travelled on the Underground or the 607 trolleybus route from west London to Uxbridge. In a press release dated 11th April 1957, London Transport announced that some routes would be *specially strengthened* over the Easter holidays. Included in the list were the 319, 348A, 352 and 394 which served popular parts of the Chilterns, together with 364 and 386, all of which were some of the most rural Northern area routes. In the southern area, the 413 was included as was the 436A to Ripley. It was also announced that there would be several more early morning Sunday journeys on many routes throughout the summer to assist holiday travellers who wished to catch long distance coaches. These included the 335 between Gerrards Cross and Slough, 347 from Harefield into Uxbridge, 406 Tolworth to Epsom, 415 Ripley to Guildford, 441 Beaconsfield to Slough, Windsor and Staines, and the 457 from Uxbridge to Slough. The success of these initiatives is not recorded, but they were not repeated in subsequent years.

Route 476 began in May 1954 with a limited service to Langley Green, a new housing area just to the north of Crawley. A new variant 476A followed in January 1956 and the route was extended on to Ifield where the original hamlet had been subsumed into the new town. Later that year it was extended south of the town centre to the new estate then under construction at Tilgate. On a snowy winter's day in about 1961, RT 1053 has just left Langley Green on a journey across the town to Tilgate.
(Peter Mitchell)

During 1957, the route network had reached a general equilibrium with the New Town and new estate routes generally established, and apart from the omo conversions there were few major changes. Some new initiatives were tried, including another hospital service (numbered 808) linking Stevenage with the old Lister Hospital in Hitchin which began in January, and in October a new local service in Orpington numbered 854 which was soon extended to the expanding Ramsden Estate. One complete failure however was an attempt to provide a Saturday shopping service for the villages of Stewards Green and Toothill into Ongar. With the 1957 winter schedules, the 381 had two Saturday morning journeys extended from Toothill to Ongar, but it was such a failure that it lasted barely 10 weeks, being cut back again to Toothill after 22nd January 1958. When the 381 had first been introduced in August 1950, there had been an intention to extend it to Ongar but this was prevented by the partly unmade state of the road between Toothill and Stanford Rivers, and by the time the extension came about, any potential passengers had disappeared.

Shortages of platform staff persisted throughout 1957, as did various degrees of unrest which led to incidences of unofficial strike action over some roster changes. The unrest though was driven mostly by increasing dissatisfaction with levels of pay, and in October 1957 the Union submitted a claim for a general increase of £1 5s 0d (£1.25p) per week across the board for all staff. At a meeting between the Union (who sent no fewer than 20 people) and London Transport Executive on 1st November 1957, LT made it quite clear that they felt the claim was entirely unjustified, and even if agreed would cost £4 million in a full year

Until the new Lister Hospital was built just north of Stevenage, the main hospital was in Hitchin. The 808 was introduced in January 1957 to provide a service from the new housing areas east of Stevenage to Hitchin hospital, and ran initially one return journey only on Sunday afternoon, allowing an hour and a half visiting time. In 1961 an evening journey was added during the week and in 1963 the route was extended to start from Chells as the housing areas expanded. It was withdrawn in 1973 when the new hospital opened. RT 1078 comes along Chells Way on what was probably the Sunday afternoon journey. (Peter Mitchell)

which was completely unaffordable. The Union's case was based mainly on their contention that wages had not increased proportionately as much as in other industries, notwithstanding that average rostered earnings for Country bus crews had gone up by between 15% and 18% since January 1955. LT however, were quite clear that only steep fare increases could pay for the increase claimed, and there was clear evidence that the five fare increases in the three years to September 1957 had led to a diminution in traffic. The only alternative to sharp fare increases would be to reduce costs by cutting services, reducing the fleet and the workforce. At a further meeting two days before Christmas 1957, London Transport proposed arbitration, but the Union rejected this out of hand.

Despite this, London Transport referred the claim to Sir Wilfred Neden who was the Chief Industrial Commissioner at the Ministry of Labour. The result of this, in March 1958, was an award of only 8s 6d per week, and then only for Central Bus crews. Green Line crews represented an anomaly since – although Country Bus staff – they worked right through the Central area on a daily basis. There were also a number of Country area routes, sections of which operated over the same roads as Central area ones. As far as the Union were concerned, to award any pay rise only to Central area crews was therefore illogical and unfair, and bore no relation to their original claim of £1 5s 0d for all staff. In any event, despite the arbitration award, the Union were not prepared to accept anything less than 10s 6d per week for everyone including garage staff. London Transport made a half-hearted concession for double-deck Green Line crews since almost all of these worked the east London routes into Aldgate which were in reality long distance Central area routes, albeit limited stop services. But this was a futile attempt and had no effect in resolving the dispute.

The winter schedules of 16th October 1957 had originally included far more greater reductions than were in fact introduced – far more in the Central area than the Country area. Stiff Union opposition to these at the time the large pay claim was made however meant that London Transport deferred many of the proposed cuts until the following spring of 1958. With the lifting of fuel rationing following the end of the Suez crisis, large numbers of passengers had inevitably gone back to using their cars, and it was clear that sizeable cuts would need to be made, although principally these would need to be across the Central area network. The pay dispute remained unresolved with both sides seemingly becoming further apart. The Government of the day also had policies to contain inflation, which included holding down bus fares. The Union were suspicious of this and saw it as a 'back door' means of holding down pay awards, but London Transport remained adamant that without fare increases, any increase in wage costs was a burden the operation simply could not afford. The Union however were in no mood to compromise, and even the Prime Minister himself at one point became involved in an attempt to resolve differences, but to no avail. After four months of fruitless negotiations, a strike seemed inevitable, and the catalyst which finally tipped the balance were the proposed Central area summer schedules which were programmed to start on 30th April 1958 with large numbers of buses cut. Perhaps the most telling statistic of the proposed cuts was that even with the summer augmentation of many routes, the total number of Central area buses required on Sundays was about 160 fewer than had been required for the *winter 1957* schedules. The Union – by now led by Frank Cousins who would later become leader of the T.U.C. – were implacably opposed to the cuts and refused to be convinced that they were solely in response to falling traffic.

Faced with these cuts, and with no agreement to their claim, the Union therefore called a full strike. The stoppage was total across the whole fleet, and from Monday 5th May 1958, not a single bus, trolleybus or Green Line coach left its garage for the next seven weeks until Saturday 21st June. Throughout the strike, whatever the rights or wrongs at the time, continuing negotiations were clouded by mistrust, claim and counterclaim, and in the end of course, neither side really won anything. The financial effects on London Transport were nothing less than disastrous, the travelling public suffered appalling inconvenience, and the actual staff themselves lost seven weeks' pay and ended up with an award much lower than they had first demanded. To what extent the Union were forced into accepting the final outcome is not known, but there were certainly large numbers of staff who felt that in the end the strike had achieved little or nothing for them. The award as eventually agreed gave Central crews 8s 6d per week, Green Line crews 7s 6d, and the rest just 5s 0d. The final agreement signed on 20th June 1958 by Frank Cousins and Sir John Elliott (the LTE Chairman) referred to some additional payments for special cases and productivity, with provision for *an upward trend*, whilst the anomaly in pay for Country Bus crews where they worked over Central area routes was referred to *in so far as Country area staff are concerned it is not the intention that any decision will leave staff in an unfavourable position compared to other road services staff or comparable grades elsewhere*. In reality of course this meant little, and staff had been badly served by their Union who had consistently rejected rises which were much greater than they eventually settled for. During the strike, traffic congestion in London had risen to levels which previously had been unimaginable. The suburban railways and Underground system were barely able to cope, and even the small number of private operators who were given temporary permission to run some services made little difference.

The new Ramsden Estate in Orpington had its first bus service in October 1958 when route 854 started, requiring one RT from Dunton Green. The route linked the estate to the town centre and the station at Chelsfield, the timetable including a couple of journeys to Green Street Green to allow crew changes during the day. The crew of RT 3507 take their short break at Ramsden Estate terminus and the picture shows the unusual rear blind in use at the time. (Peter Mitchell)

Looking back sixty years later, it is impossible to overstate the serious and lasting damage that the strike did to London's bus operations. In the weeks after the strike, revenue was around 20% less than before it began, although in a perverse way this was a blessing in the short term since staff shortages were even more serious. None of those on strike could afford the loss of seven weeks' wages so that many had left for better paid jobs in manufacturing. During all of this, recruitment had been suspended, so there was no pool of newly recruited staff coming in to replenish the losses.

Looking back sixty years later, it is impossible to overstate the serious and lasting damage that the strike did to London's bus operations. To a great extent, the whole dispute had been self-inflicted, both sides seemingly unable to accept the reality of the situation at the time. The Union simply refused to accept that widespread service cuts and job losses were necessary despite obvious evidence of reducing revenue, or that their own actions and endless disputes were exacerbating the decline in passengers who saw services as increasingly unreliable. London Transport for its part simply failed to recognize that low wages were the overriding cause of staff shortages and dissatisfaction, and had to be substantially increased almost regardless of the cost if the public were to be provided with the levels of service they expected. During the strike, the lack of trust was made worse by LT's announcement that a further 10% reduction on the Central area network was being planned, an action which only hardened the Union's attitude. Political expediency in not wanting to be seen to relent on the policy of restraining inflation also deterred the Government from making any useful contribution. If the Union's intransigence was a major factor, so too was that of Sir John Elliot who was the subject of widespread criticism for his unyielding approach and poor leadership of the whole process. Such was the criticism that in the aftermath of the strike, his contract as Chairman was not renewed. The strike solved none of the underlying issues. Recrimination and loss of trust on both sides lasted for another decade and would taint the long negotiations over widespread omo conversions during the 1960s.

In the weeks after the strike, revenue was around 20% less than before it began, although in a perverse way this was an advantage in the short term since staff shortages were even more serious. None of those on strike could afford the loss of seven weeks' wages so that many had left for better paid jobs in manufacturing. During all of this, recruitment had been suspended, so there was no pool of newly trained staff coming in to replenish the losses.

Below left The large area of woodland at Burnham Beeches had been requisitioned by the War Office in 1939, public access not being granted again until 1948. The area was extremely popular for weekend visitors, and that year a pre-war Green Line service was replaced by the 474 on summer Sundays and the 442 during the week. The 474 ran every hour in the morning, increasing to half hourly in the afternoon until early evening. RT 4107 was one a batch of ten new RTs delivered to Windsor in April 1951 to replace some of its last STLs, and is standing in Station Approach at Slough waiting for the next journey. Increasing car ownership dealt a heavy blow to tourist routes such as the 474 and it was abandoned as part of the cuts after the 1958 strike. (D A Jones)

Far right Operation of the 15T13s on route 424 was confined to the Outwood and Horne sections from Horley, but the bus was rostered to work one journey to Reigate where the crew took their break before returning to Horley. T 788 has had a serious collision with a building somewhere on its way to Reigate.

The full effects of the strike on the schedules was not immediate since the start of Country area summer schedules had been delayed by it, and the full force of cuts would not come until the introduction of the winter schedules. A new hospital service had been intended and would have linked the expanding estates at New Addington with Warlingham Park Hospital. It was intended to be worked on Sunday afternoons by a GS from Chelsham since there was a spare from the 464, 465 and 485 allocation that day. In the event, the route did start immediately after the strike, but whatever potential passengers there might have been had been deterred by the strike, and the route was a complete failure, being withdrawn on 15th October when the winter schedules came into force.

One previous summer service which was not reinstated was the 474 to Burnham Beeches, and eight further southern area RF routes shared between Dunton Green, Addlestone and Leatherhead garages were converted to omo which were part of phase four of the omo conversion programme and had already been planned before the strike. Another route whose introduction suffered from the effects of the strike was the 315 to Kimpton. Part of the Birch Brothers rural network referred to earlier included route 205 from Luton to Welwyn via Peters Green, Kimpton and Codicote, with some additional journeys on Saturdays on route 206 which took a different route through the isolated hamlet of Bendish. Until the mid-1950s the 205 maintained eight or nine journeys a day during the week and even three on Sundays, but although it connected at Welwyn with Birch's main 203 to and from London, it never served Welwyn Garden City until, in 1955, London Transport granted permission for Birch to run beyond Welwyn village, albeit prevented from carrying local traffic from Welwyn itself. This was just inside the 'special area', and London Transport had refused Birch permission to extend the 205 into Welwyn Garden City which, by 1958, had become an important traffic centre. By 1958, the Sunday service had gone and the route was in serious decline, so in April that year Birch cut the 205 back to run just between Kimpton and Luton only. London Transport replaced the Welwyn to Kimpton section with the new 315 route which ran on into Welwyn Garden City factory area. It ran only during Monday to Friday peak hours, operated by RTs from Hatfield, and the remainder of the former Birch timetable was abandoned completely. The irony of its introduction was that only three weeks after London Transport took over, there was then no service for the next seven weeks during the strike and how many erstwhile passengers from Kimpton were put off forever will never be known.

As the routes along the east to west corridor though Hertford had developed, they had become fragmented, and as Harlow and Welwyn Garden City grew, with Hertford between them, it made sense to revise the routes to provide a through east to west link. On 23rd July therefore the 372 was extended to replace the 399 to give a through service from Welwyn Garden City to Epping and Coopersale via Hertford, Ware, and Stanstead Abbots. At the same time, the 393 was extended from Broxbourne over Hertford Heath, through Hertford, and on into Welwyn Garden City in parallel with the 372. The two routes crossed each other at Tylers Cross near Harlow, and the timetable provided connections here so that journeys from Epping to Broxbourne and Harlow to St Margarets and Ware could be made by changing buses at Tylers Cross. The 393 became hourly along the whole route, and the 372 two-hourly over the Epping–Hertford section with some extra journeys. One man RFs had replaced GSs on the 393 the previous October, and with these changes the 372 was converted to omo as well. The creation of the

The 342 ran from New Barnet through Hertford to Broxbourne and was crew operated on an hourly headway. It was cut back to Hertford as part of the changes in July 1958, and the section to New Barnet withdrawn in June 1959 to be replaced by an extension of the 350 and 350A. RF 574 was one of 14 new RFs delivered to Hertford in May 1953 to replace former Green Line 10T10s on all the crew operated single deck routes. It is standing in the forecourt of Broxbourne station prior to the route's October 1957 conversion to one-man operation. (J.H. Aston)

through link over Hertford Heath allowed the 342 to be cut back to just the Hertford to New Barnet section, the conductors being removed from this route at the same time, leaving Hertford with just a few remaining single-deck crew workings. There were other improvements which resulted from this major change. The basic hourly service to the west of Hertford was augmented with a number of peak hour extras, and on Saturday the 372 and 393 were timed to co-ordinate with the 342 so that there was a 20-minute headway between Cole Green and Hertford. At main shopping times there were also several more journeys timed to run within a few minutes of the main service, because by then the growth of Welwyn Garden City was creating increasing numbers of shoppers and the basic half-hourly headway was unable to keep up with demand. Although the Epping leg steadily declined over the years and the direct link cut off from Hertford in 1960, the Welwyn Garden City to Harlow service became a mainstay of the local route network and remained so well into London Country days.

The need for economies and cuts across the network was essential following the strike, and at a meeting of the traffic committee on 23rd June 1958, Geoffrey Fernyhough, the Country Bus operating manager, outlined his proposals. In 1957, a loss of £192,000 had been incurred on Country area bus routes, and the loss for 1958 had already been estimated at £116,000 even before the strike, but would in reality be much greater. It was estimated that 35 more omo RFs on ten routes would save around £30,000 a year, withdrawing about 30 buses in peak periods would save £90,000, and cuts in Sunday and off peak services would save a further £26,600 a year. Some loss making rural routes would also be withdrawn

The 393/393A became increasingly important routes as Harlow grew. Epping had an additional bus allocated to the route on Saturdays for 'special duplicates', a GS working until 1959 when it was replaced with an RF. On a fine day in 1962, RF 633 has arrived at Harlow Bus Station and the driver fills out his waybill working duty EP203 on one of these extra journeys, probably from Hoddesden, the busiest section requiring duplication for Saturday shoppers. RT 993 behind went to Epping in June 1960 and is working the 396A town service to Old Harlow village. Some 40 years after the picture was taken, I would become part owner of this bus.
(S J Butler)

completely. A further meeting was held with the Union on 23rd July and a press release issued two days later announced that the meeting was *'to consider further proposals made by London Transport to bring its country bus services more into line with present traffic levels and other measures designed to reduce working costs'*. The press release also stated – unsurprisingly – that the Union *'were unable to support London Transport's proposals'*. Whilst the Executive expressed regret at the Union's unwillingness, it nevertheless confirmed that the reductions would proceed as planned. Passenger traffic had dropped by more than 10% since the strike, and the reductions would reduce mileage run by 9%. The press release concluded by covering in some detail five minor routes which would be withdrawn completely, and 14 which would be withdrawn on Sundays.

It was with the introduction of the 1958 winter schedules on 15th October that the widespread service cuts in the aftermath of the strike took full effect.

The 442 (Slough to Farnham Royal) was abandoned as was the 804 to the hospitals at Mount Vernon and Harefield. The 355 and 391 routes run by St Albans, which were both worked with crew RFs, were re-cast. The rural legs of the two routes were combined into one service running from Harpenden through St Albans to Borehamwood, numbered 355 and converted to omo. The two legs within St Albans itself were similarly combined into one cross City route, numbered 391 and 391A and retained crew working. This change converted 12 RF duties to omo. Amersham's RLHs on the 359 to Aylesbury were replaced with omo RFs, United Counties converting their share to one-man at the same time.

The 352 Sunday service to Berkhamsted had gone in June 1956, and now the remaining short journeys from Dunstable to Dagnall were withdrawn. The 317 Sunday service from Berkhamsted had also been cut back from six to five journeys, and was now abandoned completely as another victim of the cuts. The press release somewhat casually mentioned that Hudnall Common, left with no Sunday service, was 'within 1¾ miles of Clements End on the 337', though quite why the occasional passenger might be bothered to walk that far was unlikely. This rapid decline from ten Sunday journeys into Berkhamsted to nothing in less than three years is another illustration of just how quickly leisure traffic was disappearing. The 317A via Nettleden two or three times a day had been earmarked for complete withdrawal, but in the event survived. The 337 to Dunstable had previously had some summer Sunday journeys diverted via Whipsnade Zoo, and these too ceased although they were reinstated in later years. Tring garage lost the remaining Sunday journeys on the 387 to Aldbury, although B&B coaches ran a skeleton service to the village from Dudswell which connected with the 301 and 706/707.

The 336 (Watford to Chesham) was the Northern area's only route necessitating the use of lowbridge double deckers, and though busy during the week, had also suffered declining passengers on Sundays. From the introduction of the winter timetables in October 1956 the hourly through headway was halved on Sundays to two-hourly, and with the 335 Sunday service having been similarly halved, this reduced the Rickmansworth to Chalfont service to hourly. Some Sunday afternoon shorts were run on the 336 between Chesham and Chalfont to give a roughly hourly service, but LT felt the need to emphasise the alternative Green Line service from Amersham to Chenies which after the cuts had only six Sunday journeys on the 336. The winter 1958 roadside timetables for the 336 therefore had a note in bold type stating *'YOU MAY TRAVEL BETWEEN AMERSHAM AND CHENIES BY GREEN LINE COACH 703 FOR 10d'*. This was misleading however as the 703 ran along the main road at Chenies and did not serve the centre of the village itself!

At Hertford, the Sunday services on the 308, 308A, 329, 386 were all withdrawn and the 386A withdrawn completely. Further cuts there took out three more RFs Saturday, two on Sunday, and one during the week, together with the last RF crew duties losing their conductors. This brought to an end the crew-worked RFs on the 386 on Saturdays which had been necessary because the omo rosters had insufficient capacity that day, but which nonetheless had been an unnecessary extra expense. The 386A had always been a waste of time and money since the journey time via its indirect route through Much Hadham was almost an hour against the 30 minutes along the A10 direct via the 331 route. It was not surprising that this was abandoned in the cuts together with the Sunday service on the 386 which until then had still needed two buses to run a couple of return journeys each along the whole length of this most remote route.

Two weeks after these changes, the routes serving many Surrey Hills beauty spots also lost their Sunday service. The 422 up to Boxhill was withdrawn but covered by the 416 withdrawn from Tadworth and diverted to Boxhill instead. The 433 to both Ranmore and Coldharbour was withdrawn for the winter but was reinstated on summer Sunday, and the 448 beyond Peaslake to Ewhurst lost the Sunday service. The reduction in GSs to just one at Guildford on Sunday meant that the 448A town service would have become inefficient to run with a second GS so that too was withdrawn. The three Monday to Friday and four Saturday journeys on the 415 beyond Ripley to Ockham were withdrawn. Guildford lost one RF daily and two GSs on Sundays, Dorking an RF and two GSs on Sundays. The three 449 Ewhurst journeys were abandoned completely, and the route was reduced to become a town service between Goodwyns Farm and Chart Downs Estate. Despite the loss of the Ewhurst service however, two journeys on Monday, Tuesday, Thursday and Friday afternoons were extended beyond Chart Downs through Blackbrook to turn at the cross roads by Four Wents Pond on Holmwood Common. This was a truly rural terminus which served no habitation whatsoever, but in another example of London Transport's continued operation of loss making journeys, these were still running unaltered when London Country took over 11 years later. Dorking and Guildford's RFs on the 412, 425 and 432 were converted to omo. The two legs on the 424 from Horley out to Horne and Outwood Common were abandoned although the press release (helpfully?) stated that Horne was *'within a mile of the 409 north of Blindley Heath'*. Five months later LT granted Browne's Transport from Nutfield a licence to run a service from Outwood to Horley and Redhill although Horne remained unserved.

The 479 from Farningham to Dartford via an indirect route went, as well as the 492 from Gravesend to West Kingsdown. This latter ran just three shopping journeys four days a week but the Saturday and Sunday service on the 452 into Dartford from Kingsdown remained unchanged.

The winter schedules also included phase five of the omo conversion programme when 62 crew duties were replaced with 64 omo duties, saving £29,198 per annum, almost exactly the figure presented at the meeting on 23rd June. At Northfleet, one GS was replaced with an RF, and at a time when GS and RF omo duties were on separate rosters the summary noted that the RF duty would cost an extra £78 in a full year!

The overall effects of the cuts become more evident if the 1958 winter schedules are compared with those a year earlier in 1957. The totals allocated are shown in the table overleaf.

16th OCTOBER 1957	MONDAY–FRIDAY	SATURDAY	SUNDAY
DOUBLE DECK RT/RLH	781	737	418
RF crew	130	119	76
RF omo	31	30	21
GS	65	58	35
RT COACH	70	64	60
RF COACH	236	244	275

RT = 782 Thursday. GS = 63 Monday & Friday, 64 Tuesday and Wednesday.

10th DECEMBER 1958			
DOUBLE DECK RT/RLH	744	669	372
RF crew	57	44	32
RF omo	106	107	51
GS	57	51	20
RT COACH	70	50	61
RF COACH	241	227	252

RT = 743 Thursday, 742 Monday, Tuesday, Wednesday. GS = 56 Tuesday, 55 Monday, Wednesday and Friday

What is immediately striking is the reduction in weekend totals with a total of 75 buses being taken out of the schedules on Sundays and 73 on Saturdays. In 1957, only 20% of the RF buses were one-man operated on Saturdays, but a year later this had risen to 70% and on Sundays the proportion rose from 21% to 61% on a total which had been reduced by 14 vehicles. The number of GSs had been reduced as a result of the timetable on many of their routes being cut back. The abandonment of Sunday services had been predominantly on the infrequent rural routes, and with only 20 GSs scheduled in the October 1958 allocation, it meant that three quarters of these buses – all barely five years old – sat idle in their garages on Sundays after the cuts. It is also notable that even on Monday to Friday, 37 double deckers had been removed from the schedules, and although the RF total remained stable (in fact increasing by two), eight GSs were also removed, leaving 27 of them idle every day during the week. Another effect of the winter 1958 cuts was that numbers of RTs were rendered surplus, and so apart from Amersham's 336 allocation, some of the spare RTs were used to replace other RLHs, a move probably appreciated by passengers and conductors alike given the cramped upper deck layout of the RLH with its side sunken gangway. Amersham therefore lost four RLHs in the changes, and with other RLH duties being cut in the southern area, a total of 14 of these buses, which at the time were only six or eight years old, became surplus. This meant that the Country area's requirements for these non-standard buses had been reduced from 51 to 37 although three of the spare buses were repainted red for use in the Central fleet. There were no actual reductions in the Green Line timetables following the strike, and there was even a small increase of five RFs allocated Monday to Friday. But 17 RFs and 14 RTs had been taken out on Saturdays, and 23 RFs on Sundays which reflected the fact that although the basic timetables hadn't changed, the need for duplicates had reduced sharply as casual Green Line leisure traffic dropped away.

Stevenage's continued growth had meant that Hitchin garage had become very uneconomic. Although the small shed in Stevenage itself operated six RTs on Stevenage town services, Hitchin had an allocation of eight RTs and three RFs (all crew-operated) which were rostered to Stevenage town and works services and four RFs for the 716A. There was therefore a significant amount of dead mileage for both buses and crews to get to and from Stevenage. It also had two omo RFs for the rural 364 to Luton, one for the 384, and two GSs for the 383 and the infrequent 807 between Stevenage and Letchworth, also involving dead mileage on positioning journeys. At the end of April therefore, Hitchin and the small shed at Stevenage were closed and operations transferred to the brand new garage which was opened in Stevenage town centre. The operation of the two RFs on the 364 route was logically transferred to Luton. Prior to this, Luton had run five RTs on two semi-rural routes (356 and 376) out to Kensworth and Flamstead Village, so at the same time as the 364 was transferred, it was extended through Luton to cover these two routes, effectively converting them from crew RT to omo RF along with Luton's one remaining crew RF which had previously been rostered to the 364. The new base at Stevenage brought much greater efficiency to the operation of its growing town network, and meant that the only dead mileage then operated was to get the GS out to Hitchin for the 383, the drivers changing by travelling to and from Stevenage during the day as passengers on the 303 or 716. Stevenage also retained the 364 Tuesday and Saturday market day short journeys to Preston.

One indirect effect of the closure of Hitchin garage was the replacement of the double deck 356 and 376. Having transferred operation of the 364 to Luton, it was extended to cover both these routes, the 376 being renumbered 364A, although a few crew operated peak hour journeys remained. Before the change, a filthy RT 3617 works a journey to Kensworth. (Peter Mitchell)

By March 1959 the last 35 RFs had been converted for omo, and in May and June were used in phase 6 of the conversion programme along with many alterations to other routes in the continuing search for savings. The 'country' leg of the 447 from Redhill to Woldingham was transferred into the 440 timetable, whilst the busy town service from Reigate and Redhill to Merstham remained crew RF. In other circumstances this might have been a double-deck route, but it passed under a low bridge so that a unique feature of the 447 schedules was the allocation of one RLH to run peak hour journeys, an anomaly which lasted even after the route was finally converted to one-man operation at the end of 1966. The busy 322 between Watford and Hemel Hempstead was converted and extended up to Highfield in place of the 316 where the capacity of GSs was at times inadequate. Northfleet replaced the GS on the 452 with an RF, but retained a crew-worked RF during the week for peak journeys on the 451 and 490.

Hertford's rural routes had already suffered incremental reductions to the allocations, and now as part of the changes of 10th June 1959, the 350 and 350A became one of the last RT operated rural routes to be converted to omo RF. At the same time it was extended over the 342 to Potters Bar and New Barnet which itself had been one of the first of Hertford's RF routes to be converted to omo two years earlier. The change created one long omo route and, apart from the loss of a further eight crew duties, it reduced the number of buses required to operate the overall basic service by two as a result of timetabling efficiencies made possible by through working across Hertford. Then later that year in October, Hertford's GS allocation was cut back again. Only five GSs were rostered Monday, Wednesday and Friday, six Tuesday, Thursday and Saturday, and just four on Sunday, half the number required only three years earlier. With reductions to evening timetables, only two of these GSs remained in service after 7pm each day with a third on Tuesday and Saturday, which was the bus returning from Hitchin market day journeys on the 386. This decline was a direct reflection of the gradual reduction in passengers on Hertford's rural routes, and was a pattern repeated over the whole Country area.

The extension of the 350 and 350A south from Hertford to Potters Bar and New Barnet in June 1959 over the former 342 route meant that the 350A became the longest omo route in the Country area, with an end to end running time of two hours 11 minutes. By 1960 the service south of Potters Bar to New Barnet had been reduced to a few peak journeys during the week since it was paralleled by the half hourly 303/303A and Central area route 134. RF 593 rounds the bend at Letty Green on one of the journeys turning short at Potters Bar, having passed under the bridge which carried the former Hertford to Hatfield branch line. (Peter Mitchell)

RF 42 was one of eight new RFs delivered to Windsor in November 1951, initially for use on the 704. Fifteen more were delivered in the first five months of 1952 to complete Windsor's allocation to the 704, 705 and 718. It has come from Knightsbridge into Grosvenor Place on its way to Sevenoaks. (London Transport Museum)

Continuing reductions to some major trunk routes were typified by the time-tables for the 301 and 302 which had required much augmentation only four years earlier. By the time the winter schedules for 1959 were introduced, the Saturday supplementary journeys had gone completely, and the Sunday service on the 302 was halved to hourly so that the total 301 and 302 Sunday allocation had gone from 14 RTs for the 1955 summer timetable to only five for winter 1959. On the less busy Boxmoor and Aylesbury section there were always fewer Sunday passengers, but on the inter-urban part of the route out of Watford, the heavier loadings of the early 1950s were declining quickly. The 301C had run a limited service from Tring and Berkhamsted direct into Hemel Hempstead, since the 301 and parallel Green Line routes ran along the main A41 missing the town centre. In June 1957 an hourly service to the new Durrants Farm Estate at Northchurch had been added on Saturday to give a shopping facility into Berkhamsted and Hemel Hempstead, with even some journeys on Sunday afternoon, but did not alter the underlying declining trend in passengers along the A41 corridor. The reductions on the 301 and 302 became one of the earliest examples of how weekend traffic was beginning to fall sharply even on busier routes.

Grays operated the short 375 from Rainham station on the seven-minute run to Rainham Ferry to carry staff to and from the Enrox works, buses running a shuttle service every few minutes in the morning and evening peaks. Crew operated Ts were used since conductors were necessary to collect often a full load of fares in a short time. Attempts in May 1959 to convert the route to omo failed since it was almost impossible for the omo driver to collect fares at each end in the allotted layover time. As a temporary measure, conductors were stationed at the pick-up point to collect fares. The route was not profitable and Enrox were unable to give any guarantees of support, so that after only two months of this arrangement, London Transport withdrew the route completely, operation being taken over by South Essex Coaches on a contract basis. This removed four of the remaining 15T13s from service, leaving only two scheduled – one at Tring for the 352 and 387, and one at Crawley for 'supplementary schedule' works journeys.

The 375 required four buses to run the frequent peak service on the seven minute journey from Rainham Crossing to the Enrox works at the Ferry. It had to be converted back to crew operation after the failed attempt at omo because it was impossible for drivers to collect fares from an often full load. After Enrox refused to guarantee the route's losses, London Transport withdrew in July 1959. The 374 and 399 which were Grays's only other omo routes had to be converted back to crew operation as the standalone omo duty was not viable without omo on the 375. Some years earlier, T 795 awaits its next journey. (Alan Cross).

Despite the conversion of the last RFs for one-man operation, there was now a shortage of them across the fleet. Several were still in use as crew-worked vehicles, and so to relieve the shortage a number of spare RTs were drafted around the fleet for use as Green Line scheduled duplicates. This released enough coach RFs which could then be used as buses on the busy crew-operated routes run by Reigate, St Albans and Windsor, which between them needed 22 RFs, thus releasing enough omo buses to solve the shortage. Even so, Reigate still had to borrow some red RFs from the Central area for the summer to cover a shortage at Epping and Northfleet, both of which ran Green Line routes to Windsor, where – despite generally falling traffic – summer demand still required plenty of duplication. Windsor itself needed up to 20 additional RTs for Green Line duplication, and most of these came from Northfleet to be replaced by more surplus red buses from store – this time RTLs. The aftermath of the 1958 service cuts had left more than 300 RTLs surplus to requirements, but despite this, there would have been enough spare red RTs to send to Northfleet, so why non-standard RTLs were sent to a Country area garage is unclear. With their slower gearchange and characteristic Leyland 'hunting' on tickover they were not popular with Country area drivers, a factor which led to their short life at Hatfield a year later. Romford was short of enough RTs to run the additional schedules for the 726 to Whipsnade, and so these were taken from Stevenage who borrowed some red ones from store which were surplus following the previous year's cuts.

When a service to the LCC Estate at Merstham was planned the original intention had been to use double deckers but a low bridge meant that operation would be restricted to RLHs. This was considered unsuitable for what would be a busy route, and so the single deck 447 was extended to the Estate instead, becoming one of two busy town services which remained crew operated with single deckers until the end of 1966. In 1958, RF 555 has worked in from Merstham and approaches a stop in Redhill High Street which today would be unrecognisable from this picture (Alan Cross)

A large number of RTLs became redundant following the 1958 strike, but the decision to send some to Northfleet in the summer of 1959 to replace RTs needed elsewhere for duplicates was odd to say the least. Sending a batch repainted green to Hatfield the following year was an even more illogical decision given the large number of spare RTs then available. They were mostly allocated to the 303/303A but interworked all of Hatfield's routes. RTL 1256 heads RT 4551 on an 803, having just left the main railway station with the famous Welwyn Department Store in the background. The garage on the left has long disappeared under the new road system at this point. (Alan Cross)

As Welwyn Garden City continued to expand it became an obvious objective and in October 1959 two journeys Monday to Friday and four on Saturdays were diverted on the 388 from Welwyn Village to run into the New Town. In later years this helped sustain at least some level of passengers and was probably a factor in the roughly hourly headway being maintained through Tewin into the mid-1960s.

Green Line services were still carrying good loads, and the network had produced a substantial operating surplus year on year, amounting to almost £3.5 million in the five years 1953 to 1957, peaking at £741,000 in 1955. A substantial loss of £371,000 had been incurred in 1958 due to the strike, but another surplus was produced in 1959. Conversely, the Country bus routes had consistently lost money, the total amounting to over £700,000 for the same five-year period, with a significant deficit of £467,000 in 1958. Despite this, in the period up to the end of 1959, the Country area taken as a whole had produced an operating surplus of over £2 million. Although London Transport were making overall operating surpluses, they were not sufficient to service the capital debt to the British Transport Commission who expressed particular concerns over the financial performance of the Country bus routes. Perversely, they were also concerned at the negative effect Green Line routes might be having on parallel railway services. These concerns were expressed in a letter dated 4th July 1958 to Sir John Elliot, the LTE Chairman which suggested:

As regards country buses, I think there is a case for examining the advisability of continuing these services at least in their present form. It is not only that they lose money, but also that their existence greatly complicates the wage problems for the Commission. It might be worth considering whether these services could be taken over by provincial bus companies (Tilling and BET) or any other arrangement which would avoid the difficulties of the present situation. The problem we are interested in concerning the Green Line services is simply that of their effect upon the passenger traffic of British Railways. The 'wage problem' referred to was the differential in pay between Country area drivers and conductors who were paid 8s 6d and 7s 6d per week each more that the Tilling and BET crews who operated services surrounding the Country area into most of the towns on the borders of the LPTA.

This was an extraordinary letter. The fundamental idea of breaking up the Country bus network and dividing it amongst its neighbouring operators, with Green Line services somehow remaining as they were, would have been fraught with enormous difficulties, not least the pay cuts which presumably would have been imposed on all the Country area crews who would be forcibly transferred to the surrounding Tilling and BET companies taking over the routes. There was also no suggestion as to how the retained Green Line routes might be operated from garages which would lose all their bus operations and the proposition that railway passenger numbers were seriously eroded by Green Line was at the least fanciful.

Not surprisingly, after many meetings to discuss it, London Transport produced a report dated 12th October 1959 which roundly rejected the idea. The report set out that losses on Country bus routes could not be considered in isolation, and the bus and Green Line routes were actually one system which, taken together, made a profit. It pointed out though that revenue in 1959 had been affected by the inability to raise fares sufficiently to bridge the gap between the wage increases and subsequent cost reductions made, and that the fare increase delayed until August 1959 had cost about £50,000 in lost revenue. As to the Green Line routes, the report boldly stated *'the Green Line coaches are a classic example of facilities creating traffic'* and *'the popularity of Green Line travel is its comfort and speed, and above all else the convenience of the service'*. The report also made clear that it was a mistake to regard Green Line as a competitor to the railways; indeed, if anything the reverse was the case.

The two short legs to Outwood and Horne on the 424 were both abandoned after the strike, and the Sunday timetable between East Grinstead and Reigate was reduced by a third, saving one bus. The remainder of the service was little changed, but two years later the 30 minute Saturday headway was cut to hourly north of Horley, The route had been extended from the town to the new Stone Quarry Estate in May 1949 and RT 4537 is at the terminus there waiting to depart on one of the shortened journeys to Horley. The conductor has set the correct intermediate blind. (Tony Wild)

The 'speed and convenience' of Green Line travel would however begin to fade as railway modernisation and increasing traffic congestion took their toll, and as the 1950s came to a end, the trend of continuing decline in passenger traffic had become permanent. London Transport's 1959 report included many statistics, and on the face of it, it had been a good year. The numbers of passengers carried on Country Buses and Coaches, although significantly up compared to 1958 when the effects of the long strike had devastated numbers, were nevertheless lower than 1957. In the five-year period from the end of 1954, passenger numbers on Country Buses had gone down by about 15% despite the growth of the New Towns and the additional routes and traffic which had come from them. The report noted that the total population of the 'Outer Country Area' had grown by about 270,000 (or about 17%) since 1954. Also important was that television had taken hold and the number of households owning one had roughly doubled to about 60% from 1954 to 1959. Private car ownership had also increased rapidly and the number of households owning a car had also almost doubled in the five years to 1959. Green Line passenger numbers had fluctuated year on year, but ended 1959 at about the same level as five years earlier. But this masked the fact that new routes had been introduced so that in reality the same number of passengers were being carried by a greater number of coaches on an improved route network, although this increase in capacity was relatively small. 1959 however proved to be the last year before Green Line routes began what was to become a disastrous decline in passenger traffic in the years to come.

The financial results for 1959 were improved, but after deducting London Transport's mandatory contribution to the British Transport Commission, the net surplus of receipts over expenses was a meagre £30,000 which was insignificant when compared to the figure of around £5 million which London Transport estimated was needed for contingencies and fleet replacements. Increases in fares were therefore a necessity, and these would need to be more than they might have been but for the continuing drop in passenger numbers. An application for a fare increase had been made in 1959 but was not approved until late in the year, by which time further increases were necessary and in May 1960 short distance fares went up by between 20% and 25%. This was not enough however to pay for the 1960 pay rises and the May 1960 increase was followed by another in January 1961, and yet another in July the same year. In the space of only 15 months, the overall increase in fares was on average more than a third, which of course contributed to driving away more passengers. The well documented 'vicious circle' of higher fares driving passengers away, thus reducing income which can only be recouped by more fare increases, in turn driving away more passengers, was not of course unique to London Transport. The fare increases in 1960 and 1961 however probably represented the start of this process in earnest for the Country Bus network, and began to accelerate the loss of passengers. Even the 1960 and 1961 increases were insufficient to recoup the reductions in revenue and fund the wage increase, so that in April 1962 the short distance 5d fare went up again to 6d (a further 20%) and the 8d fare up to 9d.

The 1960s began in the same way as the 1950s had come to a close with continuing staff shortages. The annual report for 1959 noted that at 31st December that year there was a total of 3,484 'wage grade' vacancies, a number which had increased by 2,316 since the beginning of the year. The principal cause of this was stated as *a failure to attract sufficient recruits to driving and conducting* and of the total vacancies, 2,785 were in road services operation.

The fallout from the 1958 strike had left a widespread level of dissatisfaction among all staff – particularly drivers and conductors – and during 1959 London Transport had been discussing with Union ways in which bonus or incentive schemes might be introduced, both to improve staff satisfaction and attract more recruits. Little progress was being made however and any agreement seemed elusive, but it was obvious that wages would need to be increased appreciably if the lack of staffing was to be reversed. In March 1960 therefore, all drivers and conductors were awarded an increase of 10s 0d (50p) per week and, as discussions around bonus schemes dragged on without any agreement, a further 18s 0d (90p) per week increase was added in October 1960. The total increase in the year of £1 8s 0d per week, which London Transport simply awarded, was 3s 0d per week more than the £1 5s 0d increase they had so fiercely resisted only two years before and which had led to the disastrous strike. Looking back now, the original resistance of LT in 1958 seems to have been ill judged despite Government pressures to restrain wages, and to what extent the huge losses suffered by both London Transport and its staff could have been avoided or mitigated is impossible to say.

The 418 was an important route linking Kingston to Epsom and Leatherhead. Although it went via a different route to the 406, the two routes combined to provide eight journeys an hour between Kingston and Epsom all day with even more at peak times. Beyond Leatherhead, it was less busy and served the 'back road' to Great Bookham and its railway station. RT 3154 climbs away from Fetcham on a journey to Bookham. (Peter Mitchell)

Car ownership, television, and migration from London had together been a principal cause of London Transport radically reducing its Central area services as passenger numbers fell away continuously. In the five years to the end of 1959, a total of 1,134 buses had been taken out of the schedules on Monday to Friday. This represented just under 15% of the total scheduled for service at the end of 1954, roughly one bus in every seven. On Saturdays, the number was even greater at 1,266 or 18% and although the absolute number on Sundays was less at 1,043, this amounted to almost a 25% reduction against the 1954 figure. Because of the development of the New Towns, and the resultant migration from Inner London, the comparative figures for the Country area were less severe. Monday to Friday totals were only 44 fewer buses, but in a reflection of the sharper reduction in weekend leisure traffic, Saturday schedules had been reduced by 96 buses (just under 10%), and on Sundays the reduction over the five years of 161 buses represented just over 25%. The reductions in the Green Line allocation had also begun to reflect the serious loss of weekend traffic. During the week, the total coach schedules had actually risen by three where small reductions had been offset by the starting up of new routes. At weekends, the basic route timetables were almost unchanged over the five years, but the need for scheduled reliefs and duplicates had greatly reduced, and overall Green Line allocations had gone down by 30 on Saturdays and 45 on Sundays.

As the 1950s came to an end therefore, there was no cause for optimism and no reason to assume that the steady fall in demand could be halted. In reality, as we shall see, the decline proved to be inexorable and if anything accelerated as the 1960s progressed. This was a situation which beset the entire British country bus network, but London Transport's generally inflexible approach to its own network would make a bad situation worse than it might have been.

Works services were and important part of the duties of Country Buses. The 462 had the most Vickers works journeys since the route actually passed the factory. The 462B was one variant and provided a direct link from Walton-on-Thames. RT 4553 is at the roundabout by Weybridge station on a morning journey to the factory showing the later blind after the factory was re-named BAC Works in 1967. (Peter Mitchell)

P.M. times are in heavy figures	Hitchin - Buntingford - Puckeridge - Bishops Stortford Buntingford - Much Hadham - Ware - Hertford Unless travelling to or from a point beyond these limits, a passenger may not board or alight between Buntingford *Throcking Lane* and Buntingford *Jolly Sailors*.	386 386A

TUESDAY

HITCHIN *St. Marys Square*	11 13	11 18	2 13	2 25	4 4	5 44	8 10
Gt. Wymondley *Green Man*	11 21	11 26	2 21	2 33	4 12	5 52	8 18
Titmore Gr'n *H. of Redcoats*	....	11 32	....	2 39	....	5 58	8 24
Stevenage *White Lion*	..	11 40	....	2 47	....	6 6	8 32
Walkern *Post Office*	..	11 57	....	3 4	....	6 23	8 49
Cromer *Horse & Groom*	..	12 2	....	3 9	....	6 28	8 54
Cottered *Bull*	..	12 10	....	3 17	....	6 36	9 2
BUNTINGFORD *J. Sailors*	..	C12 20	....	C3 27	....	C6 46	C9 12
Hare Street	..	A	....	A	....	A	

THURSDAY

BUNTINGFORD *J. Sailors*	9 22	..	1 36	3 57	..	8 4
Hare Street	9 30	..	1 44	4 5		
Dassels *Hobbs Lane*	9 35	..	1 49	4 10		
Braughing *Golden Fleece*	9 40	..	1 54	4 15		
Puckeridge *Crown & Falcon*	9 46	..	2 0	4 21	..	8 17
Standon *Station*	9 49	11 45	2 3	4 24	5 42	8 20
Wellpond Green *Nags Head*	9 54	11 50	2 8	4 29	5 47	8 25
Little Hadham *Angel*	10 4	12 0	2 18	4 39	5 57	
Bury Green Road	10 9	12 5	2 23	4 44	6 2	
B. STORTF'D *S'thmill Rd.*	10 23	12 19	2 37	4 58	6 16	
Hadham Ford *Fox*						8 32
Much Hadham *Red Lion*						8 37
Widford *Green Man*						8 47
Wareside *White Horse*						8 53
Ware *Grammar School*						9 6
HERTFORD *Bus Station*						9 16

SATURDAY

HITCHIN *St. Marys Square*	11 13	12 9	2 13	2 24	4 4	5 2	....	7 34	
Gt. Wymondley *Green Man*	11 21	12 15	2 21	2 30	4 12	5 8	....	7 40	
Titmore Gr'n *H. of Redcoats*	STOP	12 21		2 36		5 14	....	7 46	
Stevenage *White Lion*	STOP	12 27		2 42		5 20	....	7 52	
Walkern *Post Office*	..	12 42		2 57		5 35	....	8 7	
Cromer *Horse & Groom*	..	12 47		3 2		5 40	....	8 12	
Cottered *Bull*	..	12 55		3 10		5 48	....	8 20	
BUNTINGFORD *J. Sailors*	..	1 4		3 19		5 57	7 57	8 29	
Hare Street	..	1 10		3 25		6 3		8 35	
Dassels *Hobbs Lane*	..	1 15		3 30		6 8		8 40	
Braughing *Golden Fleece*	..	1 20		3 35		6 13		8 45	
Puckeridge *Crown & Falcon*	..	1 25		3 40		6 18	8 9	8 50	
Standon *Station*	10 23	1 28		3 43		6 21	8 12 8 53	8 56	
Wellpond Green *Nags Head*	10 28	1 33		3 48		6 26	8 17	9 1	
Little Hadham *Angel*	10 37	1 42		3 57		6 35			
Bury Green Road	10 41	1 46		4 1		6 39			
B. STORTF'D *S'thmill Rd.*	10 53	1 58		4 13		6 51			
Hadham Ford *Fox*							8 23	9 7	
Much Hadham *Red Lion*							8 28	9 12	
Widford *Green Man*							8 35	9 19	
Wareside *White Horse*							8 41	9 25	
Ware *Grammar School*							8 53	9 37	
HERTFORD *Bus Station*							9 2	9 46	

SUNDAY

HITCHIN *St. Marys Square*	....	..	5 14	7 54
Gt. Wymondley *Green Man*	..	..	5 22	8 2
Titmore Gr'n *H. of Redcoats*	....	..	5 28	8 8
Stevenage *White Lion*	..	..	5 36	8 16
Walkern *Post Office*	..	..	5 53	8 33
Cromer *Horse & Groom*	..	..	5 58	8 38
Cottered *Bull*	....	..	6 6	8 46
BUNTINGFORD *J. Sailors*	12 53		6 16	C8 56
Hare Street	1 1		6 24	..
Dassels *Hobbs Lane*	1 6		6 29	..
Braughing *Golden Fleece*	1 11		6 34	..
Puckeridge *Crown & Falcon*	1 17		6 40	..
Standon *Station*	1 20 3 43		6 43	..
Wellpond Green *Nags Head*	1 25 3 48		6 48	..
Little Hadham *Angel*	1 35 3 58		6 58	..
Bury Green Road	1 40 4 3		7 3	..
B. STORTF'D *S'thmill Rd.*	1 54 4 17		7 17	..

A–Arrives Buntingsford *Station* 4 mins. later. B–Departs Buntingford *Throcking Lane* 3 mins. earlier. C–Time at Buntingford *The Crown*.

(TT.4543/2)

The 386 was the longest and most remote of all Country area routes, necessitating lengthy run outs from Hertford for buses to take up service. On Tuesdays the bus ran as a 331 to Buntingford and operated the four return journeys to Hitchin before running back to Hertford over the 331 in the evening. The three short journeys to Great Wymondley were run by the bus from the 329A. On Thursday morning the bus left Hertford at 8.06am as a 386A to Buntingford before running the day's service into Bishop's Stortford. The timetable notes the two afternoon journeys to and from Throcking Lane in Buntingford described later in the text. Two buses were required on Saturdays when service was crew operated with RFs to account for higher passenger numbers and the difference in point to point timings is notable, crew buses were allowed 14 minutes less than the omo GSs over the whole length of the route. The 386A and the Sunday service were pointless and were abandoned in the sweeping cuts of October 1958. (Author's collection)

This leaflet contains
AMENDMENTS
to the Country Bus and Coach Map published in October 1958

On and from 15 October 1958

ROUTE	ALTERATION
304	WITHDRAWN between St. Albans (City Station) and Tyttenhanger. Certain journeys operate from St. Albans to Colney Street.
309	Certain buses will run on from Harefield to Hill End.
336	DIVERTED between Chorleywood and Chenies by way of Chorleywood Station.
351	WITHDRAWN.
355	EXTENDED from St. Albans by way of Sandridge, Wheathampstead, and Batford Corner to Harpenden. ADDITIONAL SERVICE: Harpenden—Batford Estate (Pickford Hill). Journeys to St. Albans (Firbank Road) withdrawn.
385	EXTENDED in Mill Way Estate to Pinfold Road.
386A	WITHDRAWN.
391	WITHDRAWN between Sandridge and Harpenden and between Harpenden and Batford Estate (Pickford Hill). EXTENDED from Hill End to Tyttenhanger.
392	EXTENDED from Stevenage (White Lion) to Hitchin (St. Mary's Square).
442	WITHDRAWN.
444	WITHDRAWN.

On and from 15 October 1958

ROUTE	ALTERATION
705	DIVERTED between Keston Mark and Bromley South Station by way of Hayes
804	WITHDRAWN.

On and from 29 October 1958

ROUTE	ALTERATION
400	WITHDRAWN.
415	WITHDRAWN between Ripley and Ockham.
423	WITHDRAWN between Swanley and Crockenhill and DIVERTED to Swanley (L.T. Garage).
424	WITHDRAWN between Smallfield and Outwood and between Smallfield and Horne.
449	WITHDRAWN between Holmwood Common (Four Wents Pond) and Ewhurst.
467A	WITHDRAWN.
470	EXTENDED from Chelsham (L.T. Garage) to Fairleigh and to Warlingham Park Hospital.
479	WITHDRAWN.
492	WITHDRAWN.
854	EXTENDED from Orpington to Ramsden Estate.

1058/2295 S/100M.

These two leaflets were issued with the October 1958 Country Bus map. Which had been printed before all the post-strike cuts and withdrawals had been finalised.

4   The Decline Accelerates

The 385/385A served housing estates surrounding Watford and rostered seven or eight RTs. In October 1956, in typical surroundings, RT 1079 is at the terminus in Holywell Estate working a journey back to Garston garage. (Peter Mitchell)

The constant lack of platform staff referred to at the end of the last chapter continued to have an adverse effect on operations, and whilst this was greater in the Central area, the intermittent levels of service resulted in what the public saw as a poor quality service and only served to deter more passengers from using bus and Green Line routes. Garston garage suffered the worst shortages. Watford and the surrounding conurbation had many large manufacturing businesses, and combined with its proximity to London offered a great variety of employment with higher pay and fewer unsocial hours than a bus driver or conductor job. Garston's staff shortages were so great that the introduction of the summer schedules on 25th May 1960 actually resulted in cuts in services rather than the usual increases so that timetables could match the number of crews available since it had been impossible to operate the previously scheduled timetable. The main 321 and 347 trunk routes, plus the busy 306 and 311 were cut back as well as the 346 and 385 groups of Watford local services. Although Hemel Hempstead operated the 322, Garston ran some additional Saturday shopping journeys to Kings Langley which were numbered 322B and these were withdrawn completely as a result of staff shortages. It was a commentary on the reduction in Saturday shopping traffic that when the staffing shortages eased sufficiently to reverse the cuts, the 322B was not reinstated and never ran again. There were minor increases elsewhere during 1960 with town services at Stevenage and Harlow being extended further into new housing areas, while Hemel Hempstead added extra works journeys as more factories began to appear in the new industrial areas out towards the new M1 motorway which had opened in the previous year.

By 1960 thought began to be given to some Country area fleet replacement, the RFs then being about half way through their anticipated service life and the RTs slightly further on than that. The half cab crew-operated single deckers had become all but superfluous with just two remaining in service, while the non-standard GSs and RLHs were already in declining numbers and would probably not need replacing on a like for like basis as a result of general service cuts. At the time however, the main thrust of fleet replacement was in the Central area where new Routemasters were replacing the trolleybuses.

RF 700 was the highest numbered RF and along with 517 and 647 one of the last three RFs delivered in March 1953, having already been converted for one man operation. After four months at Reigate, It went to Hemel Hempstead where it spent ten months as a trainer. Late in 1958 it returned and spent the next nine years there. The majority of its time would be spent on the 322, and in the days long before Watford town centre was pedestrianised, it turns from the High Street into Clarendon Road. (Alan Cross)

After the 390 was converted to omo and extended from Hertford to Sawbridgeworth, Stevenage retained a single short journey to Aston each morning as part of a morning peak duty which ran a 384B return to Letchworth and a 303 works journey to Gunnell's Wood. RT 3169 is running this journey which, with true London Transport operating rigidness, allowed one minute less than the omo timings with only a three minute layover at Aston! (Alan Cross)

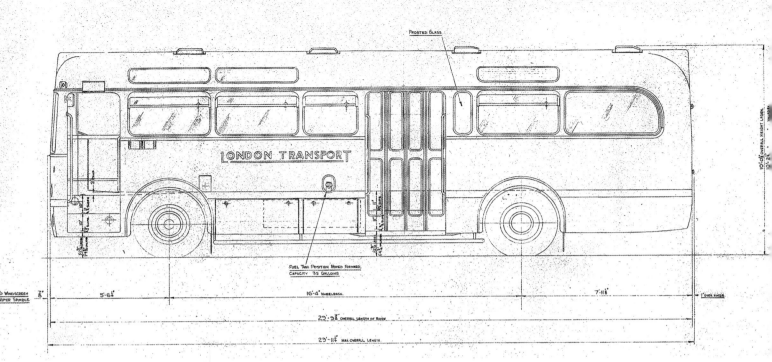

The idea of a higher capacity single decker which could be one-man operated, but where boarding and alighting times at stops could be reduced by a front entrance and a separate centre exit, was a new and novel concept at the time. Some municipal operators were just beginning to experiment with this, and London Transport ordered a small batch of three such buses to see how such buses would actually work in service. The buses which arrived in September 1960 were standard AEC Reliances with Willowbrook bodies which, although utilitarian, were not unattractive and were classified RW (*Reliance Willowbrook*) with 42 seats and a centre exit. Their first allocation was to Two Waters where they entered service on the 322 route at the end of September running alongside RFs on the route. This was a busy urban route which had been converted to omo only the previous year with a high proportion of 'stop–start' running with short distance passengers. They spent three months on the 322 before being transferred to Addlestone in January 1961 for allocation to the 427, 437 and 456 routes which ran from Weybridge to Woking by different ways and served the edge of the large LCC Estate at Sheerwater. In June 1961 they were moved to Reigate where they were mostly used on the 440 and 440A. In Redhill, the parts of the route to Salfords and Redstone Estate were busy town services, but the outer end of the 440 to Caterham and on to Woldingham, if not completely rural, represented the first time the RWs had worked a 'country' bus route. After five months at Reigate, they were moved again to St Albans to work the 355, which was a long, largely urban, route. The section north of St Albans was more rural, but served the expanding estate at Batford near Harpenden which provided a number of passengers into the town and mainline station, whilst the southern section to Borehamwood carried a great deal of short distance traffic and was generally busier. Operation of the RWs on all these routes provided useful feedback on the effectiveness of the dual entrance layout.

Although the RWs were not ordered until early in 1960, Park Royal had produced a draft design four years earlier based on the standard AEC Reliance chassis of the time. The front and rear ends, and front doors bore an obvious likeness to the RF, but the sliding window vents were very different from London Transport's standard quarter drop winding windows, while internally the floor ramped up 5ins from the front as opposed to the flat floor on the RF. The bus was designed at the time for crew operation, and a conductor's box was situated to the rear of the centre doors at the expense of an extra seat. (LT Museum)

The RLHs were never numerous in the Country area, and the 1958 strike proved to be the catalyst for significant reductions in their numbers in the service cuts which followed. The Guildford and Addlestone routes however survived unchanged, and RLH 25 has stopped at Woking station on a 436A to Ripley. The Sunday service on this route later became a casualty of the extensive reductions in the winter schedules of 1964. (Capital Transport)

During their short stay at Hertford, the RWs ran on most routes as part of the extensive cross working. RW3 has stopped the end of Fairfax Road on a 331 to Buntingford and appears to be about to change drivers. The font size for the intermediate points on the RW blinds made them appear rather smaller than the standard RF version. (Capital Transport)

The other major advancement in new vehicle design at the time, and which was to have a fundamental effect on bus operation everywhere, was the development of the rear engine double decker which could be designed to have a wide entrance ahead of the front wheels and which had obvious potential for omo, although it would be some years before this became legal. The almost complete lack of interest in these developments by London Transport for their Country area fleet was to have a profound and detrimental effect in the latter half of the 1960s.

The need to provide additional duplicates for the summer augmentation of Green Line services in 1960 once again created a temporary shortage of RTs. Having sent a batch of red RTLs to Northfleet the previous summer, the decision was made this time that a batch of 18 would be repainted green for formal transfer to the Country area. They arrived at Hatfield garage in July 1960 to release a number of RTs to Green Line duties for the summer – mostly at Windsor. Exactly how many red RTs were still surplus at this time is not known since the number fluctuated, and many of the younger ones were being reallocated to replace older roofbox RT3 versions. Nevertheless it was a strange decision to send a batch of RTLs to the Country area, particularly as they had not been well received at Northfleet the previous year. Hatfield's RTLs never appeared as formally allocated to a particular route and the allocation book dated 23rd November 1960 shows Hatfield's allocation only as 27 RTs with no mention of the RTLs. They were mostly used however on the 303 and 303A which had a Monday to Friday allocation of 12 buses. This was a long trunk route with several sections where stops were less frequent and the RTL's slower gearchange was better

Green liveried RTL 1264 is crossing the bridge over the East Coast main line, having just left Hatfield station on a journey to Hitchin, and will pass Hatfield garage a few yards further on the right. It carries a side advert for the Welwyn Department Store which was one of the largest in the Home Counties. (Alan Cross)

suited to these routes rather than the busy interurban route to St Albans and the Welwyn Garden City town services, which routes had more frequent stops. The RTLs did see some use on Hatfield's other routes from extensive cross working, but they remained very unpopular with drivers and in the end lasted just under a year before the last ones were withdrawn from Hatfield at the end of June 1961, when RTs returned to replace them. They spent the rest of their lives languishing out of use or as trainers and did not run again in revenue earning service.

Passenger numbers fell away again in 1960, and although the wage increases during the year went some way to reducing staff shortages, they were undoubtedly a factor in the loss of further traffic where lack of staff meant that the scheduled timetable could not be run. On bus routes, the decline in 1960 in passenger numbers was only about 3%, but the Green Line network lost about double this percentage. It was undoubtedly the beginning of what became an accelerating decline.

The 1960 winter schedules introduced on 12th October saw no real reductions in bus services, with Monday to Friday remaining roughly the same, and only a small reduction on Saturdays. The Sunday reductions however continued the downward trend, and a further 26 buses were taken out of the schedules. This now meant that the total number of buses rostered on Sunday was just over 45% of the Monday to Friday total – in other words more than half the fleet stood idle every Sunday. Five years earlier at the end of 1955, the Sunday total represented 60% of the Monday to Friday number, and illustrates the increasing gap between weekday and Sunday services. In particular, with the sharp reduction in less rural routes, the number of GSs rostered on Sundays had dwindled from 36 at the end of 1955 to just 14 at the end of 1960.

The schedules of the Croydon trunk routes had changed very little since 1955, but the weekend allocations were dropping away in response to falling traffic. The basic timetables were little changed although some half-hourly headways had been widened to hourly in the evenings and on Sundays on some of the outer sections, but many of the duplicates, additional peak and shopping journeys had gradually been stripped out. Compared to the summer 1955 schedules, the total number of RTs scheduled on Saturdays fell from 87 to 79 for summer 1960, but had suffered a dramatic reduction from 80 to 57 on Sundays.

The new bus station at Stevenage had opened in October 1958 and two years later, the rural 384 and 386 were diverted there having previously only served the High Street in what by then had become known as 'Stevenage Old Town' about half a mile from the new town centre. On the same date, the twice weekly 386 which had run direct between Cottered and Cromerhill through some very remote countryside was diverted to serve the tiny hamlet of Ardeley which was so small in fact that it remained one of very few places served by the Country area which had no timing point and was referred to just as 'Ardeley' in the timetable. The diversion also took the route down what was perhaps the narrowest section of road anywhere on the network, running between two low verges with open fields on either side. I well remember on an afternoon trip in 1965 the GS meeting a cyclist coming the other way. The road was so narrow at this point that the man had to get off and clamber up on to the verge to allow the bus to pass! Ardeley was already served by Smith's Coaches of Buntingford who ran a route to Hitchin which paralleled the 386 for much of the way, and had continued after the 1933 Act since the whole of the route was outside the 'Special Area'. The diversion of the 386 via Ardeley provided this tiny village with no fewer than six

The duty with running number SV 20 detailed in the text was usually worked by the spare Green Line coach. RF 54 with 716 side route boards has arrived at Stevenage bus station from Hitchin on one of the 303 journeys back from Hitchin. Its next departure will either be the 384 short to Walkern or the early evening return trip on the 807 to Letchworth. (G. Mead)

journeys into Hitchin each market day, which even by 1960 was far more than could be justified. Another small addition was at Hitchin where the 383 was extended from the town up to the new Oakfield Estate which was being developed along the road out to Great Wymondley. This created a cross town service in Hitchin between Oakfield Estate and Purwell Lane Estate, and made more efficient use of the bus between its two-hourly trips to Weston, although the timetable still required a second bus at certain times of the day with some journeys remaining crew worked. The Stevenage rosters at the time included a crew-operated RF which was used for supplementary works journeys, but on Saturday afternoons worked one of the most varied rural duties anywhere in the network. With running number SV20, the working ran as follows (*Details courtesy Laurie Akehurst*):

303	12.44	Stevenage to Hitchin	364	3.54	Hitchin to Preston
364	1.07	Hitchin to Preston		4.09	Preston to Hitchin
	1.23	Preston to Hitchin	383	4.24	Hitchin to Purwell Lane Estate
383	1.38	Hitchin to Purwell Lane Estate		4.35	Purwell Lane Estate to Hitchin
	1.49	Purwell Lane Estate to Hitchin	303	4.47	Hitchin to Stevenage
303	2.01	Hitchin to Stevenage	807	5.12	Stevenage to Letchworth
384	2.31	Stevenage to Walkern Post Office	807	6.12	Letchworth to Stevenage
	2.51	Walkern Post Office to Stevenage			
303	3.32	Stevenage to Hitchin			Finish Stevenage Bus Station 6.47pm

The 1.38pm Hitchin to Purwell Lane Estate and return ran only four minutes behind the bus which ran the route all day and was effectively a duplicate for afternoon shoppers. This duty must have been a pleasant change for the crews who, apart from peak RT workings to Letchworth on the 384 and some Hitchin journeys on the 392, spent the rest of their week toiling round and round the Stevenage town routes through endless housing estates.

By the beginning of 1961, the general pattern of new routes within the New Towns and overspill estates was established. Although populations would continue to expand, the Country area's route network had probably reached its peak, a situation which had been reflected in the allocation of buses at the New Towns which had steadily increased during the 1950s. In May 1955 Crawley, for example, needed 25 buses, which included five RTs and one T allocated to *'supplementary schedules and special duplicates'*. Five years later by November 1960, the bus allocation had increased to 30, the extra five buses all working the town services where the requirement had doubled from five to 10 RTs. In the northern area, the total number of RTs allocated to the four garages serving the New Towns had increased from 80 to 100 by November 1960.

Whilst the New Towns' expansion had to some extent offset the decline on the rural routes, the financial position of the whole Country Bus and Green Line department was now becoming more of a concern. At this point is worth summarising the population increases which the New Towns and estates had brought to the Country Bus area during the 1950s, the main figures for which are set out below:

The 369 was a short route serving Aveley estate and provided a link to the London – Tilbury line at South Ockenden. RT 4166 has just crossed the railway on its way to Usk Road in surroundings which would become developed with new roads and housing. (Peter Mitchell)

Population in Thousands

	1951	1961	Increase
Stevenage	6.8	21.6	14.8
Crawley	8.5	54.0	45.5
Hatfield and Welwyn Garden City	51.0	69.0	18.0
Harlow	4.1	18.1	14.0
Hemel Hempstead	58.0	83.0	25.0
Slough	65.0	82.0	17.0
TOTALS	193.4	327.7	134.3

It can be seen that the populations of these seven towns alone had increased by around 134,000 in ten years, while in the same period (including the New Towns) Hertfordshire's total population had risen by around 220,000, Surrey's by 156,000, and the Grays/Tilbury and Gravesend/Dartford conurbations along the Thames added many more. The major overspill estates at Sheerwater, Britwell, Aveley and Merstham, plus a great many small estates on the edge of most towns in the Home Counties had also contributed to a large increase across the whole Country Bus area. Although it is impossible to calculate the exact increase in the ten-year period, the Country Bus Department had probably an extra half a million people living in its area by 1961 compared to a decade earlier. If only 20% of

The 371B from Tilbury across Grays through Aveley was part of the frequent 371 group and terminated at Rainham where connections were made with Central area routes into east London. RT 1068 stands in the private road which was the terminus at Feenan Highway at Tilbury. The open farmland in the background would be unrecognisable today. (Peter Mitchell)

On the opposite side of the Thames from the Grays and Tilbury routes, Northfleet ran several cross town services. The Plough at Northfleet was the terminus for the 495/496, and buses turned in front of Northfleet football ground with the Pub out of the picture to the right. A former Bristol Tramways Leyland PD2 is parked behind RT 984 as it waits to return to Kings Farm estate. The timetables for these routes was unusual in that the 12 minute afternoon frequency was reduced to 15 minutes on Wednesdays to account for the lower passenger levels on early closing day. (Peter Mitchell)

these extra people had made a bus journey just once a week, then that would have meant some five million extra passenger journeys per year in 1961 compared with 1951, whereas in reality, the total numbers of passengers carried had reduced year on year. Although there are a number of different ways of measuring this, dependent on whether overall numbers or miles per passenger journey are used, London Transport's annual reports for the period show that between 1955 and 1961, absolute numbers had reduced by about 18% on Country buses and around 10% on Green Line coaches. Numbers in 1953 and 1954 had been roughly stable, but in 1952 had been about 4% less than 1951. Setting aside the

The service to Redstone Estate was an early post-war addition. Numbered 440A it was one of the shortest routes with a running time of just seven minutes from Redhill. RF 555 is pictured earlier as a crew bus on the 447, but was converted to omo in February 1959 and sent back to Reigate. It is at the Redstone terminus where buses reversed into the entrance to the cemetery on the left to turn. It has the early 'Pay as you Enter' transfer in the front windscreen.
(Peter Mitchell)

statistics, the reality was that this significant increase in population over the ten-year period had not contributed at all to the Country area network's revenue. What the higher population with its increasing affluence did contribute, however, was a significant increase in private car usage with the resultant gradual worsening of traffic conditions coupled with a steady reduction in passengers. The rapid increase in car ownership was the primary reason for the sharp decline in weekend travel, especially on Sundays, and the increasing popularity of television (ITV had begun in 1955) meant that more and more people stayed indoors rather than go out in the evenings – and even when they did they were most likely to go by car. It was also no coincidence that local cinemas suffered a similar decline at the same time. Against this background it was becoming obvious by the early 1960s that the decline in overall passenger numbers would prove to be irreversible, but during the next few years London Transport's response to this was to prove inadequate and reductions in timetables and miles run lagged behind the reductions in passenger numbers. This had the effect of each bus carrying on average fewer and fewer passengers per journey, thus gradually eating away at the overall profitability of the network.

In January 1961, the branch line railway from Dunton Green to Westerham was closed. Rail passengers who had used Westerham station and Brasted halt had a ready alternative on the 403, but the link from Chipstead to Sevenoaks railway station had consisted of a single peak journey on 454A. Southern Region therefore arranged with London Transport to introduce a peak hour service from Chipstead village to Sevenoaks station which was numbered 413B and used a single GS to cater for the few railway passengers who still had season tickets from Chipstead. These began to expire soon after the rail service had gone, after which the small number of former rail passengers found other means of transport, so the 413B quickly became superfluous, being withdrawn on 25th April.

The summer schedules for 1961 were notable for the fact that for the first time two Central area routes which had previously been extended out into the Country on summer Sundays did not run. The 93 had been extended from Epsom out to Boxhill and Dorking, and the 116 from Staines along the Thames to Runnymede and Old Windsor, but after 1960, these two routes never ran over their old extensions again as services were cut back in the face of increasing car ownership.

The east to west corridor from Welwyn Garden City to Harlow and Epping was re-cast once again in June 1961 in an effort to achieve more economies, and alternate journeys on the 393 between Tylers Cross and Broxbourne were diverted to serve a new section of route via Nazeing Gate, numbered 393A. This was not Nazeing Gate's first bus service however as Biss Brothers had begun a route from Roydon Hamlet through Nazeing to Waltham Abbey in October 1952 but it was unsuccessful, being abandoned after only 18 months. London Transport's connections on the new 393A to Harlow and Hertford were clearly more worthwhile. The total number of buses allocated to this pool of routes remained the same, but some timetable adjustments yielded savings in fuel and crew costs. Part of this network was the 380 route which ran to Sawbridgeworth along the A414 which then was a relatively minor road through the villages of Stanstead Abbots, Eastwick, Gilston and High Wych. The A414 passed about two or three miles north of Harlow New Town, but before it expanded, Sawbridgeworth was a more important objective for shoppers. Now that Harlow was becoming established, the route was diverted in October 1961 over a double run from the A414 near Eastwick to run into Harlow New Town centre and back. This added nine minutes to the overall journey time but the facility of the direct link into Harlow far outweighed any inconvenience to the few remaining passenger who wanted to travel into Sawbridgeworth from Ware or St Margarets.

Although some reductions had been made to its allocations, the June 1961 Saturday schedules for Hertford's rural routes required seven GSs, 21 RFs and three RTs plus three RFs from Epping which ran a joint allocation on the 393 and 393A. This overall total of 34 buses was only four fewer than the 1955 schedules although that had included ten RTs scheduled to routes before omo conversion. These rural services were still relatively buoyant, and their operation is interesting as it shows how varied the schedules were at garages where there was a large proportion of rural operation and interworking between routes. The seven GSs worked running numbers HG60–HG66 and ran on the 308, 308A, 329, 329A, 331, 333, 380, 386 and 388. Only one bus (HG61) spent the whole day on the same route, running the whole of the 380 timetable between Hertford and Sawbridgeworth, leaving Fairfax Road garage at 7.19am and finishing at Hertford Bus Station at 10.18pm before running light back to the garage. The other six GSs interworked between routes all day. HG64 ran the 329A to Hitchin, the 386 Great Wymondley shorts and the 329 evening service referred to earlier. The 308 and 308A had three different GSs during the day, the 388 four, and the five Chapmore End journeys on the 333 were worked by three different GSs. HG65 spent all day on the 308 and 308A before working two late afternoon shorts to High Cross on the 331. HG66 was the most varied, running a 388 to Welwyn Garden City, 333 to Chapmore End, 329 to Nup End, another 333 to Chapmore End, 331 to High Cross, 329 to Knebworth, and finally two 388s to Welwyn village.

The 21 RFs covered HG32 to HG52, and interworking of these was less complex since some of the routes had regular headway timetables which allowed several of them to work the same route all day. The 350 and 350A ran an hourly service between Barnet and Hertford, and two journeys an hour all afternoon between Hertford and Bishop's Stortford with short journeys to Widford and Much Hadham in the morning. Seven RFs (HG37–HG43) therefore spent all day working the route, and only one other RF worked an afternoon short from Bishop's Stortford to Much Hadham and back. This was HG49 which, with HG48, worked the 386 all day together with the morning and evening positioning journeys on the 331 from Hertford. HG44 and 45 ran most of the 384 and 384A while HG52 worked the 308 and 308A alongside the GSs running two journeys to Cuffley, the mid-morning 308A to Little Berkhampstead, and the early afternoon relief 308 to Newgate Street which was timed five minutes behind the GS departure to Cuffley. On its return to Hertford from Newgate Street, it then worked the 4.03pm 384 journey to Letchworth, finishing its day's work back at Hertford Bus Station at 7.26pm. HG33 and 36 ran the 333 all day, including the 333B Ware Park Hospital journeys. These were probably the most tedious duties, each bus running back and forth to Bengeo every half hour all day. Before its 333 journeys, HG33 ran an early morning short to Standon on the 331, and then in the evening it left HG36 to complete the day's service on the 333 while it was scheduled to run the 8.08pm 384 to Stevenage. This journey actually worked beyond Stevenage up to Jacks Hill at Graveley, and then ran a 390 from there to Aston, returning to Stevenage before finally running the last 384 from Stevenage at 10.32pm back to Hertford. HG46, 47, 50 and 51 ran the 390, 393 and 393A all day along with three RFs from Epping which worked EP1, EP2, and EP3, a feature of the schedules being that all three Epping buses finished their day at Hertford garage, while HG46, HG50 and HG51 finished at Epping.

On Saturday 11th July 1964, GS 64 has been allocated to HG 63. It has arrived at Hertford having run the 2.40pm 329 to Nup End and back, and the driver has changed the blind for its next journey which will be the 4.10pm to Chapmore End – one of only five journeys on Saturdays to this tiny hamlet. After this it will run two more 388 returns to Welwyn before running back to the garage at 7.15pm. (Author)

The operation of the 331 was the most mixed. HG32 and HG34 spent all day on the two-hourly round trip cycle to and from Buntingford, and these were supplemented by HG35 after it had worked the first journey out to Nup End and back on the 329. With a 30-minute headway all day, the 331 required four buses to work the basic service, and because it was busy throughout the day, two RTs were also allocated to run seven return journeys to Buntingford between them. HG26 ran two morning journeys, including the 9.05am from Buntingford which picked up heavy loads of morning shoppers for Ware and Hertford. The rest of the morning service was run with RFs, but the RT on HG26 then ran the 12.35, 2.35, 4.35 and 6.35pm journeys to Buntingford, the afternoon service being much busier. The other RT allocated was HG21, which ran the 7.16am 327 journey to Nazeing, returning as a 393A. On arriving back at Hertford, it ran back to Fairfax Road garage and was not required again until just before 1.00pm when it was rostered to work the 1.05pm 331 to Buntingford. With HG26, this meant that the two busiest lunchtime departures were both double-deck worked. The RF working HG34 had run the round trip two hours all morning, but instead of working the 1.05pm departure, it ran a High Cross short working at 1.19pm between the main service to provide yet more capacity. HG21 ran only this one return trip on the 331, and after returning to Hertford it then changed to the 310, working to Enfield so it could run extra afternoon shopping journeys between Enfield and Cheshunt before returning to Hertford to finish its day's work. In all, the 331 was operated by ten different buses on Saturday: two RTs, two GSs and six RFs which included the two from the 386 positioning journeys to and from Buntingford. Lastly, one other RT was allocated to HG27 which ran a total of ten short journeys between Hertford and Watton station on the 390 on an hourly headway during the main part of the day to supplement the two-hourly through timetable to Stevenage. There were a few additional journeys to Watton during the week which were omo worked, but Saturday traffic was much heavier. Even as late as the winter 1965 timetable, an RT was still scheduled on Saturday although the ten journeys had by then been reduced to seven. Hertford had probably the most complex schedules of any, but the interworking of buses between routes was commonplace at most garages, and as timetables began to be cut back more and more, even greater interworking became necessary to make the best use of buses and reduce running costs. Hertford's most interesting working of all however was perhaps the Saturday night staff bus which ran to Waltham Cross. One of the spare GSs was usually employed to run this, but in 1961 this was added to the public timetable, so that the 11.30pm 310 journey from Hertford garage to Waltham Cross, with a return at 12.18am arriving back at Hertford garage at 1.00am, was formally rostered for GS operation.

The winter schedules of 25th October 1961 saw some further reductions, though nothing significant. One cut however which was indicative of what was to come was the withdrawal of the 712 Green Line route during the week between St Albans and Luton except for three morning and evening peak hour journeys. The 321 and 714 provided six journeys an hour all day as far as Harpenden, and four on to Luton, so that the hourly 712 throughout the day in addition had become superfluous. The weekend service remained but even though peak hour journeys were retained, it is difficult to believe that there were passengers from the London area still wanting to commute north of St Albans on a daily basis, and the three additional journeys each morning and evening were not really necessary in terms of the additional seating capacity they provided between St Albans and

Luton. Although London Transport reacted too slowly over the following years, the reduction of the 712 was probably the first recognition that passenger numbers on sections of some Green Line routes had fallen to the point where cuts were necessary. The principal factor which had led to the reduction had begun in January 1960 when British Railways London Midland Region announced cheaper fares into London on the Bedford to London line which had been modernised with diesels replacing steam. The return fares from Luton to St Pancras were reduced from 9s 8d to 7s 6d, from Harpenden 7s 10d to 6s 6d and from St Albans 6s 4d to 5s 6d, all of which were cheaper than the equivalent 712 and 714 fares, the journey time also being much quicker. At a meeting of the Road Services Committee on 16th March 1961, it was reported that the London Midland Region modernisation had begun to abstract traffic from parallel Green Line routes, and that revenue on the 714 had reduced by 6%, and on the 712 and 713 by 8%. Routes such as the 715, 715A, 718 and 720 which paralleled similar Eastern Region routes had experienced similar drops in revenue, although the 716 and 716A had not yet been affected between Stevenage, Hatfield and London. This was perhaps the first evidence that, far from the BTC's contention that Green Line routes might have a negative effect on the railways, quite the reverse was happening and the railways were beginning to reduce Green Line usage.

The same meeting also discussed the general decline across all Green Line routes which was causing increased concern. In the space of only three years, by the end of 1962, roughly one passenger in every eight had abandoned Green Line routes compared to 1959, about half of this reduction coming in 1962 alone. Furthermore, it was evident that the mileage travelled by the average Green Line passenger was also reducing. Train journey times to London had been reduced as railway modernisation gained momentum, and following the modernisation of the London to Bedford line referred to above, the lines from Liverpool Street to Hertford East and Bishop's Stortford were electrified in 1961. The section of the Metropolitan line beyond Rickmansworth had been steam hauled requiring a change of loco at Rickmansworth, but this too was electrified in 1961, the last day of steam being 9th September. Final upgrading of the Metropolitan line was completed in June 1962 when new schedules increased frequency and reduced journey times to central London. The routes which paralleled these rail lines continued to suffer a drop in passenger numbers, with a particularly steep reduction on the 715 and 715A routes to Hertford.

Running number HG 27 was the duty for the RT on 390 short journeys to Watton. During the week, these were soon cut back and became mostly omo, but on Saturdays the RT ran hourly all day until early evening to cater for extra shoppers to Hertford. As passenger numbers declined in the 1960s, the journeys were cut back, and then withdrawn at the end of 1966. RT 3807 waits in Hertford Bus Station on this duty. (Alan Cross)

The 708 was part of the 15 minute headway between Two Waters and South Croydon referred to in the text, a level of service well justified as the routes remained busy all day until the mid-1960s. RF 183 typifies the high standard of Green Line travel at the time as it loads up at Eccleston Bridge on a journey to East Grinstead. The coach is working EG 51 which was the second coach out in the morning, so is working the 10.18am from Hemel Hempstead. These off peak journeys through London were the ones which saw a significant drop in passenger levels during the 1960s although this carries a reasonable load. (G. Mead)

The gap in loadings between peak and off peak was also widening to the point where on some Green Line routes thought was given to reducing off-peak headways. Almost all routes ran to a 30-minute headway, and hourly pairs of routes (such as the 706/707 and 712/713) ran to a joint 30-minute headway over their common sections. There were also some quite long sections where three routes ran together. From Two Waters all the way to South Croydon for example – a journey time of just under two hours – the 706, 707 and 708 combined to provide more than 70 journeys a day on a 15-minute headway from early morning to late evening seven days a week, while the 709, 710 and 711 provided the same level of service from Kennington in south London out as far as Gerrards Cross.

Operationally however, reducing off peak headways was not easy to achieve. On the majority of Green Line routes with a 30-minute headway, typically the garages at or near each end of the route sent out seven or eight RFs until about 9.00am or 9.30am every morning. Around the time the last coach was scheduled to depart from its home garage, the first coach from the other end would arrive, followed every half hour by the rest from the opposite end of the route. All of these outward journeys ran into London in the morning peak, and generally carried good loads, with several garages also running RTs as scheduled duplicates as far as London. After a 50- or 60-minute layover, the coaches all returned back to their home garage, departing between about 10.00am and 1.30pm, and arriving back between lunchtime and late afternoon. These return trips were the off peak journeys which were carrying fewer and fewer people, but having run out on the morning peak journeys to the other end of the route, the coaches all had to return back to their home garage, and this made it difficult to reduce the off-peak frequency. The same applied in the afternoon when peak hour traffic through London made the service worthwhile, and reasonable numbers might be picked up in London for evening journeys home, but the services from the opposite ends of the route into London from mid evening were becoming less and less used. Inflexible Union agreements relating to length of shifts and breaks also prevented almost all routes from being split in central London, and it would be some years before this became possible.

In January 1962, cheap fares had been introduced on routes 703, 709, 710 and 711, partly to combat cheap rail fares on lines from London to Uxbridge, High Wycombe and Amersham, but they proved unsuccessful in attracting additional custom. A report entitled *'Green Line Coaches in relation to British Railways'* was presented to the Traffic Committee in May 1962 with the results of studies of passenger numbers by rail and Green Line over comparable journeys. The study had looked at several routes into London including from Tring and Watford, Luton and St Albans, Bishop's Stortford and Harlow, and Hitchin and Welwyn Garden City. It found that only 4% or 5% of all passengers (depending on the route) travelled by Green Line between main points (i.e. railway stations), and only 15% travelled between points not actually near railway stations. The report concluded, perhaps obviously, that *'comparison of journey times and frequencies prove that British Railways possess a formidable advantage between main centres of population'*. The report also added somewhat dismissively that *'since only a small number of passengers are required to provide a profitable operation, then Green Line remains complementary to rail and should be maintained'*. Whilst the proportion of passengers using Green Line would obviously be small compared to rail, the actual figures showed that this was in fact very small. If only about 20% of Green Line passengers were using the service instead of rail for comparable journeys, then the other 80% were mostly made up from shopping, leisure, and some commuting, all of which had been showing signs of an increasing downward trend, so that the contention that Green Line was complementary to rail, whilst true, was somewhat complacent in the circumstances. It should be added however, that earlier in January that year, at a Commercial Department meeting, a discussion had taken place about the downward trend in passengers on all road services and that there was *'every need for a continuing review of services.'* Over the ensuing years though, such reviews consisted almost entirely of reducing frequencies with little reference to the relevance of the actual route network itself, so that other than the withdrawal of a few infrequent rural routes, the network itself remained unchanged. This lack of basic change was a factor common to operators across the whole country and it was perhaps one of the major factors which gave London Country such problems a decade later.

The development of a Routemaster coach is well documented, its success in service leading to the fleet of RMCs from 1962 and RCLs from 1965. CRL 4 spent short periods at Windsor on the 704 and 718, and underneath complex trolleybus overhead it turns right from Chingford Road into Forest Road on its way to Windsor. The important trolleybus routes to London Docks and Liverpool Street crossed the routes from Manor House to Woodford at this point. (C. Carter)

Despite the failure of the RT version of a Green Line coach as RTC 1 in 1948, the fourth prototype Routemaster, designated CRL 4, had been built as such and entered service at Romford on service 721 in October 1957 to work alongside the RTs on this busy route. After three months there it went to Reigate in January 1958 to work the 711, and in August to Windsor for the 704. The 704 schedules at the time meant that the first two Windsor coaches out every morning ended up at Tunbridge Wells at the end of the day, and vice versa, so that CRL 4 also spent some nights garaged at Tunbridge Wells. Working in normal service, the prototype ran an average of about 2,000 miles each week, and this proved valuable in ironing out some general mechanical and electrical faults which developed. Over the next 18 months, the coach was sent to Hertford, Epping, back to Windsor and finally Stevenage where it was withdrawn in August 1960 in order to carry out some strengthening works to the rear and modify the air suspension. However, after 200,000 miles in service this experimental coach was considered a success, and in early 1961, a decision was made to build a batch of Routemasters to full double-deck Green Line coach specification. The fleet of RFs was now over ten years old, and although solid and reliable, the image they represented needed upgrading and modernising, particularly in the face of declining traffic. The history of the RMC coaches has been well documented, but five decades after their introduction, it is difficult to recall just how much of a sensation they caused when they appeared. They provided genuine luxury with generous legroom, luggage racks, fluorescent lighting, heaters, a smooth ride from the air suspension, and with their folding platform doors they were handsome vehicles, enhanced further still by a simple but elegant livery. In service, they had a high top speed and were more than capable of maintaining time – even catching up lost time from traffic delays – and were very easy to drive. Sixty eight of them were built at a cost of just over £7,000 each, and the first was launched with suitable high profile publicity in July 1962.

Other than the east London routes, the Green Line network's busiest, and most frequent, route was the 715 from Guildford to Hertford. It had run to the same daily timetable with a 20-minute headway two months after it had been reintroduced in February 1946 and needed 21 RFs to work the basic timetable, ten and 11 from Guildford and Hertford respectively. Hertford also ran another four RFs on the 715A to London, and in the July 1962 allocations five RTs were also rostered at Hertford as duplicates Monday to Friday, two Saturday and four Sunday. The southern end of the route was less busy and Guildford had one RF Monday to Friday and one RT on Sunday for duplicates. This meant that during Monday to Friday peak hours, 31 coaches were allocated to the 715 and 715A, Hertford's RT duplicates providing an additional capacity of 280 seats over and above the scheduled timetable for the Northern half of the route. The 715 could be described as one of Green Line's 'flagship' services and the decision was made to allocate the first batch of new RMCs to this route. The 20-minute headway was obviously convenient for passengers, but reducing this to 30-minutes might not reduce convenience to any degree, and the seating capacity of two RMCs per hour was almost identical to the three RFs previously used. Thus from 29th August 1962, the RMCs took over the 715, the through headway being reduced to half-hourly, with 21 RFs replaced by 14 RMCs, resulting in a saving of one third on the costs of fuel and crews. The 715A was converted at the same time, the hourly timetable being unchanged, although because of the higher seating capacity of the RMCs, the 715A duplicate RT was withdrawn as was one of the duplicates for the 715. In the evening peak, the former 20-minute headway combined with the five duplicate journeys meant that departures from London to Hertford were frequent, and between 4.00pm and 6.00pm there had been 12 departures on the 715 and four on the 715A. The new timetable reduced this to nine and three respectively – a reduction of 25%. The greater capacity of the RMCs meant that overall seating capacity for all these peak hour departures was reduced only slightly – but the problem was the reduced convenience from a lesser number of departures. Traffic delays on through journeys coming up from Guildford also meant that on the new 30-minute headway, there might be longer gaps in the service to Hertford. Despite the impressive new coaches therefore, these reductions resulted in an immediate loss of passengers amounting in cash terms to almost a third of the saving in operating costs. The intangible effects of the damage done to Green Line's image of convenience and reliability were not it seems appreciated at the time, and whether a 'cost-benefit analysis' might have drawn other conclusions is impossible to say.

The result of the new RMCs coming into service was that the RFs at Hertford and Guildford became surplus. Between them, including traffic and engineering spares, they had had a total of 29 allocated before the changes. A decision was made that 16 of these would be converted for one-man operation and be down-graded as buses. As London Transport's policy was to keep such conversions in batches with consecutive stock numbers, the surplus RFs were variously re-allocated around the fleet so that the coaches actually released for conversion were RF 298–313 which had themselves been converted to Green Line coaches only in 1956 to cater for what was then an increasing demand and the introduction of new routes; ironically the 715A one of them.

A brand new RMC 1458 has aroused much interest as it stands on the forecourt of Guildford garage waiting for a crew to take it to Hertford. These fine coaches brought new standards of comfort and ride quality to Green Line journeys, but the timetable cuts which often accompanied them did nothing in the longer term for Green Line's reputation. Two redundant RFs stand without blinds inside the garage.
(Peter Gascoine)

While all these changes were taking place, other minor alterations were made during the year. The expansion of Penn village resulted in the GS-operated 373 from there to Beaconsfield being replaced with RTs by extending the 363 route from High Wycombe to Penn through to Beaconsfield. The 373 had been remotely operated from Amersham's 398 allocation and involved additional positioning journeys on the 398 to and from Amersham garage. The 398 was at best marginal, and by eliminating these journeys, of which most probably ran almost empty, some useful savings were made. Amersham's GS allocation was reduced by one bus and omo duty, but with adjustments at High Wycombe no extra RTs were needed there to run the extended 363.

Despite generally reducing passenger numbers, additional summer services to some places were still worthwhile. With the summer schedules on 23rd May, the 313 from Enfield to St Albans was extended non-stop to Whipsnade as usual, the rural 337 and 364A had additional journeys to serve the Zoo, and the 343 from St Albans to Dunstable also had a few journeys diverted from the main road at Kensworth run as positioning journeys for the 313. The weekend service on the 726 started at the same time with journeys during the week added in the main school holiday period. The 364A from Luton ran via the hamlet of Woodside to Markyate, then up to Kensworth with just a couple of Monday to Friday peak journeys extended to Whipsnade intended for the few zoo staff who travelled by bus to work. The Sunday extension to Whipsnade was pointless however since Luton & District service 53B ran from Luton via Dunstable to Whipsnade Zoo daily, and in 1962, the summer Sunday headway was still every 20 minutes. Despite this, the 364A retained its summer Sunday extension for another four years before finally being withdrawn at the end of the 1966 summer season.

In March 1962, RT 4738 lays over at Penn waiting to return to Totteridge. Six months later, the 363 was extended to Beaconsfield to replace the 373, although on a much reduced service, the limited former Sunday service being abandoned. The section into Beaconsfield would later suffer a steep decline, finally being reduced to just two journeys, two days a week under London Country's management. (Malcolm Papes)

In the first years of the 1960s, Bank Holidays could still be relied upon to provide many extra passengers, and several routes had an augmented service, particularly on Bank Holiday Mondays. The normal half-hourly Sunday headway from Dorking to Guildford on the 425 was increased to four journeys an hour requiring eight RFs all day, and the hourly headway on the cross country 410 from Bromley to Reigate was doubled to half hourly. In the afternoon, extra short journeys were run to give four per hour as far as Bletchingley and three per hour between Bromley and Biggin Hill. The normal hourly service south of Capel on the 414 was doubled to half hourly, and an hourly headway ran on the 416 from Tadworth to Esher together with an hourly 422 to Boxhill. The 401 along the Darenth Valley to Sevenoaks still justified a half-hourly Sunday headway, but even this was increased to four journeys per hour on Bank Holiday Monday right up to 10.00pm, requiring ten RTs all day. Many other routes with hourly headways had their frequencies doubled to half hourly, and services often started earlier than a normal Sunday timetable. Green Line timetables were unchanged, but as mentioned in the previous chapter, large numbers of unscheduled duplicates were put out. Experience from previous years, coupled with the likely weather forecast, meant that garages had an accurate idea of how many duplicates were required, and there was no need to publish a revised timetable since it was only necessary to run out the additional buses for extra passengers who could generally be guaranteed to turn out in sufficient numbers. The popularity of Windsor saw a unique addition to the 457 timetable from Uxbridge, the half-hourly normal timetable being augmented by a 15-minute non-stop service from Uxbridge to Windsor Castle all day on Sundays. Although this additional service was scheduled it was never advertised, so it could be amended or withdrawn in bad weather.

The last half-cab single decker was withdrawn from service on 13th August 1962 when T 787 ran for the last time at Crawley. For some time before, it had been used only on peak hour workings on the 853 works services and the odd run on the 426 out to Horley. The operation of this last non-standard bus had been a bit of an oddity after the bulk of the original batch of thirty had all been withdrawn by the end of the 1950s. After it was withdrawn, its scheduled working was retained with a crew-operated RF. Apart from T 787, only three others of the original 1948 batch of thirty still remained: T 785 at Abbey Wood as a staff bus and T 790 and T 792 in store at Garston.

The introduction to London Transport's 1962 annual report states with confidence 'The year 1962 was one of major decisions and achievements'. Whilst there was some truth in this – approval was given for the start of the Victoria tube line for example – there were few achievements on the Country buses, although the construction of the new Harlow garage began in January that year. Tucked away on page 10 of the report is a short paragraph which refers to improved staff levels and traffic conditions, but which concludes by saying that 'efforts were continued to match services as closely as possible to passenger demands'. This is something of an understatement and a euphemism for the widespread service cuts which the Country Bus Department made when the winter schedules were introduced on 24th October that year. These brought about a number of service cuts as well as some fundamental operational changes.

The second batch of RMCs was put into service at Epping and Windsor to replace RFs on the 718, 720 and 720A routes, and while the headways on the 718 and 720A were retained, that on the 720 was cut back to hourly. Falling passenger numbers following the electrification of the London to Bishop's Stortford railway the previous year meant that the former 30-minute headway north of Harlow could no longer be justified, although the 720 and 720A timetable still provided a half-hourly service between London and Potter Street. At the same time, the 396 parallel bus route from Epping to Bishop's Stortford was reduced with the bulk of the service running only from Harlow. Whilst the reduction north of Harlow may have been justified purely in terms of passengers carried, the service from London to Sawbridgeworth and Bishop's Stortford lost the convenience of a half-hourly headway and made it much less attractive. In addition to the timetable cuts, two of the five weekend 718 duplicates were removed as well as the two for the 720A so that the schedule changes reduced Epping's total Green Line roster from 24 to 17 coaches, a reduction of almost a third, and the RFs all became redundant. The 720 and 720A in particular had always had stiff competition from the Central Line for journeys from Epping itself into London since the Underground was much quicker, also serving Wanstead, Leytonstone and Stratford which were all important points along the route. But by 1962, other factors had come into play and the cutting of the weekend duplicates became inevitable as numbers of passengers transferred to the railway services, and leisure trips to Epping Forest fell away significantly as car ownership increased. Whilst the reductions on the 715 might have been realistic, halving a frequency from 30 to 60 minutes served only to make the timetable far less convenient, regardless of seating capacity, but this was a policy which would be repeated on other routes where the RMCs replaced RFs, and was undoubtedly a factor in driving away passengers.

Other service cuts, which on the face of it were not great, were nevertheless significant. The 306, a busy interurban route from Watford to Barnet, was cut back to Borehamwood on Sundays, and the 315A which augmented the 303 and 303A trunk route in peak hours and Saturdays, had all the Saturday journeys to Hitchin withdrawn. The Saturday service had existed to provide extra capacity for shoppers to Stevenage and Hitchin and its withdrawal reduced the through service from Welwyn to Hitchin from three to two buses an hour, removing two RTs from Hatfield's Saturday schedules. In the Chilterns the 348 and 348A were extended from Chesham over the 397 route to Tring (the 397 was withdrawn) to give one combined route and better use of buses, but the hamlets of St Leonards and Buckland Common lost their Sunday service as the route was cut back to Bellingdon that day. The double deck 362/362A routes were cut back to Chesham on Sunday, and the section up to Ley Hill converted to omo by running some 316 journeys from Amersham garage though with a reduced service. In another reflection of dwindling Sunday traffic, the whole of the 388 timetable between Hertford and Welwyn was withdrawn. Batford Estate on the edge of Harpenden lost its Sunday service, and the remaining peak hour journeys on 381 linking Roydon with St Margarets (with a rail connection to Liverpool Street) were abandoned.

The overall allocation on the Croydon trunk routes suffered a further reduction at weekends, and the total Sunday run-out was reduced again. The reduction from 80 for summer 1955 to 57 for summer 1960 had already been drastic, but from September 1962, it fell to 40 RTs – exactly half the number required seven years earlier. Dunton Green, East Grinstead and Guildford were left with just one RT each on Sundays for their contribution, whilst the totals at Chelsham had dropped from 18 in 1955 to seven for winter 1962, and at Godstone from 12 to six. The cuts on Saturday were less severe with 74 RTs required, a reduction of five on the summer 1960 schedules. Only three RTs were cut from the Monday to Friday schedules which came from reducing peak duplicates and relief journeys on the 403 and 409. Even before 1962, all of the extra Saturday shopping journeys on the 405 between Crawley and Horsham had gone leaving the basic 30-minute headway all day on the through Croydon to Horsham timetable. The winter 1962 schedules reduced the 405 Sunday timetable north of Redhill to an hourly service in the afternoon only as far as Merstham, leaving just the half-hourly service through to Croydon on the 414. The only exception to this was of two odd journeys to Croydon on Sunday afternoon to give a through journey south of Redhill. The 1.33pm from Croydon allowed a connection at Horley for the 851 to Smallfield Hospital, with a return connection back to Croydon off the 482 later. Despite these cuts, the busy section between Crawley and Redhill – which was more of a suburban service – still benefited from four buses an hour all day Saturday till late afternoon when shopping traffic still justified additional buses. However, on weekday evenings (including Saturdays) apart from one late evening journey, there was no service on the 405 north of Redhill after 5.45pm, and the Sunday headway between Horsham and Redhill was reduced to hourly requiring only three RTs with a fourth bus to run afternoon and evening short journeys between Redhill and Horley only. The parallel 414 though had seen few reductions over

RT 978 looks as if it has recently been repainted as it leave Stevenage Bus Station on a 303A to New Barnet, the timetable of which was little changed after the withdrawal of the parallel 315A on Saturdays. It went to Hatfield in June 1960 and was withdrawn early in 1963 by which time very few of the RT3 bodied buses remained in service. Spare central area RTs were repainted and transferred to replace them, and the last roofbox bodied buses lasted just into 1964. (Alan Cross)

the same period, and the 1962 winter timetable still provided a half-hourly Sunday headway all day as far as Capel, the hourly headway on to Horsham still running until late evening. The 414 remained relatively well used on Sundays, and Dorking garage was the only one whose allocation had been unaltered since 1955, still requiring three RTs seven days a week for its share of the route. The 411 Sunday service was withdrawn completely, leaving only a half-hourly service from Croydon to Godstone on the 409 and hourly onwards to Forest Row. Even though it served Boxhill, the 470 was reduced to hourly all day, although a combined 20-minute headway was retained between Leatherhead and Croydon with the 408. The 'country' section of the 403 was reduced to just an hourly Croydon to Sevenoaks service, being withdrawn between Sevenoaks and Tonbridge on Sundays, and the parallel 402 lost its Sunday service over the entire route from Bromley to Tonbridge. Only two years earlier, in the summer 1960 schedules, Dunton Green garage had run five RTs out every Sunday on the 402 and 403, and even with the reductions for the 1960 winter schedules, three were still required, but this was now reduced to a single bus. On Sundays, the whole road between Bromley and Tonbridge was now covered only by the half-hourly 704 Green Line route, and fares were reduced so that bus fares could be charged on the 704 for local traffic over this section.

The 427, 437 and 456 routes between Weybridge and Woking were mostly cut back to Addlestone, and the 462 (which paralleled the 436, 436A and 461 between Chertsey and Staines) was withdrawn beyond Chertsey except for a couple of peak journeys. In rural north Kent, the 489A to Meopham disappeared on Sundays. This was always a rather superfluous service, since Maidstone & District ran the hourly 122 through Meopham direct into Gravesend. Apart from its link to Longfield station, and the small village of Longfield Hill, the 489A had little purpose and the fact it survived several more years is indicative of London Transport's characteristic lack of response to such unremunerative routes at the time. Thames Weald, a rather eccentric local independent operator, felt it worthwhile to introduce a two-hourly Sunday service between Meopham and Southfleet to connect with the remaining 489 as a replacement, although it was 18 months after the 489A Sunday service had gone before its replacement began in May 1964. It somehow survived for three years before being withdrawn.

The most significant operational change of the 1962 winter schedules however was that they represented the first mass withdrawal of the GSs, being replaced indirectly as a result of the new RMC coaches coming into service. Chelsham and Amersham's complete allocations of GSs were replaced with the RFs which had been converted from the redundant coaches thrown up from the changeover to RMCs on the 715 and 715A. There were still a small number of routes operated by other garages where RFs were not approved due to particularly narrow roads, but Chelsham and Amersham, which then, with Hertford, had the largest allocations of GSs, were the obvious choices for complete conversion since their routes were all approved for RF operation even before this. The two garages between them had a total of 19 GSs allocated to cover 16 scheduled workings, and four of Chelsham's allocation (GS 1, 3, 6 and 7), and five of Amersham's (GS 52, 55, 56, 64 and 65) had spent their entire working lives at their respective garages. Before the change, Epping had one GS and one RF allocated for the infrequent 381/381A Monday to Friday and one GS Sunday for the remaining 381A journeys. Despite the Monday to Friday RF being spare on Saturdays, the official 381 Saturday allocation was two GSs, but in July 1962, Epping only had one allocated (GS 27), so if two were actually used, then one was probably borrowed from Hertford. The second GS was actually allocated for duplicates on the 393, so that in practice the spare RF would have been used, but whatever the reality, Epping's GS was also replaced at the same time as Chelsham's and Amersham's. Tring garage had GS 33, although it had been replaced on the 387 during June 1962 and was out of use when the October 1962 schedules began.

Chelsham's rural routes between Oxted, Edenbridge and Westerham had been established after the War. When the 706 and 707 Green Line routes were reinstated in June 1946, the 707 ran only as far as Oxted, so that the prewar section on to Edenbridge was replaced with a new bus route numbered 465, while the third route to complete the triangle was the 485 which linked Westerham to Edenbridge. While there were additional journeys from Oxted to Chart and Holland, the 464, 465 and 485 all had a basic two-hourly headway over the whole length of each route, and the 464 and 465 which ran together as far as Crockham Hill provided a regular hourly headway over that part, but resulted in an alternate 90- or 30-minute uneven headway along the legs from Crockham Hill to either Westerham or Edenbridge. The timetable also provided for the two-hourly arrival of a 464 at Westerham and subsequent departure of a 485 to Edenbridge to make the long standing connection to the 403 and 410 routes which crossed each other at Westerham at the same time every hour. When the GSs had been introduced in 1953, Chelsham required a maximum of seven buses Monday to Friday, and by 1955 a new housing estate at Hurst Green, together with some factories at Holland, justified a 15- or 20-minute headway into Oxted, plus additional shorts as far as Chart. With several school journeys as well, the timetable required all seven buses, and for another seven years until 1962 there was little change to the timetables.

The sections beyond Chart to both Edenbridge and Westerham were always less well used, and while the two-hourly headway was adequate, journeys began to run with fewer passengers. Oxted – like many other Home Counties small towns – became an affluent commuter town, and car ownership dealt a heavy

A schoolday journey on the 464 ran in a circle from Chart through Oxted and Pollards Oak Estate at Hurst Green back to Limpsfield which it had passed only 25 minutes earlier. Blinds for circular workings or where the terminal points were close together did not display the ultimate destination in larger letters, but showed the destination in the same size as the intermediate points. GS 8 displays the correct blind for this journey as it picks up a passenger near Old Oxted. It was transferred to Chelsham after its first overhaul in May 1956 and spent the rest of its days there until withdrawal in October 1962. It was sold the following year.
(Alan Cross)

blow to passenger numbers on these routes from the late 1950s. Until October 1962, three of the total allocation of seven GSs worked morning and afternoon peaks, one of these also working the late morning journey from Chelsham to Oxted and back which also doubled as a crew relief bus. Part of the roster also included leaving one of the 'spreadover' GSs parked at Oxted Station to cover for any breakdowns since the whole operation of these routes was completely remote from Chelsham garage. It was possible for one bus to work the full circle over the three routes every two hours, but until 1960, the schedules had been inefficient with longer layovers at Edenbridge, Westerham, and especially at Holland. A bus leaving Holland would not return back for just over two hours, and several were timed to stand at Holland for 15 or 20 minutes before leaving on the next short to Oxted or Chart, which meant that the total number of buses rostered to run the whole timetable was more than it needed to be. By 1960, the 15- or 20-minute headway over the Holland, Oxted and Chart section had been cut back to half hourly, and as passenger numbers fell away further, there was a need to make changes to the way these routes were scheduled. Layovers at Edenbridge and Westerham were reduced, permitting the basic all day two-hourly headway on each route to be operated by just two buses which worked each of the three routes in turn round a circle as follows:

464   Holland–Oxted–Crockham Hill–Westerham
485   Westerham–Crockham Hill–Edenbridge
465   Edenbridge–Crockham Hill–Oxted–Holland

This circuit took 1 hr 55 mins to complete, with one bus leaving Holland on the 'odd hours' as a 464, the second running round the opposite way on the 'even hours' as a 465.

Before they were replaced in 1962, Chelsham needed six GSs Monday to Friday plus a seventh for schoolday journeys. Five were rostered on Saturdays, and four on Sundays, although five were actually required since the fifth bus ran out in the early afternoon replacing one of the morning run-out which returned to Chelsham after lunch. After the RFs took over, in addition to the two required to run the basic service above, a third spent most of the day working between Holland and Chart along with the short four-minute trip from Oxted Station to the council estate at Barrow Green Road which ran only every two hours during the day with no evening or Sunday service. The seating capacity of the RFs being far greater than the GSs allowed the morning and afternoon schoolday journeys to be cut from four to two. These journeys linked the schools at Limpsfield and Merle Common with Hurst Green and Holland, running a short distance beyond Merle Common to Staffhurst Wood which was the first point where buses could turn. Before October 1962 four GS would all arrive at Staffhurst Wood within a few minutes on these school trips. The changes reduced the total number of buses needed to only three with two more for just the morning and afternoon peak, and even then one of the afternoon buses was required only on schooldays. Only three RFs were scheduled on Saturday with a fourth to work two journeys from Chelsham to Oxted as the crew change buses. The Sunday timetable was reduced to the basic two-hourly headway on each of the three routes requiring just two buses with one lunchtime crew change run to Oxted. One morning peak journey on the 464 was run from Chelsham into Oxted via Tatsfield Village to provide a commuter link to Oxted, and was worked by a 707 Green Line coach (CM36) as a positioning journey before its first run of the day to Aylesbury.

The overall effect of the new timetable was that Chelsham's omo allocation was reduced from seven to five, and to only four in the afternoons during school holidays. Two ran back to Chelsham in the early evening leaving the remaining two to work the last Westerham and Edenbridge journeys. Between Holland and Chart, loadings were still reasonably good, but beyond there the routes had become marginal at best. Edenbridge was a reasonably sized small town which attracted a few shoppers during the day, but on the leg to Westerham the route ran through woodland all the way, so that apart from Crockham Hill and a few cottages at Hosey Common, traffic potential was always limited. The problem with these three routes was that it was not possible to reduce the two-hourly headway of each route without drastically cutting the whole route pattern, so that this basic timetable remained intact for several more years despite increasing losses. Chelsham had also rostered a GS on duty CM44 before October 1962 to run some school journeys on the local 453 to Caterham, but this unusual working also ceased with the new schedules.

At Amersham, the replacement of the GSs involved only minor timetable reductions. The duplicate bus on a couple of school journeys became unnecessary with the large capacity of the RFs, combining the routes from Chesham to Tring and to St Leonards and Buckland Common into one, and the ability to interwork RFs across the whole single-deck schedules gave better use of vehicles resulting in a saving of one bus in Amersham's run-out. In June that year an experimental service numbered 372 had been introduced within the large Belhus Estate at Aveley, Grays rostering one GS. It was however unsuccessful and was also a casualty of the October changes.

In July 1962, there still been 77 of the original 84 GSs in stock. Seven had been sold in 1961, three of them to Corvedale Motors in Ludlow, a small independent

Amersham's entire GS allocation was replaced with RFs in the October 1962 changes. RF 291 heads RF 302 as they pick up passengers at the bottom of Gore Hill opposite Amersham garage, both routes having been GS operated before the change. Both RFs were part of the batch of former Green Line coaches converted to omo bus status referred to earlier following the introduction of the new RMCs. They will run together all the way to Beaconsfield, RF 291 then running back light to the garage. The 332 followed the same route as the 398 except for a short section via Stanley Hill in Amersham to serve the schools there, and this is the single afternoon 332 schoolday journey. (J.G.S. Smith)

The 372 began in June 1962 to give a daytime service for shoppers within Belhus Estate. Although a worthwhile experiment, it proved a failure and was withdrawn with the service reductions in October that year. GS 34 is empty as it runs through the dreary surroundings of the estate. (Peter Mitchell)

operator who could benefit from these small cheap second-hand buses. Of the remaining 77, two were unlicensed, and one (GS 82) was allocated to Harrow Weald Central area garage for staff transport. This left 74 GSs which were allocated around the fleet for service, but they had only a maximum of 54 scheduled workings Monday to Friday, 46 Saturday and only 16 on Sunday. The changes of 24th October reduced these to 35 Monday to Friday, 32 Saturday and just five on Sunday. Even allowing for the engineering spares, this meant that at least 25 or 30 GSs were now all surplus to requirements, even though they were all barely nine years old and little more than half way through what would be a normal service life. Not only that, but because no more than three quarters of the original total had ever been used at any one time (and many of them for only a few hours a day during the week and not at all on Sundays), their overall mileage was much lower when compared to the rest of the fleet of the same age. Whilst they were not universally popular with engineering staff – access under the lift up bonnet while standing on the front bumper leaning in over the radiator was not easy – they were economic in fuel consumption and were solidly reliable. The crash gearbox with its back to front gate could be something of a challenge for drivers, but they nevertheless represented a very attractive purchase for small independent companies. It is no surprise therefore that in the 12 months after the October 1962 changes, 20 were sold off to many small operators. But London Transport received a poor return on its original investment having purchased too many of them in the first place.

In the first few months of 1963, the sale of five GSs to Tillingbourne Valley Motors led to the running of the 448 Guildford to Ewhurst route by GSs from both LTE and Tillingbourne with whom they ran the route jointly. This well documented but unique operation lasted about 16 months until London Transport withdrew from the route in August 1964. Initially, Tillingbourne used former GS 1, 3 and 4 (which had been withdrawn from Chelsham the previous October) on the 448 as well as their own local Guildford town service to Warren Road, and what was then still an hourly rural service to Farley Green which shared much of its route as far as Albury with the LT 425 and Brown Motor Services route to Forest Green. Over time, Tillingbourne would become the largest customer for GSs, eventually buying 13, including one second hand from a fire brigade and two from London Country, GS 64 being the last one purchased in April 1971. Not all though saw revenue earning service, some being cannibalised for spares, but Tillingbourne's GSs gave many years' service lasting into the early 1970s, long after London Transport had relinquished their share of the 448 in 1964.

After all the major changes with the October 1962 schedules, a further batch of RMCs entered service a month later and were used to replace RFs on the 719, a route which had been introduced only in July 1956 as part of the expansion of the Green Line network at the time. It linked Hemel Hempstead to Watford via Abbots Langley with its expanding new estates, and on through areas of north-west London not previously served by a Green Line route. It was still quite busy and the RMCs replaced the RFs on an equal basis without any reduction in the timetable. In this case, the modern image of the new RMCs had a positive effect as passenger numbers on the route rose almost immediately following their intro-duction. Whether this was partly due to the run-up to Christmas which tended temporarily to increase passengers, and whether some passengers transferred from the 708 is unknown, but this represented at least a small positive in the face of decline elsewhere. The last of the 68 new RMCs was delivered at the end of 1962 and went to Stevenage and Addlestone to replace RFs on the 716 and 716A on 2nd January 1963, where, like the 719 conversion, the timetable was unchanged. Between London and Welwyn Garden City, Hatfield garage ran the 717 which worked to a joint timetable with the 716 and 716A, but there were not enough RMCs to convert this so that RFs on the 717 continued to run alongside the RMCs.

At the completion of the conversions, 61 scheduled RMCs had replaced 71 scheduled RFs on the converted routes, and with spare vehicles, almost 90 Green Line RFs had become surplus during the process. Route 715 lost seven coaches and the 720/A lost three. RF 298-313 as mentioned already had gone to Amersham and Chelsham to replace the GSs there, while the majority of the others were either temporarily stored or cascaded round the fleet for use as spare vehicles. Ten of the shorter private hire RFs transferred to Green Line duty in 1956 to bolster what was then an increase in the network were sold after these changes. In the last two months of 1963, ten coach RFs were sold, followed by a further ten in the first few months of 1964. Others were gradually downgraded to bus status and used to convert a number of the less important double-deck routes to omo single-deck working, some of these coming with the 1964 winter schedules.

Each morning and evening, Garston ran some 719 positioning journeys to and from Hemel Hempstead on the 347, and RMC 1504 waits in the service road beside the garage with the blinds set for such a journey. The running number GR305 was much higher than all other Green Line numbers due to the fact that when Leavesden Road's operations were moved into Garston, numbers up to 100 were needed for bus routes, and the Green Line schedules were numbered in the 300 series. (M. Papes collection)

At the end of 1962, there had been a reduction of only 20 buses in the overall total scheduled as compared to the end of 1961. This was largely due to the cuts in rural timetables across most garages, although some busier interurban routes were also beginning to have their total allocation reduced. This reduction of 20 though applied to the Monday to Friday peak schedules and masked the reduction of double this figure (around 10%) on both Saturdays and Sundays. The reductions in Green Line coach rosters also represented roughly 10% over the year, and the majority of these had come from the wider headways on routes where the RMCs had been introduced. Fine vehicles though they were – and they undoubtedly made a big impact on what had been Green Line's fading image – the service cuts and resulting deterrent to passengers which came with them proved over the next few years to more than offset any advantages their modern comfortable image might have brought about. Before the end of the decade, Green Line reductions would be so great that even some of the RMCs would be without work.

Smart new vehicles could also do nothing to prevent the worsening traffic conditions which the Green Line routes were by then experiencing. Indeed London Transport's 1962 Annual Report highlighted just how the balance of traffic between buses and cars had changed. In the five years between 1957 and 1962, the total number of LTE buses and coaches entering central London in the morning peak (7.00am to 10.00am) had gone down by 1,000 which represented a drop of just over 16%. This reduction was entirely in Central Bus schedules however since Green Line timetables were virtually unaltered during this period. Conversely, the number of cars had gone up by almost 18,000 which was an increase of 39%, while the total number of passengers carried on buses and Green Line coaches had fallen by just over 18%, about the same as the drop in the number of buses. However, the number of people in private cars had risen by over a third, and when motor bikes and scooters were included, the figures showed that at the end of the five-year period, whilst the total number of people travelling into central London was only fractionally less, the total number of vehicles carrying them had risen by 37%, which represented an absolute number of 26,200 additional vehicles. When one also considers that this 37% increase was after the 16% reduction in the total buses, then it is easy to understand just how the balance had changed and how the resulting congestion had fundamentally altered London's traffic conditions. Late running on Central Bus routes could be restored simply by turning some buses short of their outer termini so that they could pick up the correct time for the return journey. This solution was not available to Green Line routes however where the coach in most cases had to work right through. Apart from the 725, every single Green Line coach worked through central London in this peak period which was why late running had become an increasing problem for the schedules. On some routes, it was possible to turn a coach short, and St Albans and Luton crews working the early morning journeys on the 712, 713 and 714 were, for example, occasionally turned short at Leatherhead where they could take their break and pick up the correct time for the return journey. This though gave uneven gaps on the final leg to Dorking and did not help the declining public perception of the service. The congestion however was not just confined to central London and it was only on the outer ends of some Green Line routes through open countryside that lost time might be caught up. Even at the outer end, traffic could be bad, and I recall arriving mid-morning at Dorking in 1964 when it took the coach almost 15 minutes to get through the town to the Bus Station instead of the five minutes scheduled.

If a coach arrived late at the other end of its route, then this reduced the crew's break – typically 50 or 60 minutes – before they had to start the return trip. On some routes though this could be as little as 40 minutes which, on the 715 included the walking time down Fairfax Road to Hertford garage and back from the crew change point on the main road. Whilst a small delay could be overcome, there were times when, even if the crew agreed to take a shorter break (which they were not obliged to do), the return journey might leave late. For many crews with long service, it was a matter of pride that they should leave on time regardless of running in late, but this was not always the case. On some routes where the operating garage was a few miles before the end of the route, a crew from one end would change at the opposite end's garage, and a local crew would then work a 'swinger' duty to run the coach to the end of the route where only a ten-minute layover might be scheduled. They then worked back to the garage where the original crew would take their own coach back having had their break. This was the pattern for 706 journeys to Westerham for example where Tring crews came off at Chelsham. A Chelsham crew then worked to Westerham and back, the original Tring crew taking over for the return trip to Aylesbury. Some rosters scheduled a crew to work past the 'other end' garage to the outer terminal to take a short layover before returning to the garage where they would come off to be relieved by the crew who had worked the coach an hour before them. Godstone crews for example worked through to Chesham on the 709, then back to Amersham for their break. In these situations, late running meant that the outer leg beyond the garage to the terminus then either had to be abandoned, or worked by standby crews on overtime. This was not uncommon at Epping where late running Windsor crews on the 718 had to come off without working on to Harlow, and an Epping crew on standby ran to Harlow and back to give the Windsor crew

The drastic reductions to Sunday services on the Croydon trunk routes have been referred to. The 411 however did not have a Sunday service and the weekday 30 minute headway remained little changed. RT 3725 went to Godstone in August 1961 and ran on these routes until transferred away towards the end of 1965. It is descending the steep Church Hill in Caterham on its way to Reigate. This hill was designated as a 'third gear hill' and drivers were required to change down into third at the top for the descent.

The winter weather in the first two months of 1963 caused much disruption and difficulties for crews in their efforts to run as many journeys as possible. This picture of RF 588 on the way back from Aldbury illustrates the conditions which lasted several weeks, although in parts of Kent and Essex, conditions were much worse.

something like their scheduled break. On some routes the coach itself was scheduled for only a ten- or 15-minute break before running the return journey. On the 708 for example, an East Grinstead crew would have only ten minutes at Hemel Hempstead bus station, then set off on the return journey but come off at Two Waters for their break. The first two East Grinstead crews each morning were replaced by the last of the 'early turn' Hemel Hempstead crews (and the opposite arrangement at East Grinstead). If the East Grinstead coach was running too late then Hemel Hempstead kept a 'late running spare' so that its crew could set off on time using the spare coach. Thus several garages were gradually allocated these spare coaches as delays became longer and more frequent, and although numbers varied there were around 15 coaches allocated across the fleet by 1961. All this of course meant additional cost, coupled on some journeys by loss of revenue. By 1962 late running was becoming more commonplace, and beginning to seriously disrupt this simple operating system. It was perhaps the Green Line network's greatest weakness, and was a major factor in its continual decline throughout the latter half of the 1960s.

The beginning of 1963 saw the worst snow and winter conditions for 16 years, heavy snow beginning just after Christmas and causing much disruption across the whole country. Some garages faired very badly, and Chelsham could not get beyond Botley Hill crossroads for some time. This is a particularly exposed spot high on the North Downs, and Titsey Hill down to Oxted was impassable so that the 707 and positioning journeys for the 464 and 465 could not be run. This meant the links to Holland, Chart and Edenbridge became difficult until the roads became passable again. Similarly the 403 and 706 down to Westerham could not be run until the roads were cleared. When the main A11 was blocked for a few days in the first week of January, Epping could get no buses up to Harlow, so the New Town had no bus service at all until the main road could be re-opened. North Kent suffered particularly badly and buses parked outside in the yards at Dunton Green and Dartford had to be physically dug out of the snow before services could run. A GS on the lane near Southfleet became trapped in a snowdrift as did another on the 471 on the narrow road between Scotts Lodge and Cudham where it stayed for several days until breakdown crews could get to it. Although the

initial heavy snow cleared in a week or two, there were many further snow falls and severe icy weather, all of which had a depressing effect on travel and receipts for many weeks until conditions finally improved in late February.

On 16th February 1963, a new route was started between Biggin Hill and Orpington. Numbered 479, running just four journeys on Saturdays only, it was intended to provide a shopping service into Orpington and was introduced after lobbying both by the local council and local people. With council support, the Orpington Rural Transport Association had been set up in 1962 and applied for consent to start a service from Orpington to Biggin Hill via Downe. Since the route was entirely within the 'Special Area', London Transport's consent was essential, but they refused. Continued pressure however resulted in the introduction of the 479, but routed instead along Shire Lane, where there were few potential passengers, since London Transport decided that there would be insufficient demand through Downe Village and the Central route 146 ran from there into Bromley. Operation required one GS from Dunton Green which ran out light to Biggin Hill to take up service. The Saturday allocation for the 471 was one fewer than Monday to Friday, so that good use was made of the spare bus although GS 76 and later GS 19 were sent to Dunton Green as further back up. Indeed, on the first Saturday, with enthusiastic support, a duplicate GS had to be run to cater for the number of passengers. However, Bromley was a greater attraction than Orpington, and the 410 and 705 combined to provide between four and six journeys an hour into Bromley. The 479 was originally intended to start in November 1962 to take advantage of shopping traffic in the approach to Christmas, but did not start until February. Not only did this miss the potential advantage of Christmas, but when it did commence it was during the worst winter snow conditions for 15 years. It was soon apparent that there were simply not enough passengers to make the service pay, London Transport withdrawing it on 15th June after only 18 weeks, declaring the 'trial route' a failure. Consent was then granted to the Association, who began operations the following Saturday, and the route formed the beginning of what would become an expanding and successful network of routes in the area, eventually becoming part of the Metrobus network many years later.

It could be said that when London Transport were pressurised into running the 479, it was designed to fail from the beginning, perhaps so that they could justify their initial resistance to the route. During the short 18 week period of operation, GS 19 was one of the regular performers and is seen here on the main road approaching Biggin Hill from Orpington. It had been out of use at Windsor for 18 months before being sent to Dunton Green, and after the end of the 479, stayed until August 1964 when it was withdrawn and sold a few months later. (Peter Mitchell)

The Country area's need for lowbridge double deckers had never been great, and although the RLH's sunken gangway layout was unsatisfactory, they had served their purpose well. Even before the RLHs had been delivered however, the Bristol Lodekka had rendered the sunken gangway design redundant overnight when it appeared in 1949. Given its success – more than 5,200 Lodekkas were built during an 18-year production run – it was surprising that other manufacturers had not produced their versions, as many BET group fleets had the need for lowbridge buses, but were precluded from buying the state-owned Bristol/ ECW product. It would be 1956 before AEC produced their 'Bridgemaster' with Dennis introducing their 'Loline' in 1957, the latter being built under licence from Bristol to the Lodekka design. Leyland/Albion produced their 'Lowlander' in 1962, and Guy produced the somewhat eccentric (and unsuccessful) 'Wulfrunian' in 1960.

In 1962, AEC developed a further model on the Renown, and in February 1963 sent a demonstrator to Northfleet for it to be tested in service on the 480 alongside the RTs on one of the busiest and most intense Country area routes. They were hoping that the bus would create interest since only around 130 Bridgemasters had been sold in five years, and perhaps allocation to the 480 was designed to show how it performed on such a busy route. This though was not the best place to demonstrate it and they might have been better testing it with a provincial BET operator – perhaps City of Oxford or East Kent – who would have had more need for such buses. The square angular bodywork was unattractive at the very least and compared poorly against the ECW equivalent on the Bristol Lodekka or Northern Counties bodies on Dennis Lolines. In service, its performance compared to the RTs proved less than satisfactory. Despite its overall weight being less than the RT, fuel consumption was around 13% greater, and its acceleration from ten to 30mph was marginally slower despite being nominally more powerful than the RT. It was withdrawn from Northfleet in June after only four months in service and received no more interest from London Transport. The Bridgemaster and Renown saw little other success, achieving sales of only 431 between them before production ceased in 1967. Indeed, combined sales of all the alternatives amounted to only around one fifth of all Lodekkas.

The bulky angular bodywork on the AEC Bridgemaster demonstrator is well illustrated by this picture taken outside Dartford garage on one of the many short journeys on the 480 from Gravesend which turned there. The higher seating capacity of 69 was useful on this busy route, but not sufficient to overcome its lack of performance when compared to the RTs. RF 217 is behind ready for a 725 to Windsor.
(Bruce Jenkins)

The 1963 summer schedules came into operation on 22nd May, the main change being the opening of the new Harlow garage and the closure of Epping, whose operations were transferred to the New Town. Harlow had become increasingly important, and its continuing growth meant that Epping had become a remote and inefficient base from which to serve Harlow. Before Epping's closure, all of its 21 RTs allocated to the 396, 396A and Harlow Town services had to run to Harlow to take up service every morning, so that in the two hours after the first bus out at 5.37am there were 39 departures from Epping to Harlow, frequently only a minute or two apart, most running virtually empty. Several then had to run back to Epping to provide a link to the Central Line into London and even on Sunday mornings, it was necessary to run 11 journeys from Epping to Harlow. After the morning peak, a number ran back to Epping with few if any passengers, and the situation was repeated again in the afternoon, so that there was a high proportion of wasted cost in running such an inefficient schedule.

When Harlow opened, the 339 from Warley and Brentwood to Epping was extended to Harlow, and the 396 Epping to Bishop's Stortford was reduced, much of its former timetable to Bishop's Stortford being replaced with extra journeys running from Harlow using the 397 or 397A numbers, which at the same time penetrated further into the developing Passmores area in Harlow. Of the rural services, the 390 was extended from Harlow to Sawbridgeworth, but the Sunday service went. The 380 Hertford to Sawbridgeworth was withdrawn and replaced by extending the 388 from Hertford to Harlow but with one fewer journey on Saturdays, the Sunday service being reduced to only three journeys, one mid-afternoon and two in the evening. This cut the longstanding direct service from Sawbridgeworth to Ware and Hertford, but Harlow's expansion had changed

The 805 began in April 1956 to further improve services in Harlow. It ran between Potter Street on the old A11 and Little Parndon, the name given to a new housing area to the north of what had been the small hamlet of Great Parndon before Harlow expanded. The timetable was irregular at first with a limited service, but 18 months later was extended further into the expanding estate to Canons Gate and increased to a 30 minute headway, increased again to 15 minutes on Saturdays. RT 976 stands at the original Little Parndon terminus in the early days of the route. A family appears to be moving into a new house further along the road at a time when Harlow's population expanded rapidly. (Peter Mitchell)

In the changes made when Harlow garage replaced Epping, the 390 was extended to Sawbridgeworth in place of the 388. RF 269 passes the timing point at the Plume of Feathers pub at Gilston on its long journey to Stevenage. It was one of many Green Line RFs rendered surplus from service cuts and one of a large number converted to omo for bus work in 1965. (J G S Smith)

travel patterns. The Sunday service west of Hertford on the 388 to Welwyn was withdrawn. The 381 was extended to Harlow, and the service to Roydon was reduced to only five journeys to reflect the decreasing need for a link from there into Epping. Although the 381 retained a good service from Epping Green to Epping, the service to and from Harlow was used principally for positioning journeys and shopping with some long gaps, particularly on Saturdays. The savings in staff wages and fuel costs made by moving Epping's operations to Harlow came from eliminating all the positioning journeys from Epping and reducing the service to a lesser number of profitable southbound morning journeys from Harlow for commuters wanting to catch the Central Line Underground into east London and return in the evening. Two fewer RTs were required Monday to Friday, and three fewer on Saturdays and Sundays. Changes to the single-deck roster added one RF on Saturdays, and the Green Line allocation was unchanged but for the removal of a further duplicate.

The 339 timetable had regular short journeys between Epping and Ongar which remained after the route was extended to Harlow when Epping garage closed. A few years earlier, RT 1034 has turned at Brentwood station to wait for a journey to Ongar. The intermediate blind is for short journeys between Warley and Coxtie Green which the bus would have worked earlier in the day, but which the conductor has forgotten to change. The steam train in the station pre-dates the electrification of the line into London.

Other than the opening of Harlow, the 1963 summer schedules made few changes, although a few more GSs were taken out of the allocations with four Monday to Friday and three on Saturdays being replaced with RFs. The five GSs which remained scheduled on Sundays were one each at Dorking (433), Garston (309), Guildford (448), Dunton Green (471), and Northfleet (490). These however would not last, and those at Dorking, Garston and Northfleet were withdrawn with the winter schedules on 9th October. The 433 Sunday service was seasonal, but that on the 309 and 490 was withdrawn permanently. Perversely at Dunton Green, a second GS was added to run the 471 on Sunday afternoons although the timetable only required one bus to run the route. Up to this point, drivers rostered to the 471 had travelled mostly by 704 Green Line and changed over at Green Street Green with a couple of changes taking place at Orpington Station by travelling on the 431. Progressive cuts in Sunday timetables had got to the point where this became more difficult to schedule, so the second GS was used by the relief driver to change over at Orpington. There was also an odd Sunday afternoon duty on the 471 where an RT ran five short journeys between Orpington Station and Green Street Green to suit visiting times at Orpington hospital. The bus ran as a 471 from Dunton Green into Sevenoaks, then as a 431A to Orpington, reversing the process after completing the 471 hospital journeys. This duty (running number DG9) had been a real oddity for some time and was unique in the Sunday operation of what was otherwise a wholly GS operated route.

One initiative worthy of mention in 1963 was the introduction of a new express service from Watford to Windsor on summer Sundays. In previous years, the two-hourly Sunday headway on the 335 had been increased to hourly for the summer, but it was not a direct link between Watford and Windsor, taking a few minutes less than two hours end to end. The new route, numbered 375, stopped only at Croxley, Rickmansworth and Slough, and made the trip in only 55 minutes which must have been an exhilarating ride! Garston rostered two RTs for the route, one being saved on the 335 which was not increased to hourly for the summer season

The new garage at Harlow was a very worthwhile investment at the time and opened for operation on 22nd May 1963. It received 25 RTs, 9 RFs, and 16 RMCs from Epping to cover a maximum of 46 scheduled duties and gave significant savings in dead and un-remunerative mileage to and from Epping. This picture shows the impressive size of the new garage with the pedestrian underpass beneath Fourth Avenue leading to the town centre. Harlow would be the last garage built, the overall total of 29 garages becoming an increasing financial burden over the following decade. (London Transport Museum)

presumably because of the new 375. There were six journeys towards Windsor on the 375 and five back, the last bus from Watford to Windsor working back to Garston as a 335. The 375 was successful enough to warrant running again for 1964, but did not re-appear for 1965 and did not run again. The once popular 457 Sunday Express service from Uxbridge to Windsor, which had been augmented on Bank Holidays, had though become unnecessary, and the summer 1963 service consisted of just the half-hourly headway on the conventional route.

There were no major Green Line changes for summer 1963, but the seasonal 726 to Whipsnade was cut back to just one return trip Monday to Friday and two Sundays. Although this reduced the facility from Ilford and east London, the 712 and 713 had an additional service numbered 712A, running two journeys Saturday and four Sundays from London to Whipsnade. There were no other changes to Green Line schedules, having remained almost unaltered for the previous few years. Even the east London 721 and 722 routes still ran up to eight journeys an hour during the week on the joint section as far as Ilford, with six an hour almost all day on Sundays. The other east London routes from Grays however were cut significantly. Having suffered a dramatic loss of passengers after the electrification of the London to Tilbury and Southend lines, the off peak service beyond East Ham on to Aldgate was effectively halved. Following a few years of relative stability, 1963 was the last year before the process of withdrawal and thinning on Green Line schedules began to accelerate in the face of an increasing drop in passengers.

In January 1963, a new London Transport Board replaced the former London Transport Executive. Almost immediately, they began negotiations with the Union to introduce a programme of wholesale service reforms including a significant extension of one-man operation. The Union predictably responded with claims for increased pay and a shorter working week in return for any efficiencies which could be achieved. Equally predictably both sides were some way apart from the very beginning, little progress being made so that following several months without any progress or agreement, the Union instituted a ban on overtime and rest day working in October 1963. This had a far more serious effect on Central area operations, although a contingency plan was put in place to withdraw all Country area Sunday services should the Union's action continue. Clearly something needed to be done to break the deadlock and, in a repeat of 1958, the Government itself became involved in an effort to try to find a way forward. As a result of this, in November 1963, the then Minister of Transport appointed Professor Phelps-Brown from the London School of Economics to head an inquiry to review the pay of drivers and conductors, *'in the light of manpower requirements and operating conditions in London traffic'*. The terms of reference also asked the inquiry *'to pay due regard to the possibilities of increasing the efficiency of services'*. The initial report was produced very quickly on 12th December and recommended an immediate increase in pay rates which was implemented equally quickly, leading to the withdrawal of the ban on overtime and rest day working. This was only a short term solution however, and the ramifications of the whole issue of pay linked to efficiency savings would drag on for another four years until a final resolution was thrashed out, during which time staff shortages often remained critical, staff turnover increased, and both sides were party to many acrimonious discussions, all of which did nothing to resolve matters or improve either the service to passengers or London Transport's worsening financial position.

The three RWs were taken out of service at Hemel Hempstead on 1st October 1963 where they had entered service just over three years earlier. Before that they had spent a short period at Hertford where, with extensive interworking, they had run on most of the routes although one of them was generally allocated to the 333 town service to Bengeo most days. Although never officially allocated, Hertford also loaned one to Stevenage for a short period in October 1962 and saw brief service on the 383. Overall, the RWs had proved that the dual entrance layout worked well, and they provided much useful experience in service which had an influence on the eventual designs of the large capacity single deckers that would come into service in great numbers at the end of the decade. All three were sold to Chesterfield Corporation where they stayed for several years to complete a full service life.

The final change of note at the end of 1963 was the opening at last of the Dartford Tunnel more than thirty years after it had first been approved. In a fit of enthusiasm which completely over-estimated the attraction of bus services linking both sides of the Thames, a new RT-worked route, number 300, began running between Grays and Dartford every forty minutes. As if this were not enough, the 722 Green Line was also extended through Ockenden, Aveley and the Tunnel every half hour to Dartford. Whilst neither of these services was to prove a success, at least the initiative had been taken in trying to create new business. The most bizarre facility however was a service to carry cyclists and pedestrians through the Tunnel. The Dartford Tunnel company purchased a fleet of five purpose built vehicles based on Thames Trader lorry chassis with very odd looking bodies containing bicycle racks downstairs with seats upstairs for the cyclists and pedestrians. London Transport operated the vehicles, but it became obvious almost immediately that the number of cyclists who wished to travel from one side of the Thames to the other was negligible, pedestrians even less, and the facility was a complete failure. The special buses were replaced with Land Rovers carrying trailers for bicycles, a bizarre operation that met with

This picture is a perfect illustration of the change in the development of bodywork design during the 1950s. Only seven years separate these two buses, but the differences are considerable. GS 14 is pulling onto the stand at Hertford Bus Station on a journey to the garage while RW 3 is about to run a short trip to Bengeo where the dual door layout was more beneficial on a busy journey. (Michael Dryhurst)

equal failure. Quite how anybody thought that cyclists and foot traffic might justify a profitable service through the tunnel can only be guessed! The 300 and 722 routes fared no better, it becoming immediately obvious that substantial losses would be incurred. The figures for week commencing 18th November 1963 showed that only 276 journeys were made on route 300, total receipts amounting to just £53 14s 9d, nowhere near enough to cover the Toll charges through the Tunnel which amounted to £82 16s 0d. Revenue on the 722 was even less, totalling only £26 3s 9d against toll charges of £101 4s 0d. With the addition of wages and fuel, significant losses were therefore being suffered from the start of operation. Operation however continued until November 1964 when the 722 was cut back again to Corbets Tey and the 300 was replaced with a less frequent service renumbered 399, operated with a single GS which saved a little over £2,000 per annum in staff costs – but still nowhere near enough to offset the losses incurred.

The Thames Trader buses designed to carry cyclists and pedestrians – which were prohibited through the Dartford Tunnel – were among the most bizarre buses ever operated by anyone. The service ran to a 10 minute headway from early morning until late evening, seven days a week, increasing to every six or seven minutes at peak times. It was an immediate failure, as were the Land Rovers and trailers which soon replaced them. This picture of TT 1 and TT 2 shows the unique bodywork very well. (Tony Wild)

DARTFORD TUNNEL
NEW BUS ROUTE 300
and extension to
GREEN LINE COACH ROUTE 722

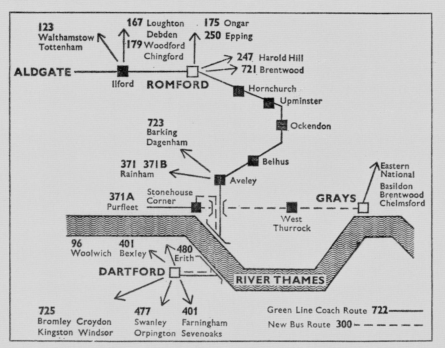

Places of Interest south of the river

	Route from Dartford		Route from Dartford
Sevenoaks, Knole Park, Darenth Valley & Eynsford	401 Direct	Orpington	477 Direct
Tonbridge & River Medway	401 to Sevenoaks, then 402, 403, 454, 704	Danson Park, Bostall Wood, Woolwich	96 Direct
Brands Hatch	401 to Farningham, then 478 or 703 or 452 Direct (Sat. & Sun.)	Bromley, Croydon, Kingston	725 Direct
		Gatwick Airport, Crawley	725 to West Croydon, then 405, 710
Ide Hill	401 to Sevenoaks, then 413/A	Westerham	401 to Sevenoaks, then 403 or 725 to Bromley, then 410, 705
Tunbridge Wells	401 to Sevenoaks, then 704	Biggin Hill	725 to Bromley, then 410, 705

Places of Interest north of the river

	Route from Dartford		Route from Dartford
Romford (for the Market)	722 Direct	Woodford & Chingford (for Epping Forest)	722 to Ilford, then 179
Epping, Theydon Bois & Abridge	722 to Romford, then 250	Walthamstow & Tottenham	722 to Ilford, then 123
Stapleford Abbots & Havering	722 to Romford, then 175, 250	Harold Hill	722 to Romford, then 247
Ongar	722 to Romford, then 175	Brentwood	722 to Romford, then 721 or 300 to Grays, then Eastern National 40
Hainault Forest	722 to Romford, then 247A		
Harlow New Town	722 to Romford, 250 to Epping, then 339, 718, 720A	Basildon	300 to Grays, then Eastern National 248
Bishop's Stortford	722 to Romford, 250 to Epping, then 396, 720	Chelmsford	300 to Grays, then Eastern National 40
Loughton (for Epping Forest) & Debden	722 to Ilford, then 167	Dagenham & Barking	722 to Aveley, then 723, 723A, B

There is a surcharge of 6d. (3d. for a child under 14) for each passenger going through the Tunnel. This will be collected by the Conductor.

1063/2859K/500

Leonard Ripley & Co., Ltd., London

Opposite RT 626 appears to have a reasonable load as it climbs up from the recently opened Dartford Tunnel. Only two cars are following with a third in the distance as the bus comes up the slip road to what was then a T junction on the main road into Dartford. At the north end, the tunnel road simply finished at a T junction with traffic lights onto the A13 Southend road, and the main dual carriageway which initially led up to the A2 but would later become part of the M25 is not yet open for traffic. (Peter Mitchell)

The start of services through the Dartford Tunnel was advertised with these posters which were added to roadside timetable frames and emphasised the new connections available for onward journeys and places of interest that could be reached. The extended 722 lasted just less than one year and both the 300 and 722 lost money from the beginning. (Alan Charman Collection)

Early in 1964, the old Thames Ammunition Works on Crayford Ness marshes near Dartford closed down. It had been served by the 475 works service which by late 1963 consisted of only one morning journey from the works to Belvedere Station, and by a few special journeys on service 486 to and from Dartford. These were worked by two of the RTs allocated to Dartford's supplementary schedules, and were all withdrawn once the works closed.

When the summer schedules for 1964 were introduced on 6th May that year, they showed a marked difference from previous years and reflected the fact that the augmentation of services for the summer months had become almost unnecessary as a result of the continuous drop in leisure traffic. The number of buses required on Sundays for augmentation of summer timetables was 10% less than 1963, saving 5,000 miles per week, and 10 peak buses were withdrawn Monday to Friday. The withdrawal from the 316, 448 and 448A described below would also save around 1.1 million miles in a full year – a very worthwhile saving on two rural routes which were marginal at best. Sunday services were withdrawn from the 355 between Radlett and Borehamwood (where it was paralleled by the 712 and 713 Green Line), and the Welwyn Garden City 324 town service to Knightsfield which was covered by other journeys on the 303 trunk route.

East Grinstead ran the infrequent 494 to Oxted which had been introduced in January 1948 after some years of campaigning by local residents along the line of the route. It paralleled the 428 from East Grinstead out to Lingfield, and then struck out through some very sparsely populated countryside to Oxted, the only villages served on the way being Crowhurst, a very straggling community, and Tandridge which was quite small. Between Crowhurst and Tandridge there was almost no passenger potential, and even in 1954 there were only six journeys on weekdays and five on Sundays. The 8.35pm from East Grinstead to Oxted and the return at 9.40pm ran seven days a week and must have carried few passengers, but were still running in 1960, although by then there were only three Sunday journeys. The winter 1962 schedules had reduced the Sunday service further to just two afternoon journeys which could be worked in with the 428 timetable by one bus. The route had been an obvious choice for GS operation, and the timetable only ever needed one bus, but its operation had been separate from the rest of East Grinstead's small single deck schedules since a GS was unsuitable for the bigger loads on the 428, 434 and 473. And so with the 1964 summer schedules, East Grinstead's GS was replaced with an RF, whilst at Dorking the 433 was again reinstated on Sundays for the summer to give an afternoon service to Ranmore and Coldharbour.

The 353 was a long cross-country route running from Berkhamsted over the Chilterns through Ashley Green, on to Chesham, Amersham and through the Chalfonts to Slough and Windsor, providing many links for commuters and shoppers as well as weekend leisure traffic to Windsor and the Chilterns. With an end to end running time of almost an hour and three quarters, it required eight RTs to run the half hourly headway, all of which were run by Amersham garage. Windsor's only contribution in the second half of the 1950s was the first morning journey from Windsor to Berkhamsted and back plus a few peak hour shorts from Slough and Windsor. Although some parts of the 353 ran through open countryside, there were also semi-rural urban parts providing consistent loads so that the timetable remained unchanged into the 1960s. In common with similar routes though Sunday passengers dropped away, so as an experiment for the 1964 summer season, the 353 had some Sunday journeys re-timed as an

'Express' service to try to induce a few extra passengers to make trips to Windsor. The 83 minutes from Berkhamsted to Windsor on the normal timetable were cut drastically to just 52 minutes, and given that the Express service covered the same roads (albeit with only a few strategic stops) this was more an indication of how generous the normal timetable was rather than how fast the new Express times were. It was a worthwhile experiment, but did not succeed. The express journeys were withdrawn on 4th October 1964, and the Sunday service was cut back again to every two hours a month later when the winter schedules were introduced. This reduced the number of through Sunday journeys to Windsor from 13 in summer 1963 to just six for winter 1964, and the 353 Sunday service never recovered. Windsor also made a contribution to the 335 which was another long cross-country route run jointly with Garston. From Watford, this paralleled the 336 as far as Chalfont before turning south for a couple of miles to Chalfont St Giles where it joined the 353 and 305 to give a frequent service into Gerrards Cross, after which it went by a different route through Fulmer before reaching Slough and Windsor. The 335 was very similar to the 353 and had an almost identical end to end running time Although it had only an hourly headway Monday to Friday, Windsor ran shorts to Chalfont St Giles, and on Saturdays there was a 30-minute headway which like the 353, required eight RTs shared equally between Watford and Windsor. By winter 1964 though, this too had to be cut back and the Sunday service was reduced to just six journeys on a two-hourly headway. Although the 335 and 353 linked Gerrards Cross to Slough and Windsor by different routes, the Sunday service between these two points dropped from a total of 21 down to 13 journeys in two years.

The text refers to the decline of the 335 and 353 during the 1960s. Although the Sunday service was halved and various short journeys were withdrawn, the basic hourly headway on the 335 survived until 1976 when the section from Watford to Chalfont was withdrawn. Fulmer retained its rural character and RT 4751 passes the Black Horse timing point in the village on the way to Windsor.
(Peter Mitchell)

After London Transport handed their journeys on the 316 to Rover Bus, the Sunday journeys were introduced to Ley Hill to replace part of the 362. The 316 ran hourly in the afternoon and evening, and RF 694 is on the road between Amersham and Chesham.

Until 1964 the 359 had been operated jointly between United Counties and London Transport after Eastern National's Aylesbury to Great Missenden route had been extended to Amersham in 1942. Other than Great Missenden and Wendover there was limited traffic potential along the route, and United Counties had given notice that they wished to withdraw from the route altogether. From the start of the 1964 summer schedules therefore London Transport took over United Counties' allocation and Amersham garage required an additional RF to maintain the previous joint hourly headway which had required one bus from each company. Since United Counties had wished to withdraw from the route, it was surprising that London Transport initially maintained the former hourly headway, but when the 1964 winter schedules began, the Monday to Friday off peak headway was widened to every two hours, with one gap of three hours between departures from Aylesbury to Amersham. The Saturday service though remained hourly throughout the day with only the last trip to Aylesbury and back in late evening being cut from the timetable.

At the same time as United Counties' half of the 359 was acquired, London Transport surrendered their minority share of the 316 to Rover Bus who had always operated the majority of the route, which was outside the 'Special Area', joint operation having begun in August 1944. London Transport's share had consisted of one GS running roughly every two hours to Chesham, with a second bus from mid-afternoon to early evening running an additional three round trips. Rover Bus had operated all the journeys via Latimer and Flaunden, together with the whole Sunday service which had remained hourly despite, by 1964, diminishing passenger numbers. London Transport's journeys had included an additional section up to St Paul's Road in Hemel Hempstead and this was retained but given the number 316B. Two omo duties were saved at Hemel Hempstead, but both GSs were retained, and rather surprisingly added to the 317 and 317A roster in place of an RF so that they were better utilised, although after the changes, the second GS was required on Saturdays only. When the crew-operated 362 and 362A had been cut back from Ley Hill to Chesham on Sundays in October 1962, the Amersham to Ley Hill section was covered by a few journeys run instead on the 316 as an omo service, and these continued after the main 316 had been taken over by Rover Bus.

In the southern area, the service along the Dorking/Guildford corridor had remained little changed until 1964, but by then the loss of passengers had accelerated, and the frequent service still operated was becoming unsustainable. The main 425 timetable remained half hourly during weekday peak hours and during the day on Saturday, but outside this and all day Sundays the service had been reduced to every hour. Despite a gradual reduction in passengers on the 448, its timetable had barely changed since prewar days, and although some peak hour and shopping journeys remained busy, and Peaslake generated some good loads, passenger levels were falling and the section from Peaslake to Ewhurst carried almost nobody. The 448A was carrying fewer and fewer people, but despite the steady decline, the timetable was completely unchanged in 1964 from its introduction 14 years earlier. In June 1963, I left Guildford on GS 25 working the 12.16pm to Ewhurst, and although this departure was only 18 minutes behind the previous one to Peaslake, the bus was almost full. The majority however had got off by the time the bus left Gomshall, and there were just four left when it arrived at Peaslake, all of whom alighted there. From there, all the way down to Ewhurst, the bus ran non-stop with me as the only passenger, and returned equally empty. The driver told me that most of the Ewhurst journeys rarely carried more than one or two passengers, and often none at all. By the time the bus reached Gomshall on its way back to Guildford, only three other passengers had been picked up.

In 1964, the half hourly headway to Peaslake still ran all day apart from two mid-morning journeys having been cut Monday to Friday. In total there were only four fewer journeys to Peaslake than had been run in 1946, and the five Ewhurst journeys remained identical to the prewar timetable. Combined with the 425, Brown Motors' route to Forest Green and Tillingbourne, the level of service between Gomshall, Shere and Guildford was by 1964 far greater than could be justified. With the gradual removal of duplicates and odd off peak journeys,

The 425 remained one of the busier and more frequent rural routes. RF 588 has stopped opposite the 'Compasses Inn', the timing point in Gomshall, sometime in 1963. One lady is paying the driver while the man waiting to get on looks at the photographer. The other lady sitting in the shelter must be waiting for the next 448 which turned right opposite the stop to run up to Peaslake. RF 588 has a GF garage code and spent 18 months at Guildford in 1962/63 before a further three years at Dorking where it would have continued to work the 425 most days. The A25 through Gomshall today suffers a constant stream of traffic, but 55 years ago, the road is empty!

After Tillingbourne took over the 448 and 448A, they continued the five journeys beyond Peaslake to Ewhurst which only London Transport had previously operated, but increasing losses forced Tillingbourne to withdraw them completely the following year. GS 25 had been transferred to Guildford after its first overhaul in 1956 and remained there until the 448 was withdrawn but was a casualty of the 1964 general service cuts and sold that year. It has arrived at Ewhurst and is about to turn right into the road in front of the Bulls Head at the terminus shared with Aldershot & District's hourly route 23 from Guildford via Cranleigh. The road on the right in the background is the former 449 route from Ockley and Forest Green. (Author's collection)

Guildford's schedules requiring four GSs had become less efficient and by 1960 the fourth GS was only required to work the 5.35pm 448A to Pewley Way plus the occasional unscheduled duplicate. The restriction limiting operation on the 448 to GSs due to the narrow road up to Burrows Cross remained in force, precluding conversion to RF which – with their greater capacity – could have allowed a reduction in the timetable. If this had been possible, the Ewhurst section could perhaps have been withdrawn, and the Peaslake service reduced to hourly. With careful scheduling, the daytime timetables could then have been worked by just one RF and one Tillingbourne bus, with peak additions being interworked off the 425 and 432 rosters. By 1964 the programme to replace the GSs with RFs was already well under way, and the continuing operation of the 448 and 448A was considered no longer viable in its current form. London Transport therefore approached Tillingbourne Valley to see if they would be prepared to take over the 448 and 448A completely. Tillingbourne were not prepared to pay a sum to purchase them, but an agreement was reached whereby London Transport would be paid a small percentage of the additional fare revenues which Tillingbourne would collect. Since London Transport had operated roughly two thirds of the 448 and the whole of the 448A, then in theory Tillingbourne should have seen a marked increase in receipts which, even after the additional running costs and London Transport's small share, should have yielded a reasonable return. The agreement having been reached, London Transport's last day on the routes was Tuesday 11th August 1964, with Tillingbourne taking over the next day to the same timetable. London Transport benefited well from this arrangement. It provided five more GSs for sale (including the engineering spare bus), saved the route's fuel costs, and cut four duties from Guildford's one-man rosters. It soon became apparent though that Tillingbourne had the worst of the deal, and the additional revenues were nowhere near the level required to make the arrangement viable. Within a year Tillingbourne found it necessary to look at not only the ex-LTE routes, but also its other rural service to Farley Green and the Warren Road town service in Guildford, both of which still ran to an hourly headway. Tillingbourne refused to pay anything to London Transport since there had been no spare income generated, indeed what little extra income there was only just covered the extra costs of running the previous LTE timetable. At the end of November 1965, therefore, Tillingbourne halved the Farley Green and Warren Road routes to every two hours, withdrew the former 448A together with the section of the former 448 beyond Peaslake to Ewhurst, and reduced the 30 minute headway to Peaslake to every 45 minutes. The Sunday service to Peaslake was cut to only five journeys between lunchtime and early evening. This halved their previous all day requirement from six buses to three, and apart from reducing costs significantly, also helped to ease the shortage of drivers which Tillingbourne were suffering at the time.

London Transport's own staff shortages continued unabated and if anything worsened during 1964. The Windsor area timetable book dated 9th September 1964 even went as far as including additional pages showing the *'Emergency Bus Service Cuts'* introduced *'owing to acute staff shortages'*. Just over 50 departures – mostly on Slough town services – were withdrawn but included several to Uxbridge and back on the 457 and 458. Windsor though was by no means alone, shortage of crews at Garston being around 15% and so severe that in September 1964 the 803 peak hour express route (Uxbridge to Welwyn Garden City) had to be completely suspended, and the parallel trunk route 321 cut back simply through lack of sufficient crews. Once again wages were the over-riding reason for the failure to attract and retain sufficient staff, and further significant increases in pay would be necessary if the problem was to be addressed. The final report by Professor Phelps-Brown was issued in April 1964 and resulted in an immediate pay rise of £1 18 0d per week (£1.90p) combined with a reduction in the standard working week from 42 to 40 hours. In return for this the Union would have to commit to accepting an extension of omo across all areas including the conversion of some crew-operated double-deck routes in the Country area to one-man double deckers. In the event, of course, apart from the temporary off peak conversion of the XFs at East Grinstead, there were no double deck omo conversions for a further eight years until London Country began introducing large numbers of Atlanteans in 1972. As discussed later, London Transport's strategy for replacing its Country area double-deck fleet throughout the latter half of the 1960s was poorly thought out and would cost the operation dearly in its drive for economies. The Phelps-Brown report was progress, at least in part, but did nothing to alleviate the immediate problems.

Despite continuous cuts, special routes remained well used. Huge crowds would attend race meetings at Ascot, and the 443 ran a service to and from Staines on race days to augment the 701 Green Line which would require many duplicates. RT 4529 has returned empty from Ascot and the driver signals to turn right into the forecourt of Staines garage for the next trip. (Alan Cross)

The 1964 summer Green Line schedules were notable for the much reduced number of duplicates scheduled, such that on Sundays only 27 RTs and 14 RFs were scheduled in total. Of these, eight RTs were at Windsor for the 704 which remained busy with day trippers, plus three RFs at Staines for the additional 725 traffic to Windsor. Harlow put out just one duplicate RF on the 718 and their total Sunday run-out of 15 was nine fewer than the 24 which had been required at Epping in 1955. When compared with the 1955 total duplicates consisting of 35 RTs and 67 RFs, the enormous reduction in the importance of Green Line travel on Sundays can be appreciated. Even greater was the reduction on Saturdays when just nine RTs and five RFs were scheduled for Green Line duplicates against 21 RTs and 44 RFs in 1955. Five of the nine RTs were at Windsor for the 704, leaving just four others across the whole of the rest of the Saturday schedules. Where once every garage had Green Line duplicates rostered at weekends, there were 11 garages in 1964 which had none scheduled at all on Sundays and twenty with none on Saturdays, one being Hertford where its duplicates had been reduced to just two for Monday to Friday peak hours. Nine garages had even lost their Monday to Friday allocations for peak hour duplicates which had once been a mainstay of Green Line services. At the beginning of 1964, Green Line duplicate mileage was about 9,000 per week (compared to almost 25,000 miles per week in summer 1955), but by the time the winter schedules were introduced, this had fallen to 5,000, and the overall timetable reductions were estimated to reduce Green Line service mileage by 12,700 miles per week.

The bus route reductions that came into effect on 4th November 1964 continued the systematic service cuts which had become a feature of the winter schedules for the previous two or three years, but these were far greater than anything which had gone before. The individual services affected are too numerous to mention here but 30 bus routes were cut back in varying ways. Five infrequent rural routes had the Sunday service withdrawn completely and while this was perhaps inevitable, it was the cuts to a number of important trunk routes which confirmed just how far the demand for some of these routes had fallen away outside of the busy peak periods.

The 303/303A followed most of the Great North Road from Barnet all the way to Stevenage and Hitchin was one of the northern area's more important routes. The 303 took the direct route along the A1 to Hatfield, its Sunday service having already been withdrawn by 1964, leaving the 303A, which diverted off the A1 via Brookmans Park, to maintain an hourly Sunday headway over the whole length of the route. The 1964 cuts saw the 303A Sunday service reduced to just the section between Potters Bar and Knightsfield just north of Welwyn Garden City centre. The whole of the rest of the route – and the facilities for through journeys – was left to the parallel 716/716A Green Line, and some fares were reduced to match bus fares to compensate short distance passengers. The less busy 341 route between St Albans and Hertford had its Sunday timetable much reduced so that combined with the reductions on the 303, Hatfield's Sunday bus allocation was halved from eight to only four RTs, although unchanged during the rest of the week.

The 347 from Uxbridge to Hemel Hempstead was cut back to Garston garage on Sundays, the Abbots Langley to Hemel Hempstead section being covered by an extension of the 318. The once important 396 route up the A11 from Epping to Bishop's Stortford was cut back to just a handful of Monday to Friday peak hour journeys, the focus of traffic having moved to Harlow, so that although the

397 ran from there to Bishop's Stortford, the through link north from Epping was provided only by the hourly 720 Green Line. The 339 provided another hourly bus between Epping and Harlow, but the four journeys an hour which had once run all day on the 396 and 720 between Epping and Bishop's Stortford had long since become superfluous.

The continued crew working of the rural 352 Saturday service by Tring garage was an unnecessary expense. After the Sunday service had been abandoned in 1956,

Saturdays remained the only day of the week when the route worked its full length from Berkhamsted to Dunstable, the Wednesday and Friday short journeys from Dunstable to Dagnall remaining to be worked by Hemel Hempstead off the 337 as referred to earlier. The Saturday crew working anomaly had continued only because of the need to balance rosters at Tring garage where the 301 allocation was reduced on Saturdays. But crew operation could no longer be justified, so the 4th November schedules saw the Saturday service converted to omo. Tring garage however only had a couple of omo duties for the local 387 so the Saturday operation was re-allocated to Hemel Hempstead, and the two-hourly 352 timetable was re-organised so that it could be interworked with the 317 which was also rescheduled to give a regular two-hour headway for most of the day. The revised Saturday timetable was organised so that a bus worked a 317 from Two Waters garage to Berkhamsted followed by a 352 from Berkhamsted to Dunstable. The bus then reversed this process back to Hemel Hempstead via Berkhamsted and required two RFs to work the two-hourly service. A third RF ran the two hourly 337 Dunstable to Hemel Hempstead Station timetable, and the 337 and 352 buses were timed to meet every two hours at Dunstable Square. The 352 ran only five return journeys on the new Saturday timetable so that where a 317 did not connect at Berkhamsted there were a couple of 317 journeys when the bus had to be run light to or from Two Waters garage. The Monday to Friday evening service to Berkhamsted on the 317 was abandoned, while the service via Nettleden on the 317A was reduced to only three journeys a day. The Sunday service on both the 317 and 337 was finally withdrawn. One Saturday afternoon in June 1965, I caught the 2.12pm 352 from Berkhamsted. This proved to be relatively well used with over 20 people boarding in Berkhamsted and almost the same number being picked up along the way to travel into Dunstable. The same bus then worked the 3pm back to Berkhamsted, but with few passengers, whilst I caught the 3pm 337 back to Hemel Hempstead. This journey would once have carried a good load, but there were just a handful of passengers boarding at Dunstable, and beyond Studham the bus ran almost empty for the rest of the journey. Running times were generous, having been unchanged from the days when many more stops were made to pick up or set down, and the bus arrived a few minutes early at Water End where the driver sat reading his paper to wait for time to avoid being early at Hemel Hempstead bus station where the inspector would doubtless note early running.

Tring garage's Saturday crew working on the 352 came to an end in November 1964 when operation was transferred to Hemel Hempstead and worked off the 317/337 allocation. On Saturday 23rd October 1965, RF 629 and 691 have met at Dunstable Square, both buses having their blinds set for the return journey. The half a dozen passengers waiting to board the 352 was by 1965 fairly typical. On arriving at Berkhamsted, RF 629 will then work a 317 back to Hemel Hempstead. The regular two hourly Saturday headway on these three routes required three buses all day plus a fourth to work some short 317/317A journeys to Little Gaddesden.
(J G S Smith)

At Hertford, the RT operated 327 was converted to omo RF as part of phase seven of the conversion programme and the timetable reduced. The route was a mix of semi-rural and urban operation, paralleled most of the way by other services and crew operation could no longer be justified. Its conversion was also notable as it was the first minor double decker route to be converted to single-deck omo. Three busy RF routes had remained crew operated, but in phase seven one of these – the 458 from Windsor to Uxbridge – was converted to omo, the Saturday frequency being reduced from five to four buses an hour. The remaining crew working on the 469 at Staines was also converted resulting in 24 omo duties replacing 23 crew duties and an overall saving of just over £19,000 per annum.

The two remaining single-deck crew-operated town services at St Albans (391/391A) and Reigate (447/447A/447B) were retained as well as Reigate's crew RF for the 406C works journeys to Windmill Press at Kingswood which was partly worked from the 711 allocation.

In the southern area, the 402 route had already been a victim of falling traffic and had lost its Sunday service two years earlier. Now the section south of Sevenoaks to Tonbridge was cut back to just a few peak hour journeys during the week although the through hourly Saturday service held on for a little while longer. On the Croydon routes, falling traffic meant that by the end of 1964, the frequencies on the 408 and 470 between Croydon and Leatherhead had been cut to 15 minutes on weekdays, the former ten-minute headway being maintained only during Monday to Friday peak times. The 20-minute Saturday afternoon service to Guildford had been reduced to half hourly, and the 20-minute Sunday service to Croydon reduced by a third to half hourly. The 414 had until then escaped major cuts but the winter 1964 schedules reduced the Sunday headway to hourly beyond Reigate all the way to Horsham, although the weekday service remained little changed. The Sunday 405 timetable lost the two odd afternoon Croydon journeys, and on Saturdays all the remaining additional shopping journeys between Redhill and Crawley were stripped out. During the week, evening services were withdrawn from 436A (Staines to Ripley) which also lost its Sunday service, 432 (Guildford to Great Bookham) and 404 (Sevenoaks to Shoreham Village). Many other timetables were reduced after the evening peaks and on Saturdays.

The shortage of bus RFs was overcome by using spare Green Line RFs on the crew operated routes at St Albans, Reigate and Windsor which had a peak requirement of around 23 buses between them. RF 113 was one of these and is reversing out of the entrance to Hill End Farm at Tyttenhamger. The conductor is just visible at the back of the bus keeping a lookout for the driver. The long standing restrictions on reversing for omo buses at many terminals was gradually lifted, and this route was no exception when it was one of the last two crew operated town services finally converted to omo at the end of 1966. (Peter Mitchell)

Inaction by the local authority in Oxted had meant that the road under the low bridge by Oxted station had still not been lowered despite constant lobbying by London Transport so that there had been no choice but to continue operating the 410 with the lowbridge RLHs. The route could still be very busy at certain times, but the sunken gangway layout of the RLHs was neither ideal nor popular. By late 1964 they were either 12 or 14 years old, and there was no intention of replacing them with similar buses when the time came. Indeed, there was no practical alternative available which would meet London Transport's standard-ised specifications, the AEC 'Bridgemaster' at Northfleet the previous year having proved unsatisfactory. With no suitable lowbridge double decker available, London Transport, having lost patience with the local authority, therefore took the decision to replace the RLHs with RTs when the winter 1964 schedules were introduced. This meant diverting the 410 route via a more circuitous, and less convenient, route through Oxted to avoid the low bridge, but it meant that Godstone's allocation could become all RT and allow more efficient interworking with the 409 and 411 schedules. It also allowed the busy Reigate to Godstone section which the 410 and 411 shared to be all worked by the same type of bus. Until the changes, one oddity had been an afternoon schools journey on the 410 which worked from Godstone garage to Bletchingley then to Purley as a 411 returning to Caterham as a 409. Although this working was entirely over route 411, and ran back to Caterham showing 409, it was worked by an RLH off the 410 roster, but other than that, the 409 and 411 had been worked entirely separately from the 410. The conversion of the 410 to RT removed 11 RLHs from service, and Godstone's overall allocation could be reduced by one bus over the three routes.

Frustrated by the long delay in lowering the road under the railway bridge in Oxted, London Transport finally lost patience and diverted the 410 away from its long held routeing in November 1964 so that the RLHs could be replaced by standard RTs. In the event, RTs ran the route for less than a year, being replaced by the Country area's first RMLs in October 1965. RT 3132 comes through Nutfield on its way to Reigate sometime in early 1965. (Peter Mitchell)

On a fine summer day RLH 37 pulls out from Bromley Road onto Westerham Green on a 410 to Reigate while the policemen holds the traffic This was always a tricky turn onto the busy A25, requiring a hill start, and, with a good load, preselective gearboxes did not provide the quickest response and acceleration for the driver! Apart from a short spell at Reigate, RLH 37 spent its entire life at Godstone on the 410, and this picture also illustrates the cramped upper deck layout of the bench seats with limited headroom. The shop on the corner is still there today, although Cullen's have long gone.
(Terry Cooper)

The change of routeing in Oxted caused much upset among local residents who lobbied the council to lower the road under the bridge so that the original route could be restored. This at last had the desired effect, the work began in 1965, and in May 1966 the 410 reverted to its original route once the road had been lowered to accommodate standard height double deckers. The changes of 4th November 1964 also brought a reduction to the 409 on Sundays which was severed in the middle by withdrawing the service south of Godstone as far as Felbridge. East Grinstead garage was left to run one RT on the isolated leg between Felbridge and Forest Row all day, the through journeys to Croydon being left to the 708 Green Line where – as was now becoming the norm – fares were reduced to the levels of bus fares for local journeys along the abandoned section of bus route. A slightly bizarre aspect of the new 409 Sunday timetable however was the one late evening journey from West Croydon all the way to East Grinstead. The last 708 left East Grinstead at 9.43pm, but London Transport felt the need to provide one later departure on the 409 to cater for any passengers needing to get to Lingfield or Godstone. This was run by the East Grinstead RT which had spent the day running the hourly Felbridge to Forest Row journeys, so the last departure from Forest Row at 10.25pm was therefore extended through to Godstone. However, as this was worked by an East Grinstead crew, it was necessary to extend an opposite southbound journey so that the Godstone crew could meet the East Grinstead crew and swap buses. Although the buses swapped garages, the crews were therefore able to run back to their home garage, and the timetable was compiled so that both buses met at Felbridge where each journey was given two minutes recovery time for the crews to change over. Given that Sunday evening passengers were by then virtually non-existent anyway, this seemed a complete waste of wages and fuel, but the facility continued for another year.

Notwithstanding the cuts to bus services, it was the reductions in the Green Line schedule on 4th November which perhaps emphasised the levels of service cuts which had become necessary. What had been previously unthinkable was the abandonment of a complete route, but from this date the 703 (Wrotham–London–Amersham) was withdrawn. The 703 had only ever run to an hourly headway in any event, but the quicker and more frequent Metropolitan Line service from

London to Rickmansworth and Amersham which followed electrification in 1961, had quickly abstracted what was left of the 703's already declining traffic north of London. A memo dated 26th August 1964 to the Traffic Committee had recommended withdrawal *'subject to final confirmation of loadings'*. Locally between Rickmansworth and Amersham, the 336 bus route had more than enough capacity, and the 703 had always used the main road at Chorleywood, thus by-passing the village centre where the station and shops were situated and where more passengers might have been found. The withdrawal of the 703 severed the link between Rickmansworth and Northwood and with it the link for visitors to Mount Vernon Hospital. Until withdrawal, Amersham had allocated a duplicate RF on the 703 on Sundays which ran two afternoon return trips to Wembley and back to coincide with visiting hours at the hospital. There was just a token replacement for this by using one RF on Sunday afternoons on a variant to the 336 (numbered 336B) which ran just four journeys from Amersham to Northwood. During the week, a handful of journeys were run from Rickmansworth up over Batchworth Heath to Northwood Station using a GS off the 309 timetable which was reduced slightly to provide gaps during which the bus could run the Northwood journeys. These were numbered 309A and later on, one morning journey was run using the out-stationed GS from the 336A since that had plenty of spare stand time at Rickmansworth. The 309A though was never more than a minimal token replacement for the hourly Green Line service it replaced. In another indication of the abstraction of traffic by the Metropolitan Line, Christmas Day services between Rickmansworth, Amersham and Chesham were discussed at the Traffic Committee meeting on 20th November where the Operating Manager considered that potential traffic did not justify a parallel bus service, despite the fact that there would be no Underground service on Christmas Day that year beyond Rickmansworth.

When introduced, the 336B terminated at Amersham, but was extended a short distance to Little Missenden to replace part of the 359 Sunday service when that was withdrawn at the end of 1966. RF 313 was one of the former Green Line coaches converted as an omo bus in 1962, and is working a journey to Little Missenden from Northwood. The route was never a success and was withdrawn in the winter 1968 cuts. (Peter Mitchell)

With the withdrawal of the 703, Amersham lost four Green Line RFs and eight crew duties from its daily allocation, together with the Hospital duplicate coach, but the southern section was retained so that Swanley garage was unaffected by the 703's withdrawal. However, rather than run a truncated 703 just between London and Wrotham, the 717 was extended from London to create a through route from Welwyn Garden City to Wrotham on an hourly headway which required Swanley and Hatfield crews to learn the new route. Traffic on the 720 and 720A had declined to such an extent that after only two years, the extra capacity of the RMCs on these routes was unnecessary although inadequacies regularly occurred at weekends after the conversion. Thus they were sent to Hatfield and Swanley for the 717 in exchange for their RFs which went back on to the 720/720A. Whilst the extra seating capacity of the RMCs was not required on the extended 717, it allowed all journeys on 716, 716A and 717 between London and Welwyn Garden City to be worked by RMCs. Swanley rostered three RTs on Sundays for Green Line duplicates, but these were mostly used only on Brands Hatch race days, and were taken from the spare RTs when Swanley's Sunday schedules required only 12 of the 24 scheduled during the week.

Traffic north of London on the joint 709 and 710 timetable to Amersham had also fallen away at weekends to such an extent that the 709 was cut back on Sundays to run only between Godstone and London, thus halving the frequency to hourly beyond Gerrards Cross where the routes parted company from the 711. The 710 was extended to Chesham to cover the loss of the 709 on Sundays, but with the abandonment of the 703 as well, it meant that Amersham's Green Line allocation on Sundays had dropped from 12 to just four RFs. In what proved to be a vain effort to avoid losing further passengers during the week, the 709 between London and Amersham was altered to an 'Express' service by omitting a number of stops and running non-stop along part of Western Avenue instead of the traditional route into London along the Uxbridge Road through Southall. Although this saved 20 minutes on the 'stopping' timetable it was not sufficient to prevent the continuing drop in passengers and lasted just a year until 30th October 1965 when the London to Chesham section was abandoned completely, the 709 being reduced to run just from London to Godstone.

The 703 was one of the less important Green Line routes, never running more than an hourly headway. The southern section to Wrotham suffered from not being permitted to run on to Borough Green as a result of the 1933 boundary, whilst the northern section suffered increasing competition from the Metropolitan line which offered much quicker journey times into central London. Its withdrawal in November 1964 represented the start of Green Line retrenchment which would continue unabated, although the southern section was retained, to be finally withdrawn as part of London Country's drastic review of the Green Line network in 1976. RF 264 was one of four new RFs sent to Swanley in June 1952, and is at the terminus in Wrotham where the coaches simply performed a U-turn in the village square to head back. It was one of those withdrawn in 1964 as Green Line cuts began to provide spare coaches. (Author's collection)

The 712 and 713, which ran to a joint half-hourly headway, were cut back to an hourly off peak frequency. However, since the two services ran via different routes between Radlett and St Albans, the former hourly service via each route became either every two hours off peak or ran to a disjointed irregular timetable at peak times. The various permutations of routeings via Shenley or Park Street and on to either Luton or Dunstable resulted in a completely confusing renumbering using 712, 712B, 713 or 713A (712A being used for the seasonal Whipsnade Zoo service) while the Sunday service was reduced to hourly, numbered either 712B or 713 with additional coaches in the afternoon between St Albans and Victoria. Despite these cuts to the timetable, there was no reduction in the total number of RFs rostered since the peak timetable included journeys just to London and back from each end, although there was a saving in fuel from the lower mileage run. Three crew duties were saved, and three more converted to spreadovers rostered to work the morning and evening peak trips to and from London. These duties however attracted additional payments to the crews who worked them, the cost of which offset some of the savings on the three duties no longer required. The overall savings from these changes could not have been large, and must have been disproportionate to the reduction in the timetable which was less attractive and difficult to remember for regular passengers, serving only to drive away a few more. The extension of the 722 through the Dartford Tunnel, which had run at a loss from the very beginning and suffered crew shortages on Saturdays, was abandoned on the same date as all the other changes.

The most notable event on 4th November in the face of all the cuts however was the introduction of a completely new Green Line route numbered 727. It ran from Tring to Hemel Hempstead, then non-stop down the M1, and into central London where it ran to Trafalgar Square, providing a link to the West End for commuters, shopping and theatres. The principle of running a limited stop express service to London from one of the important New Towns was sound and was the forerunner of what would become a network of similar routes more than 20 years later. The route ran to an hourly headway, Tring garage requiring an extra four RFs and eight crew duties daily to run the new service. The section along the A41 between Tring and Hemel Hempstead however probably served little purpose since the main line railway into Euston provided a much quicker journey and any passengers who were attracted to a quicker journey time would almost certainly have been abstracted from the 706 and 707. Despite the motorway section, only 15 minutes were saved on the journey time to central London, but this was nevertheless a positive attempt to try to overcome falling traffic. The new service received much publicity, but a significant downside was that there were no new coaches to go with the modern 'express service' image which London Transport wanted to convey. The RFs were still excellent buses, but were by then 13 years old, and on the section of the M1 motorway – which in those days suffered none of the terrible traffic congestion of today – their top speed of around 45mph simply did not take advantage of the potential of non-stop high speed running. Unfortunately for London Transport, major roadworks at the southern end of the M1 began in May 1965, only six months after the route began, and the resultant diversion and delays served to negate any advantages from the shorter running time.

After all the service cuts and withdrawals which came from the changes on 4th November, there were two small additions to the network before the year end. Rural railways were being closed in increasing numbers and passenger services

The 435 was introduced in December 1964 to the new Imberhorne Estate in East Grinstead, its start having been delayed by residents who objected to buses using the estate roads. The initial allocation was one RT, but with cross working from the 424 and 428, some journeys were worked with RFs and, later, XFs. RT 3053 arrived at East Grinstead in February 1966, and is in pristine condition parked in Garland Road opposite the garage. The side advert is for the new 727 Green Line route which started in May 1966. (S J Butler)

on the branch line from St Margarets to Buntingford were withdrawn on 15th November 1964. The Saturday service was not replaced, but London Transport introduced route 351 on Monday to Friday to run hourly in the morning peak and again from mid-afternoon to early evening, plus one final late journey to Buntingford. Hertford required two additional RFs, and the new route ran in a 'U shape' via Ware from both Much Hadham and Buntingford with the rail link at Ware roughly at the mid-point of the route, rather than to the previous branch line terminus at St Margarets since there was no easy or direct road link there. In the southern area route 435 was introduced on 9th December to serve the new Imberhorne Estate in East Grinstead, and ran six days a week with a few morning journeys and an hourly timetable in the afternoons. Most of the service was run by an additional bus rostered to the new route, but some journeys were time-tabled so that they could be worked by buses off the 428 and 424, resulting in a mixed crew double-deck and omo single-deck operation.

The RTs running the 721 and 722 east London Green Line routes to Romford and beyond were twelve to fifteen years old by the end of 1964. Although traffic had dropped away and frequencies reduced, decent loads were still carried on many journeys, and so a decision was taken to modernise the routes by ordering a second batch of Routemaster coaches. The 723, 723A and 723B to Grays and Tilbury were also to be included and so a total of 43 new Routemasters were ordered at the end of 1964 to add to the 68 very successful RMCs which had already been in service for two years. By then, the 30ft long RML version of the Routemaster had become the standard, so the new coaches were ordered to the greater length and would seat 65 instead of the 57 seat capacity of the RMCs.

As the first half of the 1960s came to an end, traffic at weekends was dropping away faster than during the week, and at an alarming level on some of the trunk routes which had always been the mainstay of the system, while falling passenger numbers on Green Line services were now a major concern. Television had dealt an enormous blow to passenger levels in the evenings; private car ownership had cut back occasional and leisure journeys by more than a third in the previous ten years, and the reduction in Saturday shopping traffic had all but eliminated the once numerous scheduled duplicates and additional journeys. After the 1964 winter schedules a total of 39 buses and 53 Green Line coaches had been cut from the Monday to Friday rostered totals over the previous five years since the end of 1959. This represented just over 7% of the total fleet, but masked a much greater reduction in the numbers which remained on the road after the evening peak period as evening services had been severely pruned back. Expansion of one-man operation had made no difference to the total number of scheduled omo buses – the reduction of 39 Monday to Friday buses having come entirely from the smaller number of crew double deckers required. The Green Line reduction represented a fall of 16% over five years, almost entirely as a result of the withdrawal of virtually all the peak hour duplicates. It will be no surprise that the reductions in Sunday schedules had been much greater over the same five-year period, the bus allocation having fallen from 470 to 314, and Green Line from 355 to 253, a fall of 33% and 29% respectively so that in all 258 more buses and coaches stood idle in their garages on Sundays compared to five years earlier. The GS Sunday allocation had fallen to just two buses, both from Dunton Green to run the 471, even one of these being required for a few hours only in the afternoon as a crew relief bus.

The 364A number was introduced when it replaced the 376 from Luton to Kensworth. RF 542 was among those sent to Luton in April 1959 for allocation to the 364/364A and shows the isolated rural nature of the route near Kensworth. (Peter Mitchell)

In 1965, in its evidence to the Parliamentary Select Committee on Nationalised Industries, London Transport submitted figures for the number of Country area buses and coaches which were being operated on loss making routes during 1964 as a whole. A similar analysis had been conducted on a sample week during the winter 1962/63 period, and summer 1963.

PROPORTION OF BUSES AND COACHES BETWEEN REMUNERATIVE AND UNREMUNERATIVE ROUTES

		Monday to Friday			Saturday			Sunday		
		No. In service	% profit making	% loss making	No. In service	% profit making	% loss making	No. In service	% profit making	% loss making
Winter 1962-63										
BUS	D/D	728	72	28	623	33	67	293	0	100
	S/D	216	12	88	200	19	81	81	0	100
COACH	D/D	123	64	36	102	91	9	95	58	42
	S/D	176	63	37	157	85	15	173	33	67
Summer 1963										
BUS	D/D	732	55	45	606	82	18	313	8	92
	S/D	215	15	85	195	30	70	89	0	100
COACH	D/D	120	88	12	100	100	0	91	88	12
	S/D	171	94	6	158	100	0	186	84	16
Summer 1964										
BUS	D/D	733	54	46	600	85	15	301	10	90
	S/D	206	13	87	191	33	67	84	0	100
COACH	ALL	286	68	32	254	100	0	271	90	10

Although by 1964 an increasing number of double deckers were running on loss making routes, events like the annual Air Show at Biggin Hill attracted huge numbers of visitors and produced a healthy profit for the special service to the event. Godstone put out as many buses as they could on such days and in the summer of 1965, RT 2153 has worked a special journey from Westerham. Other garages would also provide buses and RT 3171 has come from Grays and worked in from Bromley North. (Michael Baker)

The statistics for the winter week of 1962-63 may have suffered from the prolonged bad weather. By summer 1963, Saturday shopping traffic would have returned to normal, which together with some leisure journeys had increased the number of double deckers on remunerative routes, rising from nil to 8% on Sundays. What is notable however is the significant fall in double deckers running remunerative routes during the week, despite any additional summer traffic. The 1964 figures remained almost identical. The figures for single-deck buses are universally poor, with almost no change during the period. The decline in Green Line passengers has been dealt with frequently in this chapter, and the figures above simply confirm what was already apparent. Although Saturdays remained universally profitable, and Sundays were marginally better after the poor winter of 1962-63, the fall from 1963 to 1964 in the proportion of coaches running remunerative routes during the week is significant, driven in no small part by the railway modernisation programmes referred to earlier.

On bus routes, it is the statistics for the single deckers that are the most depressing. At best only one third of the single deckers on Saturday – still by far the busiest day – and only around one in seven or eight Monday to Friday were running remunerative routes, whilst on Sundays, every single decker had consistently been running on loss making routes.

Taken overall, the route network as a whole was, by the end of 1964, incurring losses which were gradually getting worse. Service cuts and one-man conversions had helped to produce a net surplus on bus routes in 1962 and 1963, but for a decade before that, serious deficits had resulted. An overall surplus had been made possible only by consistent profits on Green Line routes, but 1964 would be the last year during which the Green Line network produced a net surplus of traffic receipts. As 1965 began therefore, it was abundantly clear that the continuing reduction in passengers across the whole of the network was not only irreversible but was accelerating. Whilst 1962 and 1963 had seen a fairly stable balance between passenger numbers and miles run, the drop in passengers during 1964 had drastically increased. The statistics above relating to unremunerative routes support the argument that one-man conversions and cutting timetables was by no means a complete remedy for stemming the increasing losses. It was the route network itself which was the underlying issue. Other than the additional routes in the new towns and overspill estates, and a few rural routes added after the war, the basic route pattern was unchanged from prewar days, and whilst there were still passengers who travelled on them, there had never been a fundamental review of whether the routes still provided facilities that large numbers of passengers actually wanted. The overall fixed cost of the large number of garages around the system was also becoming a burden which was too great to sustain as it was, although London Transport made no attempt to reduce this and the whole garage network was unchanged when London Country took over.

These observations may appear to be over critical of London Transport's management at the time. Reducing passenger numbers were undoubtedly an intractable problem everywhere, but a thoroughly radical review of the route network and garages was not part of London Transport's strategic thinking at the time, or indeed over the following years to the end of the decade. It would be another 15 years before the focused 'Market Analysis Projects' introduced by the National Bus Company would make alterations to established route networks to reflect what the travelling public might actually use.

5   Cuts and Retrenchment

The 489/A were typical of the many single deck omo routes which were beginning to lose money. Whilst a few peak hour journeys to the station at Longfield, and to and from Gravesend carried good loads, passenger numbers during off peak and evenings were rapidly falling. The 30 minute joint headway on Saturdays as far as Longfield had been reduced to hourly in 1965 as traffic fell away sharply, and the seven Sunday journeys to Ash were cut to four in 1968. RF 659 is on the lane between Southfleet and Westwood on the way to Ash. (Peter Mitchell)

The second paragraph of London Transport's 1965 Annual report referred to the previous year and noted that: *there must be serious doubts as to London Transport's future ability to reconcile the two main duties laid on it by Parliament – to provide an adequate service to the public in the London area and at the same time to pay its way.* This obligation had been set out in the 1962 Transport Act, but by 1965 the deteriorating financial performance of the whole network was an increasing concern.

In the Central area, traffic congestion combined with continual staff shortages had led to significant delays and irregularity in services, which constrained to make bus travel less and less attractive. The Government's examination of the conditions in which London Transport was having to operate had led to the perhaps obvious conclusion that much more robust traffic management measures were necessary. In the Country area, 1964 was a pivotal year during which the financial position had approached the point where the network could not be sustained simply from fare income alone, and the frequent, and in some cases significant, fare increases from 1961 onwards, had failed to yield enough extra revenue to the point where the operation could pay its way. Indeed, the fare increases themselves were partly a cause of the loss of further passengers which had offset much of the additional revenue the increases were intended to generate. At a meeting of the Traffic Committee on 28th August 1964, statistics showing the estimated loss of traffic had compared test weeks in July 1963 with July 1964 following a further increase in the minimum fare. The total reduction in passenger numbers due to fare increases was estimated at 12.8%, with 10% being accounted for by the loss of minimum fare traffic.

Rather than an increase in fares, cheap day return fares were introduced on eight Green Line routes at the end of April 1965 in an attempt to attract extra passengers for the summer season, and the Annual Report mentions that *'some additional use of these routes appears to have resulted'*. To give quicker journey times to Windsor, duplicates on the 704 were allowed to run non-stop between Hammersmith and Windsor at the discretion of the inspectors – again in an attempt to make the service more attractive.

Paragraph 3 of the 1965 Annual Report stated: *the attractiveness of the Board's services should not be lessened (by further fare increases) and accordingly the Minister had asked the Board to agree to postpone action for fare increases, at the same time giving the Board assurances that the Board would not have to bear the loss in revenue caused by the postponement.* The postponement referred to a further increase which had been planned for May 1965. This was a significant point in the whole cycle of increases in fares since, for the first time, there was official Government recognition that some form of public subsidy was necessary if certain levels of service and investment in new vehicles were to be maintained while at the same time not deterring more passengers through increasing fares. In the Country area, the reduction in loadings on busier trunk routes and town services meant that their diminishing profit would soon reach the point where they would not be sufficient to counter the losses in the rural services. This principle of cross subsidisation had been common practice by operators everywhere since the war as a method of maintaining whole networks long after many rural routes had begun to lose money. Indeed, London Transport was probably more fortunate than many of the Tilling and BET group companies who generally had a lower proportion of profitable mileage from which the subsidy for loss-making routes could come. In late 1964, the Government nevertheless viewed London Transport's operational and financial issues with sufficient seriousness that the whole spectrum of their operating conditions was made the subject of an inquiry by the House of Commons Select Committee on Nationalised Industries which spent the first half of 1965 on its deliberations.

The reduction in the working week from 42 to 40 hours which came from the 1964 Phelps-Brown report was introduced from March 1965 and added further to staffing costs. Schedules however were not changed until later in the year, so the 42-hour week continued to be standard, but there was an additional cost in overtime rates for the extra two hours. There were also further overtime costs as various garages suffered the continuing staff shortages which appeared intractable despite sharp increases in pay. By 1965, staff costs had risen to 76% of working expenses, and the Annual Report makes clear that *'increases in productivity to offset increases in wages cannot be obtained unless and until significant changes in operating practices can be secured'*. A specific recommendation of the Phelps-Brown report had been that changes in working practice were necessary, but the Trade Union would prove continuingly intransigent in their opposition to changing anything, in particular greatly extending one-man operation. The Transport Union had already seen large numbers of railway workers lose their jobs as the 'Beeching Cuts' took effect with the closure of rural branch lines together with reducing the appalling over-manning which came from outdated working practices, and they were in no mood to agree to similar changes in bus operation despite the obvious deterioration in the financial position of all operators.

Despite the shortfalls in the Board's finances, it was nevertheless necessary to give serious thought to further fleet replacements for the Country area. Following the order for 43 new RCL Routemaster coaches for the east London Green Line routes, an order was placed for 14 AEC Reliance coaches for Green Line service. These were to be built to the then relatively new maximum 36ft length, with 49 seats, and were to be put into service to assess their performance. The bulk of the RT fleet was now about three quarters of the way through its normal service life, the great majority being between 12 and 16 years old. By the mid-1960s, those few RTs which had been replaced had been replaced by RFs (which were almost as old) in a small number of omo conversions. Early in 1965 therefore it was decided that a batch of new Routemasters would be used to replace RTs on some busy interurban trunk routes where their additional seating capacity would be useful and could enable frequencies to be reduced. One hundred RMLs were therefore earmarked for the Country area for delivery in two batches from late 1965.

London Transport had also ordered a batch of 50 Leyland Atlanteans for delivery in 1965 for service on some central London routes in order to test them for their general suitability for service in central London. Added to the end of this order were eight Daimler Fleetlines for the Country Bus area, and these were allocated on delivery to East Grinstead garage from 15th September to take over operation of the 424 between East Grinstead and Reigate. The 424 had a basic hourly headway, increasing to half hourly during peak times and Saturdays, and although the sections from Felbridge to Smallfield, and Hookwood to Woodhatch were quite rural the route provided some long established links across Surrey and carried many short distance passengers on its busier sections. The 424 schedules required eight RTs Monday to Friday of which four ran the basic all day service. The other four ran peak hour and school journeys together with a morning and evening peak journey on the 438 works service to Crawley. Some off peak journeys on the 435 East Grinstead town service were also worked off the 424 schedules and the Fleetines replaced the RTs on a one-for-one basis. The allocation was not completely converted to XF however as Reigate continued to run a handful of short journeys to Woodhatch and Horley using RTs from the 405 allocation together with a Green Line RF from the 711 allocation for a morning peak short journey to Horley. Similarly, East Grinstead's omo RF allocated to run most of the 435 also worked a couple of 424 shorts to Felbridge during the day, and so the operation of the 424 became a mix of three types of bus.

The terminus for the 424 at Reigate was in Alma Road behind the station, and in June 1967, XF 1 is at the stop having just arrived from East Grinstead. The bodywork on the Fleetlines and Atlanteans was typical of the period, which though somewhat box-like was not unattractive, and the XFs looked well in Country Bus livery. (Author)

In March 1965 the little-used branch line from West Drayton across Stanwell Moor to Staines closed, its timetable having been gradually reduced to no more than a few peak hour trains. The service was replaced by a Central Bus route between the two former ends of the line, but the local road network did not allow the new 225 route to run via the isolated hamlet of Stanwell Moor itself. In 1965, this was still a small village not then subsumed into what would become the expansion of Heathrow airport, and which, without the railway, would have been left with no transport link at all. The Country Bus department therefore began a new service numbered 444 from there into Staines, providing just a few shopping journeys on Tuesdays and Saturdays only and British Railways paid a small subsidy to provide the service. Running a service on Tuesdays however was poorly thought out, since Wednesday was Market Day in Staines, and the Tuesday service was changed to Wednesday with the start of the winter schedules from 3rd October. The obvious allocation would have been omo RF, but Staines garage only had two for the local 466 and 469 to Thorpe and Virginia Water with no capacity in their timetables for working on other routes. Until early 1965, Staines required 12 RTs for its allocation to the 441, but this was adjusted to 11 with minor timetable changes, and thus the 444 was crew operated with this spare RT.

The 444 provided a limited service for shopping in Staines with only four journeys on Wednesday and Saturday. Buses operated in a loop round Stanwell village, the round trip taking just 25 minutes. It lasted longer than might have been expected for such a minor route, not being withdrawn until October 1972 as part of London Country's cuts. RT 4518 runs through the village street in Stanwell. (Colin Stannard)

Although the 366 began as a replacement for the Luton to Welwyn Garden City branch line, it opened up new links to the towns at both ends, and proved to be a long term success. Whilst a couple of Saturday journeys were cut, the timetable during the week remained unchanged, and much later London Country added some additional journeys during the daytime to increase facilities for shopping traffic. Former Green Line coach RF 290 comes along the road past Brocket Hall estate on the way to Luton sometime in the winter of 1969. The 'limited stop' restriction on the route was later lifted when what remained of the 365 was abandoned. (J.G.S. Smith)

At the end of April, the branch line between Hatfield and Dunstable also closed, and another replacement bus service was started between Welwyn Garden City and Luton, numbered 366, and run with omo RFs from Luton garage. It was a limited stop service paralleling the existing 365 between Luton and Wheathampstead, and then running via Lemsford to Welwyn Garden City. With only eleven stops en route, the running time was only a few minutes more than the train service it replaced. The former railway timetable was largely a commuter peak hour service designed to give a link across to Welwyn Garden City and Hatfield for connections with the main line into Kings Cross. On Monday to Friday there were trains in the morning peak from Luton with evening peak returns but a very limited service at other times, although on Saturday there were a few journeys spread out during the day. Luton required four extra RFs to run the new 366 timetable, largely replicating the withdrawn train service, which meant that all four ran spreadover peak duties. This was uneconomic since all the morning journeys into Welwyn Garden City had to return to Luton carrying very few, if any, passengers, the same applying in reverse in the evening. On Monday to Friday, all four buses were back at Luton by 10.16am and apart from one lunchtime return to Welwyn Garden City there were no further departures from Luton until 3.35pm after which only three buses were needed to work the afternoon timetable. On Saturdays, only two RFs were rostered to run an irregular timetable aimed mainly at shopping facilities, though with shorter gaps between journeys than on Monday to Friday. With the introduction of the 366, the retention of the existing 365 timetable between St Albans and Luton appeared an unnecessary extravagance. The necessity for a link through Wheathampstead from either St Albans or Luton was all but non-existent, even more so since the 355 with its 30-minute headway covered the same road as the 365 from St Albans through Wheathampstead as far as Batford. With the introduction of the 366 therefore,

the 365 became virtually superfluous and its continued operation was a waste of resources. Although the 366 was as a limited stop rail replacement service, it should have been possible to make some journeys between Wheathampstead and Luton 'stopping journeys' to replace the 365, allowing its complete withdrawal and making use of one of Luton's spreadover RF workings during the day, while St Albans would have saved two RFs. The 366 timetable also missed the opportunity to provide daytime shopping journeys into Welwyn Garden City which – although these may have been restricted due to the route's initial licence – made poor use of the resources. As it was, the 365 and 366 allocation required six RFs at maximum and the combined timetable gave a total of 23 journeys between Luton and Wheathampstead during the day, which was far greater than passenger levels justified. As if this was not already a significant over-provision, Birch Brothers operated their 205 route from Kimpton into Luton via Peter's Green, which joined the 365 and 366 at Newmill End to provide even more journeys into Luton. The retention of the 365 which continued into London Country's era was surely a lost opportunity for savings at a time when any saving was worth having.

On 2nd June 1965 when the summer schedules began there were few changes. Routes 416 and 433 were reinstated on Sundays to give a service to Boxhill, Coldharbour and Ranmore, as were the journeys on the 364A to Whipsnade Zoo. At the other end of the scale, the once important 402 trunk route was abandoned on Saturdays apart from a couple of early journeys from Bromley to provide a service before the main southbound 704 Green Line service came through from London. All that was left on the 402 was the Monday to Friday hourly timetable from Bromley to Sevenoaks and a few peak journeys beyond to Tonbridge. In Surrey, the 493 to St Peter's Hospital near Chertsey was withdrawn for lack of patronage since hospital visiting by bus was becoming a casualty of increased car ownership.

The 493 was introduced in April 1953 as one of a number of new routes specifically for visitors to hospitals in an era when visiting times were strictly limited. Like all of these routes, usage was never great, car ownership and the gradual relaxation of visiting times steadily abstracting passengers. It ran for the last time on 26th September 1965, and some years earlier RT 3185 is in Staines garage having run back light before returning later to the hospital. (D A Jones)

The Croydon trunk routes had, by 1965, suffered further significant reductions in passengers at weekends. The number of RTs scheduled on Saturdays suffered a dramatic fall from 79 for summer 1960 down to 59 for summer 1965 by which time Saturday leisure and shopping travel had dropped significantly. The reductions on Sundays were equally great, the RT schedule being cut from 57 for summer 1960 to 47 for summer 1965, down from a total which had been 80 ten years earlier. Successive cuts had taken out almost a third of the 1955 weekend allocation across all the Croydon routes, much of which had come from the four garages further out or at the end of the route. Their combined Sunday RT allocation had dropped from 16 to just two, with East Grinstead and Dunton Green left with no Sunday allocation at all on the Croydon routes. On Monday to Friday after the morning peak, the Crawley to Horsham section on the 405 was reduced to just hourly, the 30-minute headway not operating until after lunch so that alternate morning journeys from Croydon terminated at Crawley. The 30-minute all day headway to Horsham survived on Saturdays, but the extra shopping journeys into Redhill had been reduced to just four nine-minute long shuttle trips to Earlwsood at lunchtime. The 414 was little changed, although on Sundays the half hourly headway beyond Reigate as far as Capel did not begin until after lunchtime. Beyond Leatherhead on the 408, the service to Guildford had been reduced to hourly Monday to Friday with a few extra peak journeys, but surprisingly, the hourly Sunday headway was increased to half hourly from early afternoon to early evening, and even the extra Sunday evening 10.30pm Epsom to Leatherhead cinema journey remained in the timetable. Conversely, the former cinema duplicate on the 414 which left Dorking on Saturday and Sunday evenings a minute or two before the through service had been withdrawn.

There was a small extension to Hertford's 331 route in June when it was extended from Buntingford village a short way up to the new estate at Greenways on the Baldock Road. Until then all buses had run as 331 despite the two different routes either via the main A10 or the more rural routeing through Braughing and Hare Street, but with the extension to Greenways, the route via Braughing was re-numbered 331A. These changes also brought timetable cuts on Saturday mornings, the headway to Buntingford being reduced to hourly, and there was a two hour gap in the morning during the week. The Saturday journeys worked by RTs remained however but new 331A blinds were not produced, buses continuing to show the 331 number until the odd double deck workings finally ended in 1975.

In June 1965, the 331 was extended a short distance from the centre of Buntingford to some new housing at Greenways, and the 'A' suffix introduced to distinguish journeys operating via Braughing and Hare Street as opposed to those direct along the main A10 via Westmill. Soon after the change, RF 569 is at Greenways terminus waiting to work a 331A back to Hertford. (V.C. Jones)

At the same all the Saturday short workings to High Cross were withdrawn which ended GS operation on the route. On Sundays the hourly service to Buntingford was cut significantly to just five journeys although two previous evening trips to Standon remained. The Thursday market day service from Bishop's Stortford to Buntingford on the 386 was also extended to Greenways removing the long standing idiosyncrasy of the two journeys on Thursday that had run up the Royston road in Buntingford to turn at Throcking Lane just outside the village, since there was no convenient turning point in Buntingford High Street. Buntingford was on the very edge of the LPTA and the route north to Royston had been handed to what was then Eastern National in 1933. What became United Counties service 188 ran into Buntingford on Wednesday and Saturday, but London Transport only ever covered the short distance to Throcking Lane on Thursday. Because this was outside the LPTA, such was the strict demarcation of the boundary that London Transport had never been permitted to carry local passengers despite the fact that there was never any competition with United Counties. Whether London Transport's drivers complied with the requirement not to carry anyone into Buntingford and back is not known but it is likely that some at least ignored it!

RMC 1469 was chosen to experiment with slight changes on the livery pending delivery of the RCLs. The cast metal "Green Line" roundel plate fixed in the centre of the between decks panel was replaced with a transfer positioned near the front and the "GREEN LINE" fleetname with letters all of the same height with no underlining. Smaller versions of the same transfers were applied on the lower deck just ahead of the platform doors. The production RCLs had only the roundel transfer on the upper deck with a "GREEN LINE" fleetname on the lower deck as illustrated on the picture of RCL 2251 on page 165. The intermediate and side blind displays on this bus were not adopted, and altered to the same width as the ultimate destination, which became the standard on the RCLs. The styles of this blind and the side blind were not adopted. RMC 1469 is alongside Chiswick works in this posed shot.

The main change to Green Line operation was the introduction of the new Routemaster RCL coaches to Romford in June and Grays in July to take over the east London routes from the RTs. There were more frequency reductions – mostly at Grays on the 723 – and 45 scheduled RT workings were replaced by only 36 scheduled RCLs between the two garages. Even allowing for their greater seating capacity, the total allocation of the new RCLs represented about a 7% cut in capacity, a reduction coming on top of the significant cut which had been made only the previous November when nine RTs had already been taken out of the two garages combined schedules. The RCLs brought new standards of comfort to these routes with their better seats, luggage racks and platform doors, but were certainly 'too little too late' to arrest the loss of passengers which had accelerated considerably after the Tilbury and Southend railway lines had been converted from steam to overhead electric during 1961 and 1962. The new RCLs cost just over £8,000 each which was around £1,500 more than the RMCs purchased only three years previously, and time would show that they were a costly replacement given the limited front line Green Line service life many were destined to have.

The winter schedules from 3rd October 1965 continued what by then was the annual culling of evening, off peak and weekend timetables as passenger levels kept falling. These revisions resulted in a round of severe service cuts which were greater than the previous two years. The Operating Manager had produced an estimate of mileage savings to the Traffic Committee on 26th August 1965, six weeks before the schedules were to come into force. Reductions in mileage on 'low earning routes' (which were not defined) would save 374,000 miles in a full year. These were to be offset by the introduction of the 442 at High Wycombe which, as a short local route, only amounted to 20,800 miles per year, while the planned augmentation of the 438 and 473 to part cover the closure of the East Grinstead to Three Bridges railway would add around 130,000 miles. The estimates also included figures for changes in 1966 when the summer programme would take out six double deckers and two single deckers, with the same again for the winter programme. This was estimated to save almost 1½ million miles per annum, and the introduction of the RMLs would save about seven buses and a further 182,000 miles in a year. There were proposals to extend Stevenage and Harlow town services further into estates during 1966, plus to extend the 322 to Grove Park at Hemel Hempstead, all of which would add some 200,000 miles, but were expected to be profitable given the likely passenger loadings on town services.

Unsurprisingly, the rural routes saw the greatest cuts. The 852 between Crawley and Horsham through Ifield Wood and Lambs Green had at best barely covered its costs even when it replaced the former Hants & Sussex service in December 1954. After the Horsham to Ewhurst section was transferred to Brown Motor Services in April 1955, London Transport had continued to operate seven journeys, six days a week between Crawley and Horsham for another eight years. This included a last departure from Crawley just before 8pm with a return from Horsham around 8.50pm which even in the 1950s was almost pointless. In 1963, the timetable had been cut to just four trips a day, but the timing of these was not ideal for shopping. By 1965 it was completely unviable and its withdrawal saw the end of Crawley's GSs which had included unscheduled duplicate GS workings on the 434 to Crawley Down.

Some of the greatest cuts were made to the rural routes in Hertfordshire. On the 388 between Hertford and Welwyn, what had been a generally hourly headway on weekdays was drastically cut back. Initially, the Monday to Friday off peak service to both Welwyn village and Welwyn Garden City was completely cut, and after the 8.33am from Welwyn village to Hertford, the next departures were not until just after 3.00pm to Welwyn North Station and 4.12pm to Hertford. Just one mid-morning journey from Hertford remained but this ran only as far Welwyn North Station. These cuts brought vociferous protests from people along the route, particularly in Tewin and Harmer Green who were left with virtually no service at all during the day, and so two extra morning journeys were added, but only on Tuesdays and Fridays. At the other end of the 388 the section to Harlow had already been reduced only four months earlier to just two journeys Monday to Friday and only one on Saturday morning from Harlow to Hertford, even this running only as a means of returning a bus which had worked an early 390 journey from Hertford to Harlow. The last remaining journeys on the 381 beyond Roydon to St Margarets had been withdrawn, but some journeys at Harlow were extended in a loop round Eastwick village just outside the town to cover the loss of the 388. Loadings on the 350 and 350A south of Hertford had dropped away dramatically, so that between Hertford and Barnet the whole of the Sunday timetable together with the evening service during the week was abandoned, and the 327, having been converted from RT to omo RF only eleven months earlier, was also cut back to Broxbourne on Sunday leaving only the 393A to provide a link every two hours to Nazeing.

Of Hertford garage's two Market Day routes to Hitchin, one was abandoned and the other halved. The 329A from Datchworth – the Country area's most infrequent route with just two journeys each on Tuesday and Saturday – was withdrawn. The other – the 386 – had the four journeys on Tuesdays from Buntingford to Hitchin reduced to two. Before the cuts, the 386 driver had taken his break between journeys from Buntingford at Hitchin, but after 3rd October the bus worked a short journey back to Stevenage where the driver took his break before working back to Hitchin for the return trip to Buntingford. This arrangement maintained the four journeys between Hitchin and Stevenage, but apart from the first short working to Great Wymondley which Stevenage took over, the other

Later in the book the text refers to the drastic cuts to the timetable on the 381/A to the point where it became a very limited service. A few years earlier, RF 658 takes its layover at Epping Green having worked a short journey through Epping from Coopersale. The routes were finally abandoned in London Country's earliest round of cuts in 1971.

shorts were withdrawn because they had been worked by the bus from the 329A which no longer ran. The four 386 Thursday journeys into Bishop's Stortford were also cut to two but the through Saturday service was basically unchanged with Stevenage taking on the operation of four short journeys between Hitchin and Great Wymondley by re-adjusting the 383 schedules. Before October, buses for the 386 on Tuesdays and Thursdays had worked positioning journeys to Standon or Buntingford on the 331 before setting off on the 386, but this changed by extending the 386 into Hertford without the need for the positioning journeys. In this way the 386 became three separate routes but provided a slight improvement in that any odd passengers from points along the 331 route could now travel through to Bishop's Stortford or Hitchin without a change of bus. On Thursdays, the link from Buntingford and Hare Street into Bishop's Stortford ceased, but this affected hardly anyone, although Braughing retained the service run by B.C. Cannon via a different route. Although the 329A to Hitchin was withdrawn, Datchworth retained a facility as the 329A route number was retained for a service from Nup End to Hertford via Datchworth on Tuesday and Saturday. This would probably have made good sense some years earlier since Hertford was closer, and with the building of the Nut Croft estate in the 1950s, Datchworth was just about large enough to warrant a limited bus service. The Thursday service on the 329 was withdrawn completely, Thursday being Hertford early closing day with minimal passengers. From Datchworth Green along the winding lane to the Great North Road at Woolmer Green the 329 picked up hardly anyone, so only seven months later, in May 1966, this section was abandoned, all journeys then running via Datchworth Village as 329 with the 329A number being discontinued.

The October 1965 cuts reduced Hertford's allocations to its rural routes considerably. One GS was taken out Monday to Saturday (reductions with the summer 1963 schedules had already removed Hertford's last Sunday GS working) while the number of RFs required on Sundays dropped from eleven at the end of 1964 to eight and from 23 to 18 on Saturdays. The Monday to Friday total dropped by three, but two additional RFs had been added to run the 351 Buntingford rail replacement route which started the previous November.

The bus service through Datchworth was served only by GSs until the 329A to Hitchin was withdrawn in October 1965. Up to that point, the route had not been approved for RF operation, but the restriction was lifted after which the route saw workings by both RF and GS. RF 605 is leaving Datchworth on the way to Nup End in Old Knebworth sometime after May 1966 when the 329A number was discontinued. It will soon run down the single track Swangley's Lane into Knebworth which had a blind corner by Swangley's Farm, but despite this hazard London Country would eventually use Leyland Nationals on the route! (Malcolm Papes)

In the North West area, the 364A summer extension to Whipsnade was withdrawn, and the remainder of the 364 and 364A Sunday service was cut to no more than a Luton town service only as far as Woodside, which was worked in with the 360 schedules so that one RT could run both routes. One very small improvement was the introduction of four shopping journeys on the 343A between Kensworth and Dunstable on Tuesday and Thursday. These were run at no extra cost (apart from fuel) since they were run by the Hemel Hempstead bus off the 337 which had long layovers in Dunstable on the days when the 352 journeys to Dagnall didn't run. Amersham lost all Sunday working on both the 348 and 394, and the once busy 336 to Watford was converted to omo RF as part of phase eight of the conversion programme, taking four scheduled RLHs out of service in the process. This left operation of the lowbridge RLHs confined to just 15 scheduled workings for the Staines, Walton and Guildford routes plus the one at Reigate for the peak hour working on the 447. The isolated Sunday section of the 409 from Felbridge to Forest Row was withdrawn leaving just the single late evening departure from East Grinstead to Godstone after the last 708 Green Line had left. Dunton Green lost the 431 Sunday service plus a running on the 403 as the section between Chelsham and Westerham was also abandoned on Sunday for the winter. The 413 timetable was cut to just two morning journeys to Chevening for churchgoers, plus a single working out to Bayleys Hill in the afternoon to serve the small isolation hospital between Cross Keys and Bayleys Hill.

In north Kent, the 452 from Dartford to West Kingsdown was abandoned on Sundays together with the positioning journeys to and from Northfleet garage. The 452 provided a link to Dartford for the small villages to the south with only Longfield of any size along the way, which in any case had the frequent 423 link to Dartford. The 452 had run to a two-hourly headway on Saturdays and Sundays

The 343A provided a couple of works journeys from Studham and Kensworth into Dunstable, but in October 1965 four journeys were added on Tuesdays and Thursdays to give a shopping service which could be run by the bus off the 337 during its long layovers at Dunstable. RF 238 was converted to omo bus format in September 1965 and is on one of the works journeys to Kensworth run by Luton off the 364 allocation. Luton was one of the garages whose one man buses carried former Green Line Setright ticket machines as can be seen on the cab door. (J.G.S. Smith)

only and that the Sunday service had lasted until late 1965 was a further commentary on London Transport's reticence to abandon loss-making routes. Apart from West Kingsdown, only the hamlet of Fawkham provided any passengers along the road as far as Longfield, and with Green Line providing an hourly service from Kingsdown to Swanley or Sidcup, the 452 was largely pointless. A different route numbered 492 had been started in May 1949 from Gravesend to West Kingsdown running three journeys Monday, Tuesday, Thursday and Friday (Wednesday being Gravesend early closing day). It was so marginal however that it had been another casualty of the cuts after the 1958 strike, while the 452 continued unchanged. Indeed, London Transport would persist with the 452 Saturday service so that it remained part of the loss-making network which London Country inherited five years later.

In Surrey, the 416 and 433 were again withdrawn on Sundays for the winter, and at Dorking, the remainder of phase eight of the conversion programme saw omo RFs replace RTs on the 429 and 439. This involved six buses (five from Dorking and one from Reigate) and significantly reduced Dorking's crew RT workings from nine to four. Dorking's allocation for the 429 and 439 had remained little changed for some years and whilst the Brockham and Holmwood short journeys remained well used, loadings on the country sections through Leigh and out to Newdigate and Parkgate had fallen away steadily. With the introduction of winter schedules in October 1962 the Sunday timetable had been cut, but its operation was wasteful and inefficient, even more so because crew RTs were retained. Although the section to Newdigate via Holmwood was withdrawn on Sundays at that time, for some reason a two-hourly 429 service to Newdigate via Brockham and Parkgate was retained. This was combined with a two-hourly afternoon and evening service on the 439 between Reigate and Dorking, timed to provide a regular hourly headway between Dorking and Gadbrook Cross Roads,

The 336 was the only northern area route necessitating lowbridge buses, although due to a temporary shortage of new RTs, Amersham was allocated more than required for this route, using them on the 305 and 359. RLH 15 was transferred to Amersham in April 1962 where it remained until the 336 was converted to RF omo in October 1965. It was withdrawn and remained in store at Amersham until sold in 1965 to Super Coaches at Upminster for use on their local route. (Alan Cross)

but the schedule was inefficient because four out of five of the Newdigate Sunday journeys had no fewer than 50 minutes layover at Newdigate so that the return journeys could maintain the even hourly headway from Gadbrook with the 439s from Reigate. Not only did the crews carry few passengers, but they then sat on the bus doing nothing for 50 minutes on the stand at Newdigate! Dorking and Reigate each provided one RT for this Sunday service, and the scheduling meant that each bus finished its day's work at the other garage, but the timetable was arranged such that the two buses met at Brockham at 10.48pm for the Dorking and Reigate crews to swap buses and return to their own garage. With strict adherence to Union agreements, the timetable notes that the two opposing journeys 'arrive at 10.46pm' which allowed the crews two minutes to cross the country lane and swap buses! This did not last long however, and within a year, the Sunday service had been reduced to just one Dorking RT working hourly as far as Brockham with alternate journeys going on only as far as Leigh, Newdigate, being finally abandoned on Sundays. After conversion to omo the previous working pattern, where a bus ran as a 429 from Dorking to Newdigate via Brockham then changed to a 439 onwards back to Dorking via Holmwood, was simplified by abandoning the 429 route number and running all journeys around the Newdigate circle in either direction as 439. New blinds were made so that no change of blind was necessary at Newdigate, thus allowing a bus to work through there without any layover. The five minutes saved allowed an omo RF to run to the same end to end timings as the previous crew operated RTs, thus maintaining the efficient scheduling of the buses working the two-hourly cycle. The only surprise perhaps was that the conversion had not taken place much earlier or at least perhaps separation of the circular service through Newdigate into a single deck omo route. It is not known whether this was considered, but in the early 1960s there had been a shortage of converted omo RFs, and this may have been a limiting factor since it was not until the service cuts in 1963 that sufficient RFs became spare for use in such conversions.

Other parts of the southern area also had extensive cuts. At Chelsham, the 453 Sunday morning service was withdrawn, and the remaining afternoon and evening service converted to omo. The remainder of the 465 Sunday timetable was withdrawn leaving Chelsham with just the one omo RF Sunday afternoon working for the 453. The withdrawal of the 465 on Sundays severed the link not only from Oxted to Edenbridge, but also to Holland, although there remained an apparent need for a limited service from there into Oxted. The 707 Green Line route to Oxted was still hourly on Sundays, and so seven journeys during the day were extended from Oxted to Holland to replace the 465. Although this proved short lived as demand fell away further, this was an innovative way of covering the withdrawn 465 and was a unique instance of a Green Line route being specifically extended to cover the loss of a rural bus service.

Many other services had the Sunday timetable cut back or abandoned completely, and the cutting of evening and odd short journeys across many routes is too numerous to detail here. Overall the number of buses taken out of the schedules during the week was not great, but many ran a reduced mileage resultant from widened headways off peak and reductions to evening timetables. On Monday to Friday 17 RTs were replaced with 13 omo RFs; the Saturday overall total was reduced by only one with 12 RTs being replaced by ten omo RFs plus, perversely, one additional crew RF at Luton Monday to Saturday for duplicates on 364 works journeys to the Vauxhall Motors plant. The 364 allocation at the

The Sunday extension of the 707 from Oxted to Holland was unsuccessful and lasted a little over two years. Sometime in the summer of 1966, RF 170 displays the blinds which were added to show the extension as it waits on the stand at Aylesbury. Some six months later, it was one of those modernised, and remained in service until October 1973 from Garston at the end of 1973. After a year in store at Garston it was sold to a dealer. (J.G.S. Smith)

The 727 Express was an innovative attempt to attract more passengers, but the performance of the RFs on the non-stop M1 section was hardly conducive to 'express' service speeds. The later roadworks dealt what proved to be a terminal blow to the route which lasted for barely one year. RF 131 on its way back to Tring perfectly illustrates the problems which came from the major works. (Bushey Museum)

time was unusual in also having one additional omo RF allocated from Engineering spares Monday, Tuesday and Wednesday, but two RTs (running number LS 9 and LS 102) allocated Thursday and Friday for the complex duplicates necessary for the large numbers of employees at Vauxhall. On Sundays a total of 26 buses was removed from the schedules after 3rd October, which although not seemingly a large number represented one twelfth of the previous Sunday total. However, the new Sunday total of 306 scheduled buses had gone down by 137 in only five years since the November 1960 winter schedules, representing a reduction of almost a third. Only three GSs were now required on Sundays – two for the 471 from Dunton Green, and one from Grays for the 399 Dartford Tunnel route. A minor change was the replacement of the single GS remaining at Hemel Hempstead for the 317/317A with an RF, leaving a maximum of 23 GSs rostered.

The winter 1965 schedules also included reductions to Green Line schedules. The 727 Express Tring to London route which had been started only the previous November was withdrawn. It had struggled from the beginning with traffic congestion, and roadworks at the south end of the M1 had required a diversion negating the reduced journey times which had been promoted as the route's main attraction. The northern part of the 709 to Chesham, which had been converted to 'express' running only the previous November, had not encouraged additional usage and so was withdrawn, leaving only the southern half to Godstone. This left the London to Amersham section to the 710 with an hourly headway, although two of Amersham's four RFs previously allocated to the 709 were retained to work peak hour 710 journeys to London in place of the withdrawn 709. To cover the loss of the service to Chesham, the 710 was extended daily from Amersham, resulting in one of the longer end to end running times on any Green Line route at three hours thirty five minutes. The Chesham extension was cut back to Saturday and Sunday only a year later. Godstone retained its four RFs for the southern half of the 709, and the new timetable perversely provided an hourly service all day south of Caterham. Prior to the cut, journeys worked by Amersham crews had all terminated at Caterham where the crew took their layover before the run back to Amersham, resulting in two separate four hour periods during the day when there was no through service to Godstone. If Amersham crews had worked through to Godstone, the additional time would have meant scheduling two additional crew duties and one additional RF. As the truncated 709 was worked now solely by Godstone, the timetable provided a more convenient all day link south of Caterham, although the improvement was only marginal – the 708 had always provided a half hourly service from Godstone to Croydon and London.

At Romford, the new RCLs had done nothing to arrest the continuing drop in traffic on the 722 (Upminster to Aldgate) which had fallen away to such an extent that a timetable which only a year earlier had been every half hour seven days a week was reduced to only Monday to Friday peak hours. One RCL was however added to the 721 schedule for some extra journeys between Romford and London to cover part of the reductions on 722. Although the 722 still required eight RCLs for the morning and evening peak, these were all spreadover duties, and at weekends, Romford's run-out had been cut from 21 to 16 on Saturdays and from 15 to 10 on Sundays. In only three years, the combined Green Line run-out from Grays and Romford for the east London routes had fallen from 50 to 38 Monday to Friday, 39 to 29 on Saturdays, and from 33 to just 19 on Sundays. The decline in Green Line passengers on Sundays as a whole was reflected in a reduction of scheduled coaches from 325 to 265 since 1960.

Despite all these reductions two new local services were introduced. The 442 ran to the new Hicks Farm Estate in High Wycombe and was perversely scheduled for GS operation, while Addlestone began running the 474 round a new housing area at Holloway Hill, and at Crawley the 476 was extended to run in a loop round the Furnace Green area as further housing was being built.

The most important change of the 1965 winter schedules was the entry into service of the first of the new RMLs. They were standard buses but with a higher ratio differential to provide faster running speeds for Country area routes, and had semi-automatic gear change as opposed to the fully automatic fitted to the Central area buses, and the Country area green livery suited them very well. The first batch were allocated to Godstone garage for the 409, 410 and 411 on 3rd October 1965 to completely replace their RTs, although on the due day a number of red RMLs were sent to Godstone since sufficient green ones had not arrived in time. Godstone's operation of these routes was almost completely self-contained and ran the whole of the timetables other than two buses each from Reigate and East Grinstead, both of which received a single RML to complete the conversion. The section from Croydon to Caterham and Godstone was still the busiest, where a 15 or 20 minute headway was maintained all day with an increase to every seven or eight minutes with eight buses an hour during peak times. The extra capacity of the RMLs however allowed the peak headway to be cut from eight to six buses an hour, since the total seating capacity of six RMLs at 432 seats per hour was not appreciably less than eight RTs at 448 seats, and the reduction in

The 474 was started on 1st November 1965 to provide a shopping service for some new housing in the Holloway Hill area at Botley's Park. The round trip took just 17 minutes and there were only four journeys, although the two afternoon runs were not operated on Wednesday to reflect early closing day in Addlestone. RF 667 with a single passenger is working a journey on the route. (E Shirras)

frequency meant that if an intending passenger just missed a bus they might wait only two or three minutes longer for the next one. Since traffic congestion along the Croydon to Purley road disrupted the regular headway anyway, then irregular gaps in the 409 and 411 service were already commonplace in peak hours and the reduction in frequency caused minimal if any inconvenience. A maximum of 33 RTs (Godstone 29, Reigate and East Grinstead two each), were replaced by 28 RMLs by reducing the peak hour requirement between Croydon and Godstone, and by removing some peak journeys from the outer 'country sections' on the 409 and 410. One bus each was saved at Reigate and East Grinstead and three at Godstone. Other than this, the combined timetable between Reigate and Godstone on the 410 and 411 was almost unaltered, as was the 410 on to Westerham and Bromley. Operation of these routes also served to test the new RMLs on the steep ascent of Church Hill at Caterham, and Redstone Hill out of Redhill, together with the long arduous ascent of Westerham Hill on the 410. The most rural part of the operation was the 409 south of Godstone, characterised by fast running with few stops through open countryside. The basic hourly headway to East Grinstead and on to Forest Row remained unchanged, though few journeys justified a crew operated double decker, the conductor being able to sit on one of the longtitudinal seats to the rear of the lower deck for much of the journey.

A few weeks later on 21st November a second batch of new RMLs went to Northfleet for the busy 480 trunk route which linked Gravesend with Dartford and Erith. For much of the day this ran to a ten-minute headway, and there were no timetable reductions despite the RML's greater capacity. The Monday to Friday allocation was reduced by only one, but on Saturdays remained unchanged, so that the 480 enjoyed a considerable increase in seating capacity from the new buses.

A week after Northfleet put its RMLs into service, the new AEC Reliance RC coaches went into service at Windsor and Dunton Green on the 705. The 14 coaches were split equally between the two garages both of which needed six to run the route, leaving one spare. At Dunton Green, the last coach scheduled for the 705 each morning was rostered to work an early journey on the 404 into Sevenoaks. Although this journey did not traverse the extremely narrow lane from Shoreham Village, it started from Twitton where the road through the village still had some narrow sections. Quite what the drivers made of having to run an RC on this journey instead of the RFs they replaced is not known, but their extra six feet length and additional width cannot have made the transition easy. The pale grey and green livery of the new RCs with the italicised *GREEN LINE* fleetname was modern for its time and the new coaches presented an impressive image which together with their greater seating capacity represented a much needed upgrade to the Green Line fleet. Sadly though, their performance in service did not match up to the image they were meant to convey, despite the fact that by the time they entered service the AEC Reliance was a proven heavy-weight chassis. They were very different to drive from an RF, and drivers soon formed an opinion that their handling and steering was too light. But their main fault proved to be the braking system which needed constant adjustment to the extent that daily maintenance was often required simply to keep them fit for service the next day.

As 1965 came to an end, the decline had accelerated and the number of passengers carried on bus routes had fallen by almost 5% compared with the previous

RML 2313 was one of the first batch allocated to Godstone in October 1965, and still looks brand new as it lays over in Station Road, Oxted. The RMLs were a fine addition to the fleet, but as discussed were the wrong choice at the time given the increasing need for greater omo. It has worked the 12.15 from Reigate which ran as an additional journey for returning shoppers at lunchtime, and was the only working which turned at Oxted before returning to Godstone. (Alan Cross)

The AEC Reliance RC coaches looked impressive when they entered service, but were perennially troublesome. Their new pale grey livery with green waistband and trim is shown well in this picture of RC 9, which is about to leave Sevenoaks for the three-hour run to Windsor. The board below the front windscreen shows the 'Express' section of the route which had been introduced in August 1963. Coaches ran direct via Chiswick flyover and Colnbrook by-pass with only 13 stops between London and Windsor saving 20 minutes on the previous running time. It was intended to encourage additional traffic but had limited success, coaches returning to the 'stopping' route on 2nd December 1967 when Tunbridge Wells garage shut and the service between London and Windsor was reduced by a third.

year. The decline in coach passengers however was greater still, but a worse statistic was the fall in passenger miles paid for which was 10.2% and 11.9% less than 1964 for buses and Green Lines respectively. Not only were passenger numbers continuing to fall away, but the average passenger was travelling a shorter distance, worsening falling revenue still further. By now the average age of the fleet was well over an acceptable norm despite the introduction of 122 new buses and coaches during the year. At 31st December 1965, 643 out of 697 (92%) double deckers scheduled on bus routes were either RT or RLH which were between 11 and 17 years old, whilst the entire 223 scheduled single deckers were RF or GS which were between 12 and 14 years old. On Green Line, 166 (60%) from a total of 276 scheduled were 14 year old RFs with a few equally old RTs for duplicates. The fleet's average age would reduce only marginally throughout the rest of the decade, and would prove a serious issue for London Country when they took over the network four years later.

The cost of wages had also become an increasingly serious burden. The combination of increases in rates of pay, more holidays, the shorter working week and 'productivity' bonus payments had increased the overall costs of wages by more than 20% in the space of around two years from early 1964. During 1965, working expenses had risen to such an extent that for the first time (apart from the adverse effects of the 1958 strike) they exceeded traffic receipts resulting in an operating deficit of £932,000. Other income, plus the £3.85 million paid by the Minister of Transport in compensation for deferring fare increases, just about equalled the interest on the capital loans which had been made to London Transport, so that overall the whole operation had made a final loss of almost £1 million. Of London Transport's total capital expenditure in 1965 roughly two thirds was accounted for by the new Victoria tube line, the Minister of Transport therefore having to make a further £18 million loan to cover this expense. London Transport had spent much time and effort since the 1962 Transport Act arguing that the obligation imposed by the Act to pay its way was simply not possible, and at last there was Government recognition that this was the case. The fares increase which had been deferred from the previous year was brought in on 16th January 1966 and although short distance bus fares were unchanged, the intermediate 'half mile' fares were increased to the next stage up, having the effect of coarsening fare scales. At the same time, the minimum Green Line fares were increased from 1s 3d to 1s 6d (up 20%) for five miles and from 1s 9d to 2s 0d (up 14%) for seven miles. London Transport had estimated that the increases would provide an extra £5 million revenue in 1966, but this proved insufficient to offset increases in general running costs throughout the year. These increases were also poorly received by passengers. However, even with Government subsidy, the January 1966 increase was a financial necessity.

The year 1966 began with further new RMLs coming into service, seven going to High Wycombe in February to cover the six buses which worked the busy 363, a town service which included the ascent of one of the steepest hills in the Country area up to Totteridge requiring the buses to have specially uprated fuel pumps for the climb. At the other end of the route there was a long steady climb out of High Wycombe up to Hazelmere where the 363 turned off the main Amersham road into the large village of Penn, and the RMLs were ideal for such a busy route. A month later, more were sent to Garston to take over the 306, 311 and 347. These were all very busy interurban services which linked the large conurbation of Watford to Barnet, Shenley, Borehamwood, Hemel Hempstead and

Uxbridge and between them took 25 RMLs, only one fewer than the 26 RTs scheduled before the conversion. The 347/347A was the longest route to be converted in this change with an end to end running time of an hour and forty minutes and had eleven RMLs rostered six days a week, with as many as seven still required on Sundays. Garston garage though was still suffering from staff shortages, and there were insufficient crews to work the whole of the scheduled run-out. In order to ease the problem slightly, it was necessary to transfer three crew duties to Hemel Hempstead, but that garage had no spare capacity. Tring garage did however, and so two buses from Hemel Hempstead's 301 and 302 allocation were transferred to Tring to create the space for the two 347 duties and one 318 duty there instead.

Windsor allocated RMLs to Slough town services, including the cross town 407 and 407A between Langley and Cippenham. Joint working with Thames Valley across Slough had been agreed in December 1957, and in January 1966, Thames Valley's 60 and 69 were extended to Langley in a joint timetable with the 407. The 407A was a peak hour service via Slough Trading Estate at Salt Hill. RML 2309 has arrived at Langley Village and swings round the island at the road junction to the stand. An unidentified RF is behind on a 458 from Uxbridge surrounded by two Ford Anglias and a Mini. (Capital Transport)

The 445 was a very minor omo route, and until the end of 1966 operated by GSs. There was however an early morning crew operated positioning journey to get a bus to Datchet for a 484A peak journey into Slough, and RT 1146 is working this as it approaches the green in Datchet village. (Capital Transport)

This left the final 19 RMLs which went into service at Harlow and Windsor in May. At Harlow they were used to replace eight of the 21 RTs allocated to the complex schedules for the 396/397/397A routes between Epping, Harlow and Bishops Stortford, and included several runnings on the 804/805 town services. At Windsor, they were principally allocated to the 446 group of Slough town services, plus some of the 484. These routes included a number of Monday to Friday peak hour and works journeys for Slough Trading Estate which, because these did not run at weekends gave some spare RMLs which were then rostered instead to the 417, 457 and 457A on Saturdays and Sundays.

With the completion of the conversions, 90 scheduled RMLs had replaced 104 scheduled RTs. Of the newer green RTs replaced, a number which were now surplus to the Country area's needs were repainted red and transferred to the Central fleet to replace older RTLs and RTWs, the last of the latter class being withdrawn during 1966.

The new RMLs updated at least part of the double deck fleet and were undoubtedly fine buses. But they were also the wrong buses for the time. By 1965, the rear engine front entrance double decker had become well established with substantial numbers in service across the country; some of the BET companies such as Trent, Devon General and Maidstone & District having put large numbers into service to replace traditional front engine half-cab buses. One-man operation of double deckers would not become legal until July 1966, and Brighton Corporation were the first to convert a cross-town service to double deck omo on 11th September 1966, ironically at first using some traditional half cab Leyland PD types which they had converted to front entrance and altered the front bulkhead to allow the driver to turn round and issue tickets. Having recognised the advantage of large capacity double deckers which would be capable of conversion to omo when legislation allowed, operators which already had Atlanteans and Fleetlines in service had buses which could be readily used on omo work as the need arose and when agreement could be reached with the Union to operate them as such.

Harlow's RTs were only partly replaced with new RMLs in 1966. Eight RMLs were rostered along with 12 RTs to the 396 and 397 routes, the schedules of which included most of the workings on town and works services. RML 2353 is operating a journey on the 397A to Templefields and will work to Bishops Stortford on the 397 at some stage during the day. (Simon Butler)

London Transport were by no means alone however, and many operators continued buying half-cab traditional double deckers in what was to prove an expensive and very short sighted policy. Tilling Group companies for example, some of which operated the most sparse and unprofitable country bus routes anywhere, continued to buy Bristol FS and FLF Lodekkas right up until production ceased when the last FLF went to Midland General in September 1968. As many as 372 FLF types were delivered in the final two years of production. Tilling Group however were prevented by statute (apart from small concessions) from buying buses other than from Bristol and Eastern Coach Works, and were unable to purchase rear engined buses until Bristol's version (the VR for *vertical rear-engine*) came into production in 1968, and even then only 80 were delivered that year. The VR, although suffering a number of early teething problems, became a rugged and reliable industry standard in the National Bus Company years, over 3800 eventually being produced. By the early 1970s the majority of operators had far too many half-cab crew operated double deckers.

Despite omo conversion of some minor crew operated routes, the 421 retained RTs having been converted to double deck in May 1955 to increase capacity as Kemsing and Otford expanded after the war. The service to Kemsing was two buses an hour during the day, but beyond there, along the narrow lane to Heverham, the service was only every two hours with odd extra peak journeys. Heverham was one of the smallest hamlets served by RTs, and on 9th October 1968, RT 3120 waits at the terminus to work the 3.42pm back to Sevenoaks. It was a route which could have been converted to omo, but it was January 1972 before London Country did so, abandoning Heverham at the same time and diverting it to serve new houses at Noah's Ark in Kemsing. (Author)

The 710 suffered competition from faster and more convenient train services, particularly over its southern leg to Crawley. The headway had never been better than hourly, passenger levels declining rapidly from about 1963 leading to the withdrawal of the London to Crawley section as discussed later. A few years earlier, RF 112 is waiting on the stand at Crawley bus station for the 3 hour 20 minute run to Amersham. (Omnicolour)

The seeds of this situation had been sown after the war when the country's entire fleet of double deckers had been almost completely replaced in just a few years. Since all those buses were new in a relatively short timescale, they became due for replacement in an equally short timescale from around 1960 onwards, by which time, the rear engined double decker – which had first appeared in 1958 – was becoming a tried and tested product. Their seating capacity was greater than the conventional half cabs they replaced, and this could permit a reduction in frequency on some busy routes without affecting the level of service to any great degree. Despite this, half-cabs continued to be purchased in large numbers, so that by the late 1960s when the need for one-man operation was becoming paramount, operators everywhere found themselves with large numbers of relatively new buses which had at least another ten or twelve years' normal service life, but which could only be worked by a two-man crew. This was to prove an enormous financial burden particularly for London Transport's Country fleet.

The Union was predictably opposed to the principle of one-man double deckers and would put many obstacles in the path of negotiations to put them into service. Indeed London Transport experienced difficulty in 1965 in getting the Union even to agree to crew operate the Atlanteans in the Central area. Country bus crews however had separate agreements relating to operating different buses on routes and to one-man operation. The introduction of larger numbers of Fleetlines, even though crew operated initially, would not have been the major stumbling block it proved to be in the Central area, and so the opportunity for substantial savings was lost.

The summer 1966 schedules, like the previous year, brought about little real change but included the customary reinstatement of a few Sunday services, and some journeys on the 712 and 713 were again extended from St Albans to Whipsnade Zoo. A plan to extend the 390 from Sawbridgeworth to Lower Sheering did not materialise, but the 390 timetable was adjusted to allow what would have been the four minutes extra running time for the short extension. Although this extended the end to end running time through to Stevenage by only a few minutes, it was enough to disrupt the easily memorised regular two hourly headway and perhaps didn't help to retain the already fragile passenger numbers.

After only a year in service, it was obvious that the RCLs had not had the hoped for effect of encouraging more passengers to the east London Green Line routes. As noted, the 722 had already been reduced to a Monday to Friday peak hour service, and the RCLs were completely wasted on this route. When they had first gone to Grays, it was discovered that their longer wheelbase prevented them from safely running through the dip in the road under a bridge with limited clearance in South Stifford on route 723B. The four RCLs for the 723B were therefore exchanged with four RMCs from Hertford's allocation for the 715A. Passengers on the 715A were falling equally dramatically, so its four RCLs, together with Romford's allocation from the 722 were therefore transferred to Tunbridge Wells and Windsor to run the 704 where they could be much better justified. Four of the RFs displaced from the 704 went back on the 715A, but in a completely retrograde move, RTs went back on the 722 whose timetable was reduced again, to the extent that the eight previously scheduled RCLs were

The temporary transfer of Central area red RTs to Country area garages is referred to in the text, frequently being used in the summer to release green buses for Green Line reliefs, or at other times to cover overhauls. They were frequent visitors to Stevenage who received no fewer than 23 of them in January of 1966 when a similar number of its buses were due for overhaul or transferred elsewhere. One was RT 1382 seen here leaving Stevenage bus station with a full load on the 809 town service. (Capital Transport)

replaced by only five RTs. This change was a tacit recognition that the 722 was by then in terminal decline, although the route somehow survived for another two years until final withdrawal in August 1968. On a positive note, two new town services had been introduced experimentally in May. The 380 at Harlow and the 389 at Ware were both small routes each requiring one omo RF and were designed to provide mainly daytime shopping facilities to parts of the towns not previously served.

Prior to the summer schedules, 16th March 1966 was a notable day for the Green Line network. At the start of 1966, a total of 146 Green Line RFs remained rostered to provide the basic service on the routes still operated by them, with a further 15 for duplicates and late running spare coaches. They were fine vehicles which by then had given 15 years of virtually trouble-free service, but by the mid-1960s they looked tired and outdated. Given the gradual contraction of the Green Line network at the time, London Transport was rightly cautious about its future. Compounded by early doubts about the performance of the RCs this led to the decision to experiment with refurbishing some Green Line RFs, both to improve their image and to extend their life for a few years while the future of the Green Line network could be clarified. In July 1965 therefore, RF 136 had been taken out of service for refurbishment, and its reappearance in March 1966 was a revelation. The modernisation of the Green Line RFs has been written about in great detail elsewhere, but when RF 136 re-appeared the new image it presented, both inside and out, was an outstanding example of careful design, and to the uninitiated, it was very easy to mistake this 15-year old coach for a new vehicle. RF 136 was allocated to Dunton Green so that it could run alongside the RCs on the 705, also running from Tunbridge Wells on the 704. The project was an outstanding success, and authority was given almost immediately for a programme to convert 174 more RFs, commencing in August 1966 and taking

RF 285 waits at Ware station for a journey on the 389 which started in May 1966 along some residential roads north of the town centre which previously had no bus service. It ran to an hourly headway in each direction round a circular route and was economic since it operated only at off-peak times, and used an RF which would otherwise be idle in the garage during the day. It was reasonably successful, but withdrawn by London Country in 1975 (S. Butler collection)

eleven months to complete. The total of 175 refurbished coaches covered the 146 rostered for daily service, 15 for duplicates and late running, plus 14 for engineering spares. Over time, history would prove that the £142,000 (£816 per coach) cost of the refurbishment programme was one of the best investments ever made in the fleet, and many of these RFs gave a further eight or ten years' service with a few running even longer. Indeed, of the last five RFs still in service with London Country at the beginning of 1978, four (RF 125, 175, 183, and 202) were from the modernised batch and were in their 27th year of service. Once the programme had begun, it was decided to wait until sufficient numbers were completed to convert an entire route, most of which still required an allocation of between 12 and 15 RFs. The first conversion however was contrary to this principle when Dartford and Northfleet received enough for their allocation to the 725 in September, while Staines at the other end of the route did not receive any until a month later, but by the year end enough refurbished RFs were available to convert all of the 706, 707, 708 and 710.

Equally important for Green Line in 1966 was the introduction on 10th July of a completely new route numbered 724, running from Romford right across the northern area of the network to High Wycombe. It was the northern equivalent of the extremely successful 725 in the south, but rather than running through London suburbs, the 724 was further out and linked a number of important towns, which encouraged passengers to use the route from the moment it began. With an hourly headway, the route required seven RFs, three at High Wycombe and four at Romford, bringing some much needed additional work to this garage given the continuous cuts to the 721 and 722 which otherwise was Romford's only work other than the seasonal 726 to Whipsnade. The 724 was also a fast limited stopping service, with stops only at major points along the way since there were frequent trunk routes which paralleled sections for most of its length and provided facilities for short distance journeys. At 70 miles and with an end to end running time of 3 hours 1 minute, and only 26 stops on the route, the limited stop basis was key to maintaining the tight timetable. This however proved to be slightly ambitious, so that after a month's operation, end to end running time was extended by 15 minutes and two addi-

The start of the 724 on 10th July 1966 was an important innovation for the Green Line network which by then was beginning to suffer an increasing decline. This leaflet contained the timetable, fares and list of all the stops en-route, and although the initial running time proved unworkable and had to be extended that did not detract from the route's immediate success.

tional stops added. The most significant feature of all though was that the 724 was one-man operated from the start. Although final agreement had not been reached on additional productivity payments for omo drivers on Green Line routes (and would prove very elusive over the following two years), the Union had accepted the change in principle at a meeting on 10th June, a month before the route started, thus allowing the quick introduction of the 724. The route was an immediate success and still runs in much the same form today, despite the many changes in ownership and route networks which followed privatisation more than twenty years later. A more mundane, but nevertheless useful extension to another Green Line route happened on the same day the 724 started when the 706 had some journeys extended from Westerham three miles further on to Winston Churchill's house at Chartwell, and despite further retrenchment on the 706 over ensuing years, the Chartwell extension was maintained.

London Transport's much vaunted 'Reshaping London's Buses' plan was published in September 1966, and was intended to combat the four elements which had dogged the operation of London's buses for some years, namely traffic congestion; staff shortages; heavy peak demand; and the trend towards shorter journeys. The great thrust of the Plan therefore was the re-organisation of many Central area routes into a number of shorter more manageable ones which could be centred on 'hubs' such as main Underground stations and which, because of their shorter length, would be subject to much less traffic disruption. These new routes would also be accompanied by the introduction of large capacity single deckers which would be one-man operated thus reducing the requirement in overall staffing numbers. The Country Bus area was hardly mentioned although staff shortages were constant and traffic congestion worsened almost daily. The only mention of the Country area was in section 6 (v) of the Plan which included the broad statement that *'Country bus routes will, in the main not be altered, but one-man working will be much extended...'*, and Section 6 (vi) added that *'Green Line coaches will continue to provide an express service, probably developed with new cross connections. The coaches will be one-man operated'*.

The extension of the 706 to Chartwell proved a long term success and RF 46 displays the blind used as it makes its way through Watford with the conductor standing by the front step in the customary position. It was sent to Tring after modernisation in 1966 and illustrates the striking difference when compared with the old livery.
(P. J. Relf)

To put the plan into action, decisions had to be made as to the design and type of new single deck vehicles to be used, and the AEC 'Merlin' bus which had been successful on the central London 'Red Arrow' routes was the obvious choice. During 1965 and 1966, the Atlanteans had entered service on selected Central area routes, and the experimental front entrance Routemaster FRM 1 had been completed. The FRM design had commenced in September 1964 and had taken some time to develop. In other circumstances it might have been the forerunner of a large fleet of London Transport designed front entrance rear engined buses, but it was June 1967 before FRM 1 went into service alongside the Atlanteans for comparison. Following the recommendations of the 1964 Phelps-Brown report, at one stage a plan was formulated to build almost 3,000 FRMs to replace RTs, of which 460 would have been for the Country area. As time moved on however, the Reshaping Plan with its emphasis on large capacity single deckers became the overriding strategy, and plans for a fleet of FRMs came to nothing. In 1968, plans for large numbers of one-man double deckers for the Central area were revisited, resulting instead in the Daimler Fleetline DMS. It is also interesting to speculate what the Country Bus area would have done with a large number of FRMs from about 1968 onwards. If nothing else, significant savings in operating costs could have been made four years earlier than was eventually the case, and the fleet would have had a large number of one-man double deckers based on a proven reliable design, since the FRM had around 60% of components in common with the standard rear platform RML. The scrapping of the FRM programme proved to be a further lost opportunity to renew the Country area double deck fleet and accelerate the progress towards increased one-man operation and the consequent much needed economies.

Following the Reshaping Plan therefore a plan was approved in December 1966 for 468 full size large capacity single deckers which would start delivery in late 1967. Included in this total were 75 for the Country area, some as conventional omo buses, and some with standee layouts for conversion of town services from crew operated RTs.

London Transport was faced with implacable Trade Union resistance to the new buses which was centred around lengthy negotiations on increased pay rates and bonuses. Throughout 1966 and 1967 no progress was made on agreements to operate them and extend one-man operation despite the Union's commitment made following the 1964 Phelps-Brown report. In a repeat of 1958, London Transport was being squeezed between the Union demanding more than was affordable (or probably justifiable) and a Government who by then wanted to impose severe pay restraint. The Prices and Incomes Board had been set up as a result of a 1966 Act of Parliament, and so it too became involved in the negotiating process, doing nothing to assist matters. In May 1967, the Union's position hardened, and while payments in return for productivity increases were acceptable in principle, the Union insisted that any payments must be linked to all staff rather than just drivers and conductors. Arguments continued until Union leaders accepted an offer in principle in August 1967 which was put to the workforce at large, but in the event rejected out of hand. With no more progress, in December the Prices and Incomes Board recommended increases for all platform staff of 10s 0d (50p) a week and a payment which would have given Country area drivers an extra 15% for one-manning large single deckers, and 20% for one-manning on Green Line routes. The Union would still not accept this and continued to press for more in return for what they saw as the large savings which would accrue from the introduction of the large capacity Merlins and the spread of omo. One of the main objections of the Union was London Transport's insistence on paying drivers of buses with automated fare equipment less than the full omo drivers' rate, a proposal which the Union – quite reasonably perhaps – refused to accept. Plans to introduce the new single deckers, and to convert the single deck Green Line routes to omo therefore had to be deferred into 1968, and with orders committed to large numbers of Merlins, a situation developed where the new buses began to arrive in late 1967 but with no agreement to operate them.

The introduction of the five-day working week involved significant changes to schedules, and it was 30th December before the 1966 winter revisions came into force. They brought about – inevitably – another collection of cuts to services, too numerous to detail. A total of 11 routes had the Sunday service (or what by then remained) completely withdrawn, while another three routes had part of the service withdrawn, and three routes were completely abandoned on Saturdays. Of these the 459 (Uxbridge to Richings Park) was really only a Monday to Friday peak hour service, the need for Saturday shopping journeys having long since passed, and the 461 (Walton–Addlestone–Staines) was paralleled by either the 436/436A or the 461A and 463, all of which provided an adequate alternative Saturday service. The third route abandoned on Saturdays was the 433 (Coldharbour–Dorking–Ranmore), whilst the 412, had a bizarre reduction to the Sunday timetable which left just one single journey just before 5.00pm from Holmbury St Mary on Sunday afternoon with a late return from Dorking, just after 11.00pm. This was retained so that the Holmbury driver could provide a duty from Dorking; staff shortages made Sunday rostering difficult without an extra duty. Nevertheless, running this one journey was probably one of the more pointless operations of the period despite the scheduling issues. The changes also brought an end to regular all day single deck crew operation when the 391 and 391A at St Albans and 447 at Reigate were changed to omo. For many years, Reigate also had one RLH rostered for a peak hour working on the 447 on duty RG34, which oddly was retained after the RFs lost their conductors. The only rostered crew RF workings after 30th December were four buses, one each at Stevenage, Crawley, Northfleet and Guildford. The Stevenage and Crawley buses

Before the war the route from Uxbridge to Richings Park had been operated by the Central area from Uxbridge. When reinstated in July 1950, it was operated by the Country area from Windsor garage. The 459 left Uxbridge along the same road as the 457 rather than the pre-war routeing via Cowley and since this was a "Country area road" it was less expensive to operate as the rates of pay for Country crews were less than in the Central area. Operation meant running a bus out from Windsor, and as the route was always marginal it was rarely profitable. After the Saturday service was abandoned, the limited Monday to Friday timetable continued for a few more years until London Country finally abandoned what was left. In October 1967, RF 541 is approaching the stand at Uxbridge station for the return journey to Richings Park. (J G S Smith)

ran peak hours works services, Guildford's was rostered for peak duplicates, and Northfleet's worked a couple of peak journeys on the 451 and 490. These minor crew RF workings however changed frequently to balance out crew rosters and at East Grinstead for example a crew RF was added in July 1967 to the 438 schedule Monday to Friday and 435 Saturday while Northfleet's crew RFs were increased to two at the same time. There were also a number of odd crew worked journeys on omo routes at many garages which were used to balance rosters, a practice which continued into London Country days. The introduction of these winter 1966 schedules, following on from previous years, reduced the maximum number of GSs to only 15 from just eight garages through a series of timetable cuts, route withdrawals and conversions to RF operation. The conversion of the 471 from GS to RF at Dunton Green left just a single GS scheduled on Sundays for the 399 Dartford Tunnel service, and that only lasted for four more months.

These omo conversions were the tenth and final phase of the plan begun in 1955 although there had been many variations from the original. The table overleaf summarises the overall changes and savings achieved and provides an interesting insight into this long drawn out process. The figures have come from London Transport's own summary sheets which were updated as each phase took place, and grateful thanks are due to Alan Charman for providing these from his records.

The use of one RLH for peak workings on the 447 was an oddity. The working remained even after the route was converted to omo at the end of 1966, but was withdrawn when new MBs replaced RFs in 1968. A few years earlier, RLH 41 is on the stand in Manor Road working RG 34, the regular running number. (Alan Cross)

PHASE NO.	DATE	NUMBER OF ROUTES	S/D CREW BUSES	D/D CREW BUSES	OMO RFs ADDED	NET GS CHANGES	CREW DUTIES SAVED	OMO DUTIES ADDED	ANNUAL SAVINGS ACHIEVED
1	May 1955	2	-2		2		10	12	3016
2	July 1956	12	-17	+1	12	+2	25	27	10972
3	Oct 1957	22	-27	-1	34	-5	53	57	34000
4	July 1958	11	-23		22		46	51	18200
5	Oct 1958	19	-26	-6	38	-6	62	64	29198
6A	Apr/May 1959	15	-13	-5	19		33	37	14345
6B	June 1959	13	-8	-4	15	-1	24	27	9197
7	Nov 1964	3	-6	-6	13		23	24	19130
8	Oct 1965	3		-10	12		22	23	18200
9A	March 1966	1		-2	1		3	2	1500
9B	May 1966	2		-5	6		12	13	9400
10	Dec 1966	8	-1 -	10	17	-5	22	23	19100
TOTALS		111	-123	-48	191	-15	335	360	£186258

(1) The savings for phase 8–10 are only partially recorded – the totals shown are approximate and from the author's own estimates.

(2) The net changes to the GS allocation relate only to alterations connected with each phase and do not include all changes

(3) The number of routes in each phase includes suffix numbered routes.

(4) The saving of 335 crew duties (and consequential reduction in conductors) was of course in addition to the greater reductions in drivers and conductors from the continuing service cuts referred to throughout.

(5) Taking the annualised savings from 1955 onwards, the cumulative savings by the end of 1966 were around £1.1 million per annum without inflation in wages which had been in excess of 20% over the decade before 1966.

The 327 was one of the early double deck routes converted to omo in November 1964. The previous turning point which had required a reverse off the main road was considered hazardous for omo buses, and the route was extended a short distance into the village to turn where RF 666 takes its break. The terminus was later renamed Nazeingwood Village. (J G S Smith)

RF 56 was one of the modernised Green Line coaches downgraded for bus work, the repainted livery being similar to the MB and MBS, with the waistrail repainted yellow and green fleetnames applied. It was one of three sent to Hatfield in the last months of 1969. The 315 peak hour service to Kimpton was formally rostered for RTs and the bus is crew operated, having picked up passengers on Black Fan Road in Welwyn Garden City's factory area for an evening journey to Kimpton.

On 2nd January 1967, the railway line between Groombridge and Three Bridges was closed to passengers. This had been one of the better used lines, providing a cross country link from Tunbridge Wells to East Grinstead and the London to Brighton line at Three Bridges. It had enjoyed an hourly frequency during some parts of the day, but despite this it was another victim of the 'Beeching Cuts' although its closure caused relatively little inconvenience since there were existing bus routes which paralleled the whole line. Maidstone & District route 91 ran hourly from Tunbridge Wells to East Grinstead, and the 434 and 473 provided an hourly alternative between East Grinstead and Three Bridges. There was though a need to provide a small number of extra peak hour journeys to replace the lost train service which were run as 438A and required an additional two RTs – one each from Crawley and East Grinstead.

In central London, the end of December also saw the withdrawal of the last RTWs a process which had been assisted by the transfer of some Country area RTs made spare from the RML conversions referred to earlier. This came as part of one of the largest cuts ever made to Central area schedules with nearly 600 buses being taken out of the Monday to Friday schedules, over 650 on Saturdays and just a few below that on Sundays, all of which was the reaction to a disastrous year on year drop in Central area passenger numbers of well over 7%.

Operation of the 438 works services from East Grinstead to Crawley and Manor Royal industrial area was shared between Crawley and East Grinstead. Most of the timetable was crew operated but occasional scheduling changes included odd omo working of some journeys. RF 311 was originally RF 530 but was one of those renumbered in the complicated changes in 1962 when several former Green Line coaches were demoted to buses. It has just left the stop after the railway bridge in East Grinstead on an afternoon journey from Crawley. (Alan Cross)

In the Country area during 1966, what was previously unthinkable had come about when Saturdays had ceased to be the busiest day of the week as passengers continued to abandon buses in favour of their cars to go shopping, for leisure or to get to sporting events. From 30th December, the total number of buses scheduled on Saturdays had fallen to under 700 for the first time, and the figures below shows the rapid decline since the beginning of the decade.

November 1960	867	November 1964	751
October 1961	856	October 1965	718
October 1962	819	December 1966	686
October 1963	803		

Each year, the winter schedules had brought successive cuts, and one fifth of buses had been withdrawn on Saturdays over the six years to the end of 1966, two thirds of this reduction coming in only the previous three years as the decline accelerated. In October 1956, a total of 1,094 buses had been scheduled every Saturday, so that almost 40% of that number had been removed in less than ten years, but with fewer passengers per bus and fewer miles per journey, the real fall in Saturday passengers was over 50%. These figures starkly illustrate the necessity for the levels of service reductions between the mid-1950s, when the network was buoyant and profitable, to a decade later when the situation had been completely reversed. Crucially though, no attempt had been made to critically review a route network which was becoming less relevant.

1966 also saw further Green Line reductions. The 709 which had been truncated to work just between London and Godstone only 14 months earlier was reduced to just peak hour journeys on Mondays to Fridays, plus two return trips on Sundays timed principally to suit visiting times at Caterham Hospital. The 710, which had been extended from Amersham to Chesham to cover the loss of the 709, was cut back to Amersham during the week. Hertford's runnings on the 715A were cut back to Monday to Friday peak hours and Saturday daytime only. The off peak service during the week, together with Saturday evenings and all day Sunday were all withdrawn. The 715A had only been introduced in August 1956 but traffic congestion and competition from the railways had turned it from being profitable to virtual extinction in only a few years, even the Saturday daytime shopping service lasting only another eighteen months until June 1968.

Despite the increasing decline of Green Line services, it was something of an anomaly that for Christmas Day 1966, services were run on no fewer than 20 Green Line routes requiring 87 coaches and crews to run them. With only one or two exceptions, all the coaches on the long cross London routes ran one single journey ending up at the garage at the other end of their route. The timetables consisted of only three or four journeys starting generally between 8am and 9am, and most coaches were back in the garage by mid-afternoon. For passengers living at or near the outer ends of routes, the timetables allowed a journey as far as the London suburbs and a two-or three-hour gap before the last coach back which gave time to visit friends or relatives on Christmas morning. Travelling within London, or outwards from the suburbs however, was impossible unless a one way journey was made, and so the special service provided only a very limited facility. The Christmas Day duties were unique in that each crew worked only a certain distance along the route before meeting the coach coming the other way where they changed over to return home. Thus on the 704 the three Tunbridge Wells and Windsor crews met at New Cross to change, and on the 705 the two Windsor crews worked all the way to Keston, but only one Dunton Green crew was needed to work from Sevenoaks to Keston and back twice. On the 706 and 707 two Tring crews worked from Tring to Victoria and back whereas the two other crews who worked the morning journeys from Aylesbury to Westerham or Oxted travelled only as far as Cricklewood to change with the northbound Chelsham crews. On Boxing Day 1966 all routes apart from the 709, 715A and 722 had an hourly service all day and the 707 – having been extended on Sundays to Holland to cover the 465 bus route – even had three journeys to Holland run as 'shorts' from Chelsham garage. These were undoubtedly a complete waste of resources, but were repeated again for Boxing Day 1967. By Christmas 1968 however, the Holland extension had been withdrawn, and the entire route was withdrawn in February 1969, so this unique Green Line service ran for just two Boxing Days.

The modernisation programme for the Green Line RFs continued rapidly in the first few months of 1967. High Wycombe and Reigate received theirs for the 711 in January, Northfleet and Staines in February for the 701 and 702, and Dorking, Luton and St Albans in March for the 712, 713 and 714, this latter conversion being quite large requiring a total of 28 for the basic service plus three duplicates at St Albans and four more for spares. Hertford and Harlow then received some for the 715A and 720 in April. The 724 introduced only six months earlier was already omo and so the allocation for the 724 at Romford and High Wycombe was changed over in February with modernised coaches already so fitted. With the success of one-man operation on the 724, there was anticipation of Union agreement for universal omo of all single deck Green Line routes, so from February 1967 onwards all the remaining modernised RFs were so equipped. In the event though, as noted earlier, the wholesale conversion of Green Line routes became enmeshed in the negotiations surrounding the Reshaping Plan and no further routes were converted in 1967. Indeed it would be a further two years before Green Line omo conversions were completed. There was however one

The 715A enjoyed only a relatively short period of operation, its final withdrawal in February 1969 coming after successive timetable reductions as traffic congestion and parallel railway services dramatically reduced its passengers. In 1966, RF 141 is about to leave Hertford bus station for a journey to London as the conductor waits for any last passengers. The 715A was the only single deck route which remained crew operated as the date of conversion of the remaining routes coincided with its final day of operation. (J G S Smith)

exception to this which was perhaps the most notable event of the 1967 summer schedules. The new 727 route commenced on 13th May 1967 and was a western orbital route running from Luton to Crawley by way of Watford, Heathrow and Gatwick. Following the success of the 724, and the earlier agreement, it was also a one-man operated limited stop 'Express' service, with 12 modernised RFs specially altered to provide luggage capacity at the rear with seating reduced to 35. The new route was even longer than the 724 with an end to end running time of 3 hours 28 minutes for the 74 mile route, and required eight RFs; four each from Reigate and St Albans. There were only 25 stops in total, and the timetables of the 724 and 727 were co-ordinated to provide a regular 30-minute headway most of the day between St Albans and Rickmansworth over one of the busiest sections of the routes. The only small disadvantage was that the route had to terminate in Luton town centre rather than run out to Luton Airport since this leg was outside the LPTA boundary and thus prohibited. Had it not been, it would have allowed a direct connection to Luton Airport at a time when it was expanding rapidly with the package deal holiday market, and thus some potential revenue was lost. This situation was remedied with the advent of the National Bus Company when the LPTA boundary was dismantled, the route being extended to the Airport in 1971. Nevertheless the 727 was, like the 724, an instant success and created additional demand. With a high scheduled speed, and sections where traffic congestion could be a problem, the route was however something of a challenge for the drivers, and the RFs had to be driven hard most of the way to maintain time, although a few minutes recovery time was built in at Watford Junction, Heathrow and Gatwick.

Although the RCs provided greater capacity on the busy 727 route, their allocation in June 1969 described later was unsuccessful due to their constant unreliability. RC 7 is at Heathrow on the way to Crawley, and would soon be replaced with RFs. (Alan Snatt)

At the other end of the scale, the 1967 summer schedules saw two more GSs removed when Garston's allocation to the 309 was converted from three GS to one GS and one RF as the timetable was also reduced. The 399 through the Dartford Tunnel was finally withdrawn along with Grays's one GS following constant losses which had been more than £3,000 in its last year of operation. Eastern National extended their Southend to Grays route 2 through the Tunnel to Dartford on a limited basis, which in turn was replaced with a limited stop service numbered 402 twice a day in October 1968, being extended on into London at the same time.

ROUTE
399 to DARTFORD Limited Stop   Via Dartford-Purfleet Tunnel

In addition to the points shown in the timetable below, there are also stops at South Stifford (Mill Lane), West Thurrock (Fox & Goose) Aveley, (Stonehouse Lane) Tunnel Approach Road, (Tunnel Cement Works) Tunnel Approach Road (Administrative Offices) Tunnel Approach Road (Brent Bridge).

A 6/- ROVER TICKET will take you as far as you like on this and on nearly every other Country Bus route. Ask the conductor for details.

Weekdays

Grays War Memorial	0656	0756	0856	0956	1156	1256	1356	1500	1600	1700	1800	2000	2100	2200
Stonehouse Corner	0705	0805	0905	1005	1205	1305	1405	09	09	09	09	09	09	09
Dartford Princes Rd, Pilgrims Way	17	17	17	17	17	17	17	21	21	21	21	21	21	21
Dartford Market Street	0721	0821	0921	1021	1221	1321	1421	1525	1625	1725	1825	2025	2125	2225

Sunday

Grays War Memorial	0900	1000	1200	1300	1400	1500	1600	1700	1800	2000	2100	2200	.....	...
Stonehouse Corner	09	09	09	09	09	09	09	09	09	09	09	09	.....	...
Dartford Princes Rd, Pilgrims Way	21	21	21	21	21	21	21	21	21	21	21	21	.....	...
Dartford Market Street	0925	1025	1225	1325	1425	1525	1625	1725	1825	2025	2125	2225	.....	...

This service is operated with Pay As You Enter buses. Please have your fare ready as you get on.

ROUTE
399 to GRAYS Limited Stop   via Dartford-Purfleet Tunnel

In addition to the points shown in the timetable below there are also stops at Tunnel Approach Road (Brent Bridge), Tunnel Approach Road (Administrative Offices), Tunnel Approach Road (Tunnel Cement Works), Aveley (Stonehouse Lane), West Thurrock (Fox & Goose), South Stifford (Mill Lane).

Weekdays

Dartford Market Street	0726	0826	0926	1026	1226	1326	1426	1530	1630	1730	1830	2030	2130	2230
Dartford Princes Rd, Pilgrims Way	30	30	30	30	30	30	30	34	34	34	34	34	34	34
Stonehouse Corner	42	42	42	42	42	42	42	46	46	46	46	46	46	46
Grays War Memorial	0751	0851	0951	1051	1251	1351	1451	1555	1655	1755	1855	2055	2155	2255

Sunday

Dartford Market Street	0930	1030	1230	1330	1430	1530	1630	1730	1830	2030	2130	2230	...	...
Dartford Princes Rd, Pilgrims Way	34	34	34	34	34	34	34	34	34	34	34	34	...	...
Stonehouse Corner	46	46	46	46	46	46	46	46	46	46	46	46	...	...
Grays War Memorial	0955	1055	1255	1355	1455	1555	1655	1755	1855	2055	2155	2255	...	...

NOTE—This timetable does not necessarily apply on Bank Holidays. While every effort will be made to keep to the timetables, London Transport does not undertake that its buses will be operated in accordance with them, or at all. London Transport will not be responsible for any loss, damage or inconvenience caused by reason of any operating failure or in consequence of any inaccuracies in the timetables.

LONDON TRANSPORT, 55 BROADWAY, S.W.1   ABBey 1234   2.6.65

365/956F/550 (100)   L689   Reliance Printing, Woolwich

This June 1965 panel timetable for the 399 shows the service running hourly seven days a week. It was worked by a single GS from Grays garage. When it was finally withdrawn in May 1967, the service had lost more than £3000 in its final year of operation (Alan Charman collection)

There were few other changes for summer 1967. The 712/713 and 313 were extended to Whipsnade, and the 726, although it ran again, commenced much later and ran only during the week in the summer school holiday period. At the southern end of the 712/713, cheap return fares were introduced on Sundays to attract passengers to Boxhill and Dorking. The 360 Luton town service had two afternoon journeys extended from Caddington to Dunstable to provide a shopping facility, but the 455 along the main road from Uxbridge to High Wycombe was abandoned completely on Saturdays except for a single late evening departure from Uxbridge. The parallel 710 and 711 Green Line routes had some fares reduced on Saturday to compensate for the loss of the 455 which had already been withdrawn on Sundays three years previously. At the start of the 1960s, the 455 had run hourly on Saturdays, and with the 711 gave three journeys per hour all day along the A40 to High Wycombe, but a parallel Saturday bus service was now superfluous. In the Southern area, a further reduction came with the withdrawal of the remaining 405 Sunday timetable north of Redhill, leaving the route to Croydon to the half hourly timetable on the 414.

The Green Line RF modernisation programme came to an end in July 1967 and had involved progressively taking a number of RFs out of service while they were converted, and generally moving the remainder round the fleet to cover for them. Prior to the conversion programme, 24 of the original 263 Green Line RFs had already been withdrawn between October 1963 and October 1964 in response to service cuts, so the 64 RFs which had not been modernised or required for Green Line service were all progressively downgraded to bus status. They were fitted for one man operation for use in the continuing process of converting some of the less busy RT routes. Twenty-four of the refurbished coaches were also later downgraded to bus status.

The 1967 winter schedules started on 7th October with fewer reductions than in previous years. The services between Walton and Woking which were more suburban than rural, were cut back at weekends. Addlestone garage lost some Saturday workings on 420 and 456, and Sundays on the 463 through to Guildford, which removed two RLHs – one each from Addlestone and Guildford. Dunton Green lost the one Sunday afternoon journey on the 413 to Bayleys Hill which had been run for visitors to the Isolation Hospital beyond Cross Keys, the terminus being about half a mile beyond the hospital as this was the first point where the bus could turn. This was hopelessly uneconomic to run as the bus ran light back to Sevenoaks Bus Station after reaching Bayleys Hill, then light again an hour later for the return journey back into Sevenoaks. Of the small number of hospital visitors, the majority not travelling by car would have reached Sevenoaks by train, but in London Transport's typically inflexible fashion, the 413 journey left from the bus station, which was at least a fifteen minute walk from the railway station, thus ensuring that these few people would be deterred from using it. This single journey had been introduced after the five Sunday journeys between Sevenoaks and Brasted had been abandoned in October 1965, and was undoubtedly loss making from the first Sunday it ran. At the same time, the remaining Sunday service on the 471 was withdrawn, leaving Dunton Green with only two RTs on Sunday and no single deckers at all. In the northern area, the road north of Harlow to Bishops Stortford was left just to the hourly 720 Green Line on Sundays after the 397 was withdrawn that day. One change of note was the final severing of the rural link on the 352 between Berkhamsted and Dunstable, the remaining Saturday service being reduced to a two hourly short working from

Dunstable to Dagnall, being worked off the 337 timetable in the same way as that on Wednesday and Friday. The 702 beyond Staines to Sunningdale was already marginal, and staff shortages at Staines which had come about from an increase in annual leave allowance earlier in the year had forced the withdrawal of the service west of London on Saturdays for two months from mid-August. Although this was restored on 7th October, any regular Saturday passengers would by then have found other means. Similar staff shortages on the 714 rosters at Luton and Dorking had resulted in the timetable being temporarily halved to hourly at the same time.

On 2nd December 1967, Tunbridge Wells garage closed after 37 years. It had been opened by Autocar in 1923, and never operated anything other than the Green Line route. Tunbridge Wells's share of the half-hourly 704 had remained unchanged since the route had been reinstated in March 1946, and with its scheduled run-out of just seven or eight RFs had always been the smallest Country area base. The section of the route south of Tonbridge formed only a small part of the frequent service between there and Tunbridge Wells, which was Maidstone & District's territory, and was an anomaly from the pre-war purchase of Autocar. Tunbridge Wells was uneconomic to keep open, so it was logical to transfer its workings into Dunton Green. The lengthy common section between Bromley Common and Windsor on the 704/705 had run to a 15-minute headway since 1946, but with falling passenger numbers, this was now cut to 20 minutes. This probably made little difference north of Bromley, but the 705 was reduced to hourly so that south of Bromley Common through Biggin Hill and Westerham, the service was halved and became much less attractive. The revised timetable also meant that instead of the previous regular half hourly frequency on the 704 via Farnborough, the timetable now had alternate gaps of 20 and 40 minutes, and only one coach per hour ran beyond Sevenoaks to Tunbridge Wells, all of which reduced the total allocation for the 704 and 705 from 26 to 22. Cuts in Grays's Green Line schedules at the same time, plus some RMCs from Stevenage, released enough RCLs for Windsor and Dunton Green so that the 705 could be converted, thus allowing the whole of both routes to be worked with RCLs, their greater capacity presumably being a factor in the widened headway.

Two buses maintained the 413/413A timetable all day which included two short journeys just to Cross Keys on the edge of Sevenoaks. Buses had to negotiate a nearby narrow estate road to complete a loop since it was too dangerous to reverse at the cross roads. RF 658 has a surprising number of passengers for the eight minute journey as it loads in Sevenoaks bus station. (Malcolm Papes)

A batch of 15 experimental standee buses was delivered in 1966, XMB 15 being the last, and in the event, the only one to enter service in the Country area. It spent a long period in testing and evaluation, before being sent to Tring where it entered service on the 387 on 15th February 1969. It was renumbered MBS 15 in July 1971, and stayed at Tring until the end of 1973 when London Country exchanged it for MBS 4 from London Transport. On its first day in service the driver turns out of Tring garage while a couple of onlookers appear confused, having presumably never seen such a bus before. Red staff bus RT 1890 stands at the bottom of the yard.
(Michael Beamish)

The conversion of the 705 ousted the troublesome RCs from the route after only two and a half years in service. Six weeks before this, an Engineering Department report dated 12th October 1966 headed 'Experimental Buses' began *In general it may be said that our experience with the experimental XA, XF, RC, and XMS has been disappointing from the engineering point of view, especially so with the Atlanteans.* The XFs had displayed similar faults to the XAs – brakes, electrics, and doors – but were generally less troublesome. As to the RCs, the report stated that *From their introduction, the RCs have given a great deal of brake trouble, around half of all faults reported, and considerable effort is expended in the continuous adjustment of these brakes.* The handbrakes were ineffective and could not always be relied upon to hold the bus on an incline, and to compound matters there were *'suspension faults linked to brake shudder'.* If that were not enough, the report concluded that *The relatively high incidence of suspension trouble is somewhat troubling as is the large number of electrical defects reported.* On Green Line service, the RCs had covered an average of 1,500 miles each week and the report concluded that the RCs were simply *'not up to the job'* where such a high level of reliability was essential. Following their temporary withdrawal, they underwent a thorough engineering assessment to try to improve their reliability and did not see Green Line service for another six months before being returned to work. After much modification to brakes and suspension, three were allocated as duplicates for the 725 for a period in 1968, and in June 1969 they were all allocated to the 727 to give more capacity on the busy route and to test out the effectiveness of the modifications. It soon became apparent however that they were simply not reliable enough on such a busy, tightly timed route, and within a few weeks all but four were withdrawn again following repeated complaints from drivers. After yet more modifications, RC 10 was tried again on a 727 test run but failed at St Albans. Eventually, as noted later, they were put on to the 723 which was much easier with no steep hills and involved less weekly mileage than most routes.

The XFs, although not wholly reliable, had nonetheless performed reasonably well. With an average weekly mileage of around 900, their fuel consumption was good, but the irritation was the frequent failure of the door gear which the report concluded again was *'not up to the job'*, although the engineering staff at East Grinstead became adept at running repairs to the XFs doors to keep them in service.

In another Green Line reduction as part of the December 1967 changes, the 717 was reduced to run just between Wrotham and London, cutting the service between London and Hatfield from three to two coaches an hour on the 716 and 716A. Hatfield, having lost their share of the 717, had Stevenage's share of the 716A transferred to compensate, Stevenage's Green Line allocation being halved to just its share of the 716. Swanley's RMCs for the truncated 717 lasted only four weeks as on 30th December those, plus the RMCs at Garston for the 719, were exchanged for the RFs on the 708 from Hemel Hempstead and East Grinstead. In a repeat of other conversions from RF to RMC, the 708 timetable was reduced to hourly. This in turn resulted in an alternate 15 or 30 minute headway over the lengthy common section with the 706 and 707. The timetable for these routes could have been adjusted so that a regular 20-minute headway could be worked with the 708, but this would have resulted in an uneven 20 or 40 minute headway along the sections of the 706 and 707 from Titsey Hill to South Croydon and the longer run from Two Waters out to Aylesbury. Whilst this uneven headway is exactly what had resulted from the cuts to the 704 and 705 timetables, it was probably thought that as the common sections of these routes were much longer, they were better left at the established half-hourly headway.

Towards the end of the 1960s, Green Line relief journeys were becoming far less common, and such a journey on the 709 would have been extremely unusual. The route had been reduced to work just between London and Godstone in November 1965, and only 13 months later reduced to Monday to Friday peak hours with two Sunday journeys. RML 2312 has just left Godstone garage and is about to traverse the roundabout at the junction with Oxted road to work to London, although the reason for this working is not known. (S J Butler)

The 718, because of its links through Hampton Court and on to Windsor, had managed to retain its half-hourly headway throughout at weekends during the summer of 1967, but the northern leg from London to Harlow had been cut to hourly off peak during the week since, even in the summer school holidays, the once popular day trips out to Epping Forest had largely disappeared. In October however, the whole timetable was cut to hourly throughout every day once the extra summer traffic to Windsor and Hampton Court had fallen back. The cuts were though a little premature as conductors had to turn passengers away on some journeys after the hourly headway began before demand had dropped off sufficiently. This, plus the cuts to the 704, 705, 708 and 717, were further examples of what London Transport saw as essential economies in the face of the continuing fall in Green Line passengers. But the cuts themselves continued to be a factor in reducing passenger numbers still further on routes which were becoming less and less relevant to the changing travel patterns of the time.

A week after all the Green Line changes at the beginning of December, a new Hemel Hempstead town service numbered 344 was introduced up to Grove Hill. Three weeks later on 31st December, London Transport took over the town service run by Bream's Coaches to Long Chaulden and Apsley Mills, absorbing the timetable into the 314, which had previously been a joint service with Bream. On the same day, the Central area 215 route from Kingston to Ripley was cut back to Church Cobham leaving the route beyond there to Ripley solely to the 715 Green Line route. This section of the 215 had never been better than hourly and, other than the odd passenger for the stop by the lakes at Wisley, had been an almost non-stop run after Cobham down the A3 through open country into Ripley. In the heyday of profitable operation after the war, the 215 Central route and 415 Country route might have been linked to form one route between Kingston and Guildford, but the post-war demarcation at Ripley prevented this. The 715 had never served Kingston (although it did later) and so the opportunity for a through service from Kingston to Guildford had never been taken. By the end of 1967 however, the 415 ran just a handful of peak journeys to Ripley plus a morning positioning journey for a 436A to Woking, and the 215 no longer justified itself.

After the 215 to Ripley was withdrawn, the road south of Cobham was left to the 715. Some years before RMCs took over, RF 611 pulls away from the stop by the lake at Wisley heading for Guildford along a part of the A3 unrecognisable today. The bus has a good load on board, and the crew have time to look at the camera. This stop and the vista across the lake are no longer visible from the fast dual carriageway and slip roads from the M25. (London Transport Museum)

Negotiations to operate new large capacity single deckers dragged on without progress for the first half of 1968, and by March almost 150 new Merlins had been delivered but stood idle for want of any agreement to put them into service. Despite this though, the Country Bus department were able to begin operating them in a small way on a route which was already one-man operated with RFs, since the Union agreement in the Country area permitted a change of type. On 9th March therefore, 11 new MBs were put into service on the 447 which linked Reigate and Redhill to Merstham. The actual Monday to Friday allocation required eight buses all day – which became MB – plus three more for peak times which remained RF so that there were three MBs as spares, while the Saturday schedule required only eight MBs. At the same time, the 430 Reigate to Redhill local route was converted from crew RT to omo MB on Sundays when the 447 required only a single bus, so that the spare MBs could be allocated to the 430. Reigate's remaining oddity – the lone RLH which worked 447 peak journeys – also went when the MBs came into service. The 447 linked the vast LCC Estate at Merstham to Redhill, from where the routeing ran in a circle via Earlswood to Reigate, then over Batts Hill back to Redhill. The MBs were built to the maximum

The sheer size of the new MBs compared to RFs is well illustrated in the picture of MB 88 as it turns from Bell Street into Reigate High Street to run up to Red Cross terminus. Their manoeuvrability became an issue on many routes, and the structural weaknesses in the chassis which soon became evident did nothing for their long term reliability. (Capital Transport)

dimensions then permitted and were six feet longer and 8½ inches wider than an RF. Although their capacity was much greater, their manoeuvrability in residential estate roads with parked cars was an immediate problem. The much longer front and rear overhangs were more difficult to judge, and a sharp left turn would result in the rear overhang swinging out into the path of any unwary overtaking vehicles on the offside. Their greater length also made it much more difficult to pull into stops especially if cars had parked close by, so that the estate roads through Batts Hill and the relatively narrow residential roads into Reigate from Earlswood were difficult for drivers to negotiate. I travelled on MB 83 shortly after the route was converted from RF, and the driver that day had some fairly graphic observations about the size of the new buses which were far from complimentary! Visually however, the new buses were quite impressive, and the new livery with a wide yellow band below the windows and the non-underlined 'London Transport' fleetname in green looked very modern for the time. In operation however, the Merlin's heating systems proved to be troublesome, and the rear overhang on the chassis developed structural weaknesses in supporting the weight of the engine and gearbox. A start had been made however, and later in the year, conversions of town services began to oust RTs across the Country area as the Reshaping Plan had intended.

The summer schedules of 15th June 1968 were the first of three major changes in the year. The Monday to Friday timetable on the 702 had already been cut in May to just two morning and two evening peak journeys out to Sunningdale, and now the combined 701 and 702 off-peak through service to Gravesend was cut to hourly during the week, while at weekends the first 702 did not leave Sunningdale until 10.12am. This cut four RFs from the 701/702 allocations. On the same date the Saturday shopping timetable on the 715A was withdrawn leaving just two morning and evening peak trips Monday to Friday, cutting 4 RFs from Hertford's Saturday Green Line rosters and one during the week. Despite the large estates at Hurst Green, further reduction in the already meagre passenger numbers had rendered the Sunday extension of the 707 from Oxted to Holland unprofitable and this too was withdrawn. The withdrawal of the Holland journeys on the 707 reduced Chelsham's Sunday crew RF requirement by one, and a second duty was lost when the scheduled Sunday duplicate for the 706 was not reinstated for the 1968 summer schedules. To balance this for the summer therefore, two crew RFs were added to the 403 Sunday allocation, to run the supplementary 403 journey from Croydon to Chartwell but remained only until the winter schedules on 5th October. Northfleet exchanged one GS working on the 451 and 490 for an RF, and reduced the Sunday RML allocation on the 495 and 496 Town Services from ten to eight to reflect further losses in passengers. Staines lost two Saturday RT workings on the 441, and Stevenage similarly lost two RTs on weekdays to reflect cuts in the 800, 801 and 802 Town Service network. Reductions to the combined 409, 410 and 411 schedules at Godstone took out two RMLs on Saturdays and one on Sundays. Godstone's Sunday run-out on these routes was now only nine buses, half that of 1960 when the three routes – in particular the 410 – still carried heavy loads of Sunday day trippers. Indeed, the 410 Sunday allocation was now reduced even for the summer period to just two buses, which in 1960 had required 8 RLHs to work an all-day half hourly headway. Addlestone garage reduced its Saturday run-out by two RTs with the withdrawal of the remaining 420 timetable that day, and cuts to the Weybridge/Woking corridor on the 427, 437 and 456 also removed an RF. The combined 436 and 463 run-out that Addlestone shared with

Guildford lost two more RLHs on Sundays. At Amersham, the 336B Sunday service which had provided a skeleton replacement to Northwood Hospital for the former 703 Green Line was withdrawn, but curiously in one of the odd scheduling anomalies of the time, a crew RF was added to the 305 Monday–Friday roster. The rural timetable for the 332, 398 and 398A had an RF removed weekdays, leaving just a single RF allocated on Saturdays. The schedules for the 307, 317, 317A, 337 and 352 at Hemel Hempstead were cut, reducing the Saturday RF run-out from six to five. Finally, Garston's busy 306 and 311 routes lost two RMLs Saturday and three Sunday when the timetable that day was almost halved. Although the overall reductions in buses scheduled was not great and the examples are not exhaustive, the recurring theme was of reductions to Saturday and Sunday schedules.

By 1968 weekend leisure traffic had fallen dramatically, but there was nevertheless a creditable attempt to run additional buses on bank holidays where extra passengers might result. On August bank holiday the Surrey Hills routes saw considerable augmentation. The 425 normal hourly Sunday service had additional journeys between Dorking and Shere all day to give two buses an hour, and the 416 and 422 ran hourly to Boxhill from Leatherhead. The remaining single Sunday journey on the 412 from Holmbury St Mary remained, but on bank holiday Monday, three journeys were run from Holmbury into Dorking with a late 10pm departure back. Whilst London Transport deserve credit for such initiative, the actual timetable for the 412 seemed at odds with the needs of likely passengers who would want to travel out to Holmbury St Mary for the afternoon and back early evening. This could have been better run with a bus from Dorking garage, but instead the timetable was run with the outstationed bus which didn't leave Holmbury St Mary until 2.25pm. This meant the first journey from Dorking was not until just after 3pm, and the maximum time anyone could stay in Holmbury St Mary little more than two hours.

The text refers to the odd single Sunday journey on the 412, run principally so that the outstationed driver could provide an additional duty from Dorking, but which provided a facility only for the very few people who wished to go to Dorking on Sunday evening. It was withdrawn soon after this October 1967 timetable was published. (Author's collection)

Dorking - Holmbury St. Mary - Sutton — Route 412

This route is operated by Pay As You Enter buses. Passengers are asked to have their fares ready as they get on.

Passengers may not both board and alight on any one journey between Sutton *The Volunteer* and Sutton *Forge*.

For complete service between Dorking North Station, Dorking Town and Westcott see Summary.

WEEKDAYS / SUNDAY (TT.L98)

						MF	MF		MF				SUNDAY
DORKING NORTH STATION		08 53	10 37	12 47	15 03	15 32	16 37	17 03	17 42	19 03	20 03	22 03	23 07
Dorking *White Horse*		57	41	51	07	36	41	07	46	07	07	07	11
Westcott *The Green*		09 05	49	59	15	44	49	15	54	15	15	15	19
Wotton *Manor Farm*		11	55	13 05	21	50	55	21	18 00	21	21	21	25
Parkhurst Corner		18	11 02	12	28	15 57	17 02	28	18 07	28	28	28	32
Holmbury St. Mary *Royal Oak*	07 58	24	08	18	34		A	34		34	20 34	34	23 38
SUTTON *The Volunteer*	08 03	09 29	11 13	13 23	15 39			17 39		19 39		22 39§	

						MF	B		MF			SO	SUNDAY
SUTTON *The Volunteer*	08 08	09 36	11 20	13 44	15 46			17 46		19 46		22 44	16 51
Holmbury St. Mary *Royal Oak*	13	41	25	49	51	MF		51	MF	51	20 41	22 49	57
Parkhurst Corner	19	47	31	55	57	16 02	17 11	57	18 12	57	47		17 04
Wotton *Manor Farm*	26	54	38	14 02	16 04	09	18	18 04	19	20 04	54		10
Westcott *The Green*	32	10 00	44	08	10	15	24	10	25	10	21 00		
Dorking *White Horse*	40	08	52	16	18	23	32	18	33	18	08		18
DORKING NORTH STATION	08 44	10 12	11 56	14 20	16 22	16 27	17 36	18 22	18 37	20 22	21 12		17 22

A—Arrives Parkhurst Corner *Belmont School* at 17 04.   B—From Parkhurst Corner *Belmont School* at 17 09.   MF—Monday to Friday only.   SO or §—Saturday only.

The decline of the 726 is mentioned in the text, and the start of the 712A to Whipsnade for the 1963 summer season effectively killed off the 726 since by then traffic from east London was minimal. On a sunny afternoon, RCL 2228 stands next to RCL 2225 at Whipsnade waiting for the late afternoon journey back to Romford. These fine coaches were perfect for such a route, but sadly passenger levels rarely justified their use. It has a board under the canopy telling passengers that it serves Romford Market which was carried on its mundane daily work on the 721. (John Boylett)

With the extension again of the 712 and 713 to Whipsnade, the need for the other long standing link from London on the 726 was hardly necessary, and for 1968 just one bus was rostered to work a single return journey from Romford to Whipsnade Monday to Friday and Sunday with no service on Saturday. Even this did not start until 22nd July and ran for a few short weeks just during the school holiday period. It was a long way from the six buses rostered at weekends a decade earlier for a service which had also run for many more weeks during the summer season. After the last journey ran back into Romford garage on Sunday 6th September 1968, the 726 was not reinstated for 1969 and never ran again. A day's work on the 726 over the years must have been a welcome relief for the Romford crews who otherwise spent every day up and down the A12 into east London battling with ever worsening traffic conditions. Like Tunbridge Wells, Romford had only ever operated Green Line routes, but its importance had been progressively eroded over two decades as both of its routes became less and less frequent with an unrelenting drop in passengers. A small respite had come with the introduction of the 724 in 1966, but made little difference to Romford's slow demise. The 722, once requiring 12 buses to run a 10 or 15 minute headway, had by 1968 been reduced to an allocation of only four RTs Monday–Friday which between them ran four morning and three evening peak journeys into Aldgate, some buses being parked at Bow garage during the day between peaks. This too was abandoned after the last RT arrived back at Romford at 6.36pm from Corbetts Tey on Friday 2nd August. Once the 726 had finished four weeks later, Romford garage was left with only 13 RCLs for the 721, and five RFs for the 724, a huge reduction from the 36 RTs scheduled in 1950.

On 5th October 1968, the winter schedules brought about more reductions, again too many to detail, but what went almost unnoticed was the withdrawal of all but two of the last GSs from service. On 4th October the 433 (Ranmore–Dorking–Coldharbour) and the 308A (Little Berkhampsted – Hertford) were withdrawn, both of which had been GS operated, although the 308A always had some RF workings from cross scheduling with other routes. After this, Hertford's two remaining GSs were scheduled for only a few Monday to Friday workings on 329, 386 and 388 plus odd Chapmore End journeys on the 333. These lasted only another three weeks when RFs were officially rostered in their place. These final GS workings from Hertford were perhaps the last truly rural ones for which the GSs had been originally intended. Northfleet retained a last GS for a few journeys to Longfield and Hartley Court on the 451 and 490, an allocation which lasted for a further year until October 1969 when it was formally replaced with an RF. Although unconfirmed, there is a suggestion that the GS was in fact used occasionally a little longer, but was withdrawn by the year end. Garston had retained two GSs, one each for the 309 and 336A, the one for the 309 workings lasting only until February 1969. After Northfleet's had gone, Garston remained the last garage to operate them. The 336A had only ever been a very limited commuter and shopping service to Rickmansworth, the Saturday service having been abandoned in October 1961. In the allocations for 5th October 1968, the 336A was the last remaining single-deck route not approved for RF operation owing to an extremely tight narrow turn into the lane that went to Loudwater Village. Although in February 1969 the restriction was lifted to permit RFs, this in fact never happened, and legend has it (unconfirmed) that an attempt to take an RF round the route to test for the possibility of replacing the GS almost ended in it becoming stuck on that particular corner. So it was that the last GS continued to work the 336A until the route was withdrawn on 29th March 1972

After Hertford's last GSs were removed, Northfleet and Garston retained the last ones. Northfleet's last GS workings almost lasted into London Country's takeover but ceased a few weeks before the end of 1969. GS 53 spent its whole life at Northfleet and was withdrawn in May 1967, but not sold until the latter half of 1968. It has arrived at Gravesend's Clock Tower and turns to run back to the garage. (David Christie)

There were a number of rural routes where the timetables were gradually cut back, but too often the same timetables continued unaltered long after they could be justified, and the 433 was perhaps one of the worst examples. In 1955, there had been ten journeys to Coldharbour Monday to Friday, and 12 on Saturdays. The Ranmore leg had six journeys six days a week, and the lack of potential passengers between Ranmore Common and the isolated terminus at Ranmore itself has already been referred to. At the other end of the route, Coldharbour was the only real source of passengers, with a population of fewer than 1,000, many of whom lived some way beyond the terminus opposite the Plough Inn. When the Saturday service was abandoned at the end of 1966, the number of journeys, and even the timetable, had been virtually unchanged since 1954, only one Saturday evening journey having been cut, and when the remaining Monday to Friday service went, there were still the same 10 journeys to Coldharbour and six to Ranmore. Even in the late 1950s, the number of people who needed to commute to London or worked in Dorking was minimal, and these declined to almost nil along with a steady drop in the small number of passengers who used the route to go shopping in Dorking. I had first travelled up to Coldharbour in August 1962 on the 3pm from Dorking, which was timed to take a few shoppers back from the town. There were only five passengers, and two of these got off on the edge of the town before the bus set off along the narrow lane to Coldharbour. The 3.30pm return from Coldharbour ran empty (apart from myself) all the way back into Dorking where it picked up a few schoolchildren and a couple of ladies in Dorking for the journey to Ranmore. Over the next six years I made several journeys to both Coldharbour and Ranmore, and in three trips to Ranmore, only once was a single passenger carried beyond the few cottages at Ranmore Common to Ranmore itself.

GS 39 arrived at Dorking in February 1963 and spent the next four years on the 433. One day in 1966 it has picked up a passenger at Dorking Bus Station and sets off for the climb to Coldharbour – the longest and steepest hill on any route. The driver is smartly turned out in full uniform and cap, typical of Country area crews who still took much pride in their service. The 433 timetable continued unchanged for almost 15 years despite significant reductions in passengers, the remaining weekday service to Coldharbour lasting until October 1968. In the background, an RT waits in the Bus Station for the long trip to Chelsham on the 470. (Capital Transport)

On fine days in the summer, some journeys might have good loads to Coldharbour, but this was the exception, and the summer Sunday service had last run in 1966. Loadings were always small, and one afternoon in June 1965 on an empty trip to Ranmore, the driver said he couldn't remember the last time he'd taken anyone up to Coldharbour on the 10pm from Dorking. Although the route was always scheduled for GS operation, it had been approved for RFs by 1964, and a reduced timetable could have allowed most journeys to be worked in with buses from the 412 and 425 schedules giving better use of buses. Indeed, after October 1965 when the 429 and 439 were converted to omo RF, even greater flexibility would have been possible. After the 433 Saturday service was withdrawn in December 1967, Surrey & Sussex Coachways began running on Saturdays from Capel via Ockley and Coldharbour into Dorking to provide a limited shopping service, but even this failed, lasting less than two years. With commendable enthusiasm they also ran two Sunday journeys for the summers in 1967 and 1968 but this was an equal failure. Withdrawal of the Ranmore leg on Saturdays was long overdue, and nobody else was interested in replacing it. The Ranmore end always carried fewer passengers, and so the greatest surprise when the 433 was finally withdrawn was that the Monday to Friday Ranmore service was retained by extending the 412. Even more surprising was that all six journeys continued, including the late evening one operated by the Holmbury St Mary outstation bus before it ran back home through Dorking.

ROUTE **433 to COLDHARBOUR (Leith Hill)** via Dorking North Station & Dorking Town

A 6/- ROVER TICKET will take you as far as you like on this and nearly every other Country Bus route. Ask the conductor for details.
This service is operated with Pay As You Enter buses. Please have your fare ready as you get on.

433 to RANMORE via Dorking Town & Dorking North Station

Part of this service is operated with Pay As You Enter buses. Please have your fare ready as you get on.

NOTE : This timetable does not necessarily apply on Bank Holidays. While every effort will be made to keep to the timetables, London Transport does not undertake that its buses will be operated in accordance with them, or as all. London Transport will not be responsible for any loss, damage or inconvenience caused by reason of any operating failure or in consequence of any inaccuracies in the timetables.

LONDON TRANSPORT, 55 BROADWAY, S.W.I.   ABBey 1234   6.5.64

264/491F/400 (75)   Leonard Ripley & Co., Ltd., London

This 433 timetable had been operated continuously once the GSs took over the route, although the Sunday service ran only in the summer after 1958. The timetable remained almost unchanged despite unrelenting reductions in passengers and the eventual cuts became inevitable. The summer Sunday service last ran in 1966, and the entire Saturday service was abandoned at the end of the same year. The unchanged Monday to Friday service was then abandoned in October 1968, although the Ranmore section was retained by extending the 412. (Author's collection)

RF 593 has just left Ware Park Hospital on one of the few remaining journeys which ran there. In 1955 there had been six journeys for visitors on Saturday – including a duplicate – and no fewer than 14 on Sunday afternoon. Visitor numbers declined rapidly however, and a decade later only a small number remained. The last of these were withdrawn in June 1974, and the last two staff journeys two years later.
(Peter Mitchell)

The October 1968 cuts made more inroads into Sunday timetables leaving some garages with little or no Sunday work on bus routes. Successive timetable cuts at Amersham had reduced their run-out so that with the start of the winter 1968 schedules, there was no Sunday service at all on any of the rural routes, only three RTs remaining scheduled for the 353 and 362. The Saturday schedules had suffered reductions to the point where the run-out was eight fewer buses than Monday to Friday, but the oddity of the crew RF allocated to the 305 on Sunday remained to balance rosters. Chelsham's Sunday run-out was reduced to three RTs for the 403, 408 and 470 and one RF for the afternoon service on the 453. Dorking retained its three RTs on Sunday for the 414, but with no service on 412 or 439 just one RF was rostered for the 425. Dunton Green's Saturday allocation on the 471 was cut to one RF as the headway was reduced to every two hours in each direction round the circular route, and along with East Grinstead it now had no buses out on Sundays at all. Elsewhere, Sunday run-outs were down to equally minimal levels. Hatfield put out just a single RT for the 341, and High Wycombe ran only two RTs on the 362 to Chesham and one RML on the 326 and 363 town services. Even Hertford with its large weekday allocation was reduced to seven RTs (and five of these were on the 310/310A trunk route) while the rural schedules were down to only three RFs. Staines was left with just two RTs for the 441. The Sunday timetable on the once important 301 and 302 had been cut to such an extent that only two RTs remained to run an hourly service from Watford to Hemel Hempstead, leaving Tring to run just one RT on a few afternoon trips into Hemel Hempstead on the 312. Even this was soon transferred to Hemel Hempstead leaving Tring with no Sunday buses at all.

In the three years following the heavy cuts of October 1965, Hertford's rural routes had continued to suffer more and more timetable reductions. The routes served some of the more remote parts of the network, and passenger numbers had fallen to the point where many journeys were carrying minimal numbers, some even occasionally none. It is worth detailing some of the reductions to show just how much rural services across the network had to be cut back in the face of such rapidly decreasing usage.

The 384A had run two afternoon journeys Monday to Friday out to the isolated hamlet of Great Munden, but the December 1966 cuts reduced these to just Wednesdays only for Hertford Market Day. In order to avoid what would effectively be empty dead mileage on the late afternoon return journey, the 5.34pm 384 departure to Stevenage was diverted on Wednesday via Great Munden, from where it doubled back to Dane End to continue to Stevenage. This resulted in the bus running 25 minutes later from Dane End to Stevenage on Wednesdays, representing some inconvenience to any regular passengers from Hertford, but the saving in running costs was essential. Although savings were made by reducing the weekday service just to Hertford Market Day, the four Saturday journeys to Great Munden had continued including the last journey just after 7pm from Hertford, although this cannot have been worth while. With the winter 1968 schedules, the Wednesday service went and the Saturday service was halved from four to two journeys. The December 1966 cuts also removed the Sunday service from the 384 and the remaining 390 between Hertford and Stevenage together with what was left of the Sunday evening timetable on the 333 town service. By March 1967, this had been reduced to two morning journeys for anyone going to Bengeo Church, with six hospital journeys in the afternoon and evening, but such was the lack of hospital visitors, these had been cut to just two journeys by October 1968. The 388 through the narrow lanes via Tewin to Welwyn had been cut to just two journeys on Tuesdays and Fridays to Welwyn Garden City, and although these were later restored to run every day, Welwyn village had no link to Hertford after around 8am until late afternoon. This had been an hourly service for most of the day only three years earlier, so this represented one of the most dramatic reductions. After the 1965 cuts had severed the Market Day link to Hitchin on the 329A, the remaining service on the 329 into Hertford was gradually cut. By March 1967 the 329 had just three journeys on Monday, Tuesday, Wednesday and Friday, plus five on Saturdays, but the 1968 winter schedules reduced this to three journeys to Nup End Tuesday, Thursday, Friday and Saturdays only. Two journeys were run on Wednesday morning as far as Datchworth but survived for only another year, being withdrawn with the winter 1969 schedules. The 331 had always enjoyed a half hourly headway to Buntingford on Saturdays, with the crew RT journeys remaining in the schedules for many years, but the rapid drop in shopping traffic brought cuts when the winter 1969 schedules finally removed the RT workings and reduced the headway to hourly. The direct route via Westmill was completely abandoned on Saturdays at the same time, but because the end to end omo running time via Braughing was 58 or 59 minutes, in order to run the basic service with only two RFs and schedule the minimum five-minute layover at each end, the actual service interval became every 63 or 64 minutes instead of the previous regular hourly headway. This was hardly convenient to passengers previously used to a regular timetable which could be easily memorised. All these incremental cuts gradually removed buses from Hertford's rural operations.

Just over the Hertfordshire border into Essex, the 381 and 381A to Coopersale and the small hamlet of Toothill had suffered equally severe cuts despite serving Epping with its Underground link to London. In October 1968, the Coopersale and Toothill legs were linked whereby a journey to Coopersale continued back to Epping via the main road, running through the town 20 minutes after its first journey before continuing out to Toothill. This reduced some dead mileage, and the Saturday shopping service was cut to just two morning journeys to Toothill. Between Epping and Tylers Cross the 15 weekday journeys run in 1965 had gone down to 11, while on Saturdays the 13 journeys run three years earlier had been drastically cut to only six, with the last journey from Epping just after 4pm.

In October 1968, Birch Brothers' rural routes from Hitchin were acquired by United Counties, but one – the 204 from Hitchin to Whitwell – was inside the LPTA and was absorbed by London Transport into the 304. Prior to the end of Birch's operations, London Transport had run only two or three evening journeys at weekends beyond Whitwell into Hitchin which served little purpose, but had preserved their running rights over the route. During the week, the 304 from St Albans terminated at Whitwell and was timed to connect with Birch's 204, but after 14th October, the 304 was extended into Hitchin every day, initially continuing the former Birch timetable, necessitating an additional RF at St Albans. Some oddities in St Albans's crew rosters at the time meant that a few 304 journeys to Whitwell had been crew worked, despite it being a very rural route, and after taking over the Birch journeys, this continued with odd journeys crew operated all the way to Hitchin. Although Kimpton and Whitwell were large villages, much of the 304 was along narrow lanes and at best marginal, so the use of conductors could hardly be justified. Despite this, occasional crew working on the 304 lasted several more years, even after the BNs replaced RFs in April 1973, and lasted until St Albans double deck routes were finally converted to omo by London Country in late 1977. Les Bland, a St Albans conductor, remembers being able to sit down and watch the scenery on most of these duties as there were so few passengers.

The 356 was introduced at the beginning of 1969 and consisted of just one early Sunday morning return journey from St Albans to the hospitals at Hill End and Shenley. It was intended as a facility for hospital staff to get to work before 7.00am on Sunday morning and for night shift staff to return to St Albans. RF 72 has arrived at Shenley Hospital and waits for the 7.15am return departure. (Eddie Shirras)

The 1968 winter schedules had reduced the number of buses rostered on Sundays to 211, fewer than half of the 429 at the beginning of the decade. Given the alarming fall in passenger numbers though, and the desperate need for economies, perhaps the most startling aspect of these reduced numbers was that 172 out of the 211 were still crew operated double deckers. Perhaps the greatest irony of this was that the tiny number of double deckers which could be one-man operated (the XFs at East Grinstead) were all idle in the garage on Sunday, although there would have been no work that day for them anyway. This surely was an inordinate waste of an opportunity to make savings since a great number of routes which were double-deck crew worked in the week could easily have been converted to omo single-deck on Sundays. Although this did come about in a limited way during 1969, it was perhaps later than could have been the case.

Following the eventual agreement for the extension of one-man operation, and thirteen months later than originally planned, the first stage of conversion of single deck Green Line routes took place on Saturday 23rd November 1968 when routes 701, 702, 710, 711, 714, 719 and 720 were all changed over with accompanying cuts to the timetables. The southern half of the 710 was withdrawn completely, and when Crawley's RF 191 arrived back at the garage a few minutes after 1am on that Saturday morning, Crawley's Green Line work had come to an end. The northern half from London to Amersham remained, but the Chesham extension was abandoned. The 711 timetable was reduced to every hour plus peak hour shorts from both ends into London, although on Saturdays the half hourly frequency was retained albeit only from late morning to early evening. The 710 and 711 shared a common section from London as far as Gerrards Cross and with both routes running hourly, it would have been sensible to timetable a joint half hourly headway over this part, but instead there was generally an alternate 20 or 40 minute gap between coaches. In fact, the joint timetable had all sorts of irregular gaps throughout the day, and on Saturday afternoon there were gaps of 10, 30 and 20 minutes, none of which can have helped to maintain passenger satisfaction. The 714 was cut to hourly every day with no additional peak hour journeys, and the 719 was extended from London to Wrotham to replace the crew operated 717, which was withdrawn. Less than three months later, on 15th February 1969, the remaining crew worked single deck Green Line routes were converted. The 707 leg down to Oxted had been carrying minimal passengers for some time, so was withdrawn, and although the 706 leg to Westerham carried few people, there were just enough left to justify three morning and evening peak journeys beyond Chelsham. Thus the 707 route number disappeared, and the 706 became Chelsham to Aylesbury every half hour plus the Westerham peak hour journeys. The 712 and 713 had the remaining peak journeys beyond St Albans to Luton reduced to two, and the through service became hourly with extra peak journeys, although the Saturday half hourly headway between Dorking and St Albans was retained. The skeleton peak hour timetable which was all that was left of the 715A was finally abandoned at the same time.

In converting routes to one-man operation, the end to end running times had to be increased to allow for extra boarding times for the driver to take fares. Thus the 711 from Reigate to High Wycombe for example which had been timed at three hours and one minute was extended to three hours and 20 minutes. Similarly the 714 from Dorking to Luton went from three hours 12 minutes to three hours 25 minutes. Since the war, running times had been identical regardless of time of day or day of the week, and so a coach running into and through London in the morning rush hour had exactly the same running time as one on a Sunday evening. Whilst this was a benefit to both crews and passengers in memorising a standard timetable, it had become increasingly irrelevant, and so running times were adjusted to account for when traffic conditions were lighter in the evenings and on Sundays. The 711's newly extended running time for example was reduced by increments up to a total of 15 minutes in the evenings, and all day Sundays. The extension of end to end running times caused a scheduling problem for the joint section of the 706 and 708. Before conversion, the 706 and 708 running time from Two Waters to South Croydon had been one hour 58 minutes, but after conversion, the 706 running time over this section was increased by 16 minutes during the day. The 708 had been converted to RMC only at the end of 1967, and there had been no plans to convert this, but if it had remained crew operated the 708 timetable would not have required the additional 16 minutes, so the joint regular headway could not have been maintained. The 708 was therefore converted from RMC to omo RF at the same time.

These conversions and service cuts reduced the total scheduled RFs by only eight. Indeed the 701, 702, 706, 708, 712 and 713 required additional coaches to cover the increased end to end running times, although the mileage run by a number of them was less when rostered only for peak hour journeys. The greatest loss from the conversion however was around 220 conductors who became surplus to requirements. The single deck Green Line crews, the majority of whom had worked together for years, had built up a rapport with several of their regular passengers, and the loss of the conductors – although a financial necessity – took away one of the indefinable aspects of Green Line travel which had once been its attraction. There were many idiosyncrasies amongst the crews, such as a Hertford

The text refers to the introduction of MBS standee buses at Windsor on many of the Slough local routes. Before the conversion, RT 1021 is at Slough station on the circular 400 route while RT 1007 behind is on the 417, also converted in the changes.
(Capital Transport)

conductor who always wore a bow tie, and another who always completed his waybill in fountain pen. An elderly Dorking crew who had probably worked together since the War were known to many passengers by their first names, and the conductor never used the bell, always tapping a coin on the cab door with the words 'right away' or 'next one George'. Such charming touches were lost forever, and with worsening congestion, the one-man drivers spent most of their shifts constantly checking their watch in a losing battle against the traffic.

With the removal of the RMCs from the 708, there was no Green Line work left for them. They were only six years old, but had become victims of a level of retrenchment in the network which could hardly have been foreseen when they came into service. They were far too good to cast off however, so they were relegated to bus routes and went to Hatfield for the 303/303A and Addlestone for the 461A to replace RTs. Their comfortable seats, platform doors and luggage racks brought a new level of comfort, in particular to the Barnet to Hitchin trunk route which still enjoyed some heavy loads and longer distance passengers, and in the end they would put in another ten years or more of hard work on bus routes.

At least the one-man conversions led to a small improvement in staffing, although services had continued to be affected. Worst had been Windsor where shortages led to all the 704 short journeys to Sevenoaks worked by Windsor crews being withdrawn. This meant that there were two four hour periods during the day when the three journeys per hour between Windsor and Bromley were cut to two (giving a disjointed 20 or 40 minute headway) and the two between Bromley and Sevenoaks to one. More confusing for passengers was that the periods during the day when the timetable cuts were made were not at the same times in both

A number of RMCs became redundant from Green Line routes following the cuts at the end of 1968. Some of them were sent to Hatfield where they were allocated to the 303/303A. By then, the 315A had been reduced to a Monday to Friday peak hour service with just five journeys from Hatfield and Welwyn Garden City which ran to Mardley Hill, just north of Welwyn, only two of which ran a short distance further to Woolmer Green where RMC 1509 has just reversed into Wickfield Close at the terminus. It displays a 303 blind above the platform since these journeys were worked from the 303 rosters and the conductor has forgotten to change it. (Capital Transport)

Before the 430 became the first route converted using new MBS standee buses, one was parked in Redhill with a notice in the window telling passengers of the impending change. The Autofare equipment was both confusing at first to passengers, and often unreliable in service, but the removal of crew operation was paramount in the face of increasing losses. (Alan Cross)

directions since the Windsor crews worked 'blocks' of consecutive journeys along the route. The reductions of the previous December had resulted in the irregular headway between Bromley and Sevenoaks, and did nothing for passenger loyalty, but worse still these ad-hoc cuts lasted all through the summer when the 704 could still rely on some extra passengers. As staffing eased slightly, the winter schedules on 4th October nevertheless cut the Windsor to Sevenoaks journeys completely from the 704, which was reduced to an hourly Windsor–Tunbridge Wells service, and the schedules adjusted to give a 30-minute headway with the 705 over the common section. In less than a year, the service on these routes which had consistently been some of the most popular and busy of all Green Line services had been halved. Six more RCLs became spare and went to Grays, replacing RMCs which in turn were reallocated to bus routes.

In July 1968, the long and fraught negotiations for widespread omo and the operation of the MB types finally came to an end with an agreement, a full year later than London Transport had first planned, and almost four years after the Union had first accepted the principles contained in the Phelps-Brown report. In the Country Bus area, this at last allowed a start to be made on the large scale introduction of Merlins to replace RTs, and the first conversions were introduced at the same time as the first batch of Green Line routes were turned over to omo. The first of the new 'standee' layout buses – the MBS – went into service at Reigate where the 430 became the first town service to be converted from RT. Amersham and High Wycombe put MBs onto the 305 and 455. Amersham also used spare buses on Sunday for the long 353 to Windsor. These were the first of many conversions as a large number of new standee MBS buses began to enter service, replacing RTs in the new towns as well as at Northfleet and Windsor, where they also replaced some RMLs.

The Slough local routes were all converted to omo standee buses in March 1969, Windsor receiving ten new MBSs. Not long after the change, MBS 412 picks up at 'The George' on Farnham Road for a journey across Slough to Langley Village. It stayed at Windsor for 10 years on these routes before withdrawal at the end of 1978. (Capital Transport)

The conventional 45-seat MB version came into service to convert some semi-rural/interurban RT routes, Dorking receiving a single MB to replace its RT on the 449 town service, and Crawley three for the 434 and 473. This latter came about because the Crawley to Horsham leg of the 405 was replaced by extending the 434/473 in a reversal of the change 12 years earlier when extra double deck capacity had been necessary to replace RFs. The Crawley to Horsham section still carried heavy loads on many journeys however, and the new MBs replaced part of the RF allocation to give more capacity on some of these journeys, although on the rural stretch to East Grinstead, the winding road down from Turners Hill and the narrow railway arch at Kingscote were not ideal for a bus as large as an MB. Conversions proceeded quickly, and the allocation book for 22nd March 1969 shows a maximum of 61 MBSs and 31 MBs scheduled for service, the number of RTs having reduced by almost the same total since the previous October. The RFs made spare from some of these conversions (like the 391/391A at St Albans) were used to convert some other lesser RT routes to omo. Reigate's last works journeys on the 406C to Windmill Press at Kingswood were abandoned on the same date as the 430 was converted to MBS, releasing another RF.

Belatedly, during 1969, some crew operated trunk routes were at last converted to one-man operation on Sundays. The 405 and 414 into Croydon were converted with eight RFs replacing eight RTs, and the 406 and 418 into Kingston also changed over. This converted all of Dorking and Reigate's Sunday crew work so that both garages needed no conductors at all on Sundays for the first time. The 414 had been partially converted on Sundays in October 1968 by splitting the route at Dorking with the section to Horsham changing to omo but now the whole route was converted although with no increase in the end to end running time. Windsor converted the Sunday 457A service to Uxbridge from RML to omo RF on a 30-minutes headway which was a long way from the 1950s when the route was heavily duplicated on Sundays to cater for large numbers of passengers to Windsor. So great had the demand once been on busy summer Sundays that Windsor used every available RT for Green Line duplicates, often having to borrow red RTs

The Sunday service on the 405 was converted to omo in March 1969. Reigate rostered four MBs for the 405 and 414, while Crawley rostered a single MB, and on a cold Sunday, Crawley's MB 92 takes on a few passengers in Croydon bus station. (Norman Rayfield/ 2RT2 Group)

from Uxbridge garage to supplement the 457. St Albans converted its three Sunday workings on the 338, 358 and Crawley put one RF on to the 476 town service. These changes replaced 27 RTs with an equal number of omo RFs, but still left 102 crew operated double deckers rostered on Sundays for bus routes with 55 more for Green Line. In 1969, perhaps belatedly, several routes were converted to omo on Sundays, almost all of which were in the northern area. At various times during the year, Sunday omo working went onto the 302, 306, 311, 312, 339, 345, 385, and 385A. These were all converted using RFs spare on that day except the 306, part of the 311, and the 345 hospital service. On the 385/385A, the RFs initially proved inadequate though with some standing passengers, especially when returning from hospital visits. The only southern area route to change over was the 472 to Netherne Hospital requiring only one bus. Although these changes provided a useful saving in operating costs, it was nowhere near enough to counter the overall losses incurred across the network on Sundays, and instances of overcrowding did nothing for passenger satisfaction when some were left behind.

Later in the year, the winter 1969 cuts saw the end of the remaining service from Sevenoaks to Four Elms on the 413A. This had been one of the most infrequent routes, even in the late 1950s running only four or five journeys a day to Four Elms. Originally, it had run on from Ide Hill village a mile or so down the road towards Edenbridge to terminate at Scollops Road which was no more than an isolated road junction where buses reversed to turn. A terminus at Cooper's Corner, half a mile further on would have made more sense since there was a pub, shop and a few cottages, but this was just beyond the 1933 LPTA boundary, and West Kent Motors operated a service to Four Elms and Edenbridge. Although West Kent's routes were acquired, London Transport did not have rights to run beyond the LPTA boundary, but in 1949 dispensation was granted to run on to Four Elms to maintain the former link to Sevenoaks.

The Sunday service 414 was converted at the same time as the 405. Dorking scheduled one RF and one MB for its share of the route, and RF 255 from Dorking has arrived at Croydon Bus Station on the same stand as MB 92 on the previous page. The inspector looks on as a few passengers wait to board. (Norman Rayfield/ 2RT2 Group)

In extending the 413A to Four Elms, the sensible arrangement would have been to run on into Edenbridge. This was prevented by the boundary with Maidstone & District who ran an hourly service into Edenbridge on their 93 route from Tunbridge Wells, and none of the 413A journeys was timed to give a convenient change to the M&D service for any prospective through passengers. So rigid was the boundary that London Transport was not even permitted to operate over the cross roads at Four Elms to stop a few yards further on where the M&D 93 buses stopped. London Transport's buses could then have gone another 100 yards to reverse into a side road to turn, but the reality was that they had to turn right at the village crossroads and run half a mile along the lane towards Crockham Hill before reversing into the lane which led up to Chartwell. The bus then ran back to the crossroads to stand, a strict condition being that no passengers could be carried from the crossroads to the turning point and back, though it is unlikely this was always adhered to.

The timetable for the Scollops Road journeys was extremely inconvenient since, having terminated there, the bus then worked a short journey back up through Ide Hill Village to Sundridge Hospital (or 'Ide Hill Institute' in the 1948 timetable) a mile or so down the narrow lane from Ide Hill. Having arrived there, the bus then worked from the Hospital back via Ide Hill to Sevenoaks without serving Scollops Road. This meant that there was a direct service from Sevenoaks to Scollops Road, but the journey into Sevenoaks could only be made by travelling via Sundridge Hospital. Similarly, apart from an early morning staff journey, there was no direct service to Sundridge Hospital from Sevenoaks, it being necessary to travel via Scollops Road first. Without a through service or connection to Edenbridge, the 413A beyond Ide Hill was a long 'dead leg' and apart from

Two Waters also received new MBSs in February 1969 to replace RTs on some town services. MBS 295 in Hemel Hempstead bus station waits to work a journey on the 314C works service to Long Chaulden as a schoolboy with hooped cap looks on. The 1950s Ford Popular in front is illegally parked on the stop. (Michael Beamish)

The 413A was a loss making route from the early 1950s but continued nevertheless to provide a limited service to Coopers Corner and Four Elms, its demise being long overdue by the time it was finally abandoned. Buses ran into Ide Hill village centre and RF 687 is about to swing round the island by the village green to run back to the village hall before the long descent on to Four Elms. (Peter Mitchell)

the dozen or more cottages between Ide Hill village and Cooper's Corner, there was almost no other potential traffic all the way to Four Elms. Although Four Elms itself was a reasonable size, M&D's 93 to Edenbridge and Tunbridge Wells offered better facilities than the infrequent 413A, so the service was marginal even from its inception. The five weekday journeys continued unchanged until 1965, although anyone catching the 1.02pm from Four Elms into Sevenoaks during the week could not return until 6.28pm since there was no afternoon service, with perhaps the most pointless departure at 8.28 every evening from Sevenoaks which surely carried hardly a soul and must have run back empty. At the end of 1966, the Four Elms service was reduced to only three shopping journeys on Saturdays, but in what must be one of the most pointless changes, the Monday to Friday timetable was reduced to just one single journey which left Sevenoaks at 12.18pm and returned from Four Elms at 1.02pm The reason behind retaining this one trip is unknown since it served no purpose whatsoever apart from anyone wanting to make a one way journey. Even more bizarre was that in 1968 the restriction on carrying passengers to and from the turning point at Four Elms was lifted so that buses operated in service to Chartwell Lane turning point, waited three minutes and then returned to the crossroads to stand – but at least passengers no longer had to walk the half mile into the village! The Four Elms service was another example of a route which could have been abandoned much earlier, and when it was finally withdrawn in June 1969, the two remaining short journeys to Scollops Road went as well. This halved the service between Sevenoaks and Ide Hill, but the two-hourly 413 to Ide Hill and Brasted continued, despite the fact that it had equally run at a loss for some years. It did not last long after London Country took over.

The one-man conversions made possible by the new MBs had, at least by the end of 1968, helped to ease a worsening staff position. For the first time in a number of years, bus miles run had fallen more than the drop in passenger miles travelled. London Transport's 1968 report highlights that although the total number of Country bus passengers fell by 2.1% from 1967, total miles paid for went up by just over 1% with a reduction of 1.6% in miles run. On Green Lines, both passenger numbers and miles paid for fell by nearly 5% from 1967, but continuing service cuts had reduced miles run by almost 10%. These statistics provided a small respite from the downward financial spiral which had characterised the 1960s, but masked the reality of the continuing drop in passengers. In 12 years, Green Line passengers had fallen from 37 to 21 million, and bus passengers from 98 to 60 million. The proportionate fall in Green Line miles run was similar to the fall in passengers following drastic timetable cuts, but the 40% fall in bus passengers had been reflected in only a 20% fall in miles run. This was perhaps the most alarming statistic. Frequencies had been reduced across most bus routes, but had been nowhere near enough to counter the fall in fare revenues. The fixed overhead of garages had remained almost unaltered, and administration staff had not fallen by the same proportion as bus crews.

Fare increases proposed for 1968 had been delayed as part of the Prices and Incomes Board restraints, and although they yielded an extra £1.7 million in the last few months of the year, London Transport described them as *'too little too late'* to avoid an operating deficit for the year. Green Rover tickets had also been increased from 6s 0d (30p) to 7s 0d (35p) at the end of June but, with increasing fares, still represented good value for a day out and for some longer return journeys. A comparison of some Country bus fares over the period from 1961 to 1968, examples of which appear overleaf, illustrates just how much they had increased.

Route		1961	1968	
353	Berkhamsted to Windsor	3s 9d	5s 6d	
384	Hertford to Walkern	2s 4d	3s 6d	
386	Buntingford to Stevenage	2s 1d	3s 3d	
403	Westerham to Sevenoaks	1s 2d	1s 9d	
421	Heverham to Sevenoaks	1s 2d	1s 9d	
414	Capel to Horsham	1s 4d	2s 0d	
412	Dorking to Sutton	1s 4d	2s 3d	

		Summer 1948	Summer 1963	October 1969
704/705	Victoria to Windsor	2s 8d	4s 0d	6s 0d
712/713	Victoria to Boxhill	3s 0d	4s 5d	6s 0d
720	Epping to Bishops Stortford	1s 6d	2s 8d	4s 0d
706/707	Watford to Tring	2s 3d	3s 2d	4s 6d
708	West Croydon to East Grinstead	3s 0d	4s 0d	5s 6d

The increases in bus fares were all around 50% in a period of only seven years, while the increase in Green Line fares had been slightly less between 1963 and October 1969 just before London Transport's final increase. The comparison with 1948 however shows that Green Line fares had roughly doubled since the war. London Country would raise fares much more significantly to counter its losses and the effects of high inflation in the mid-1970s. By May 1977 for example, the fare from London to Windsor had increased to 75p (15s 0d), two and a half times the fare of 6s 0d which had applied only eight years earlier.

In the spring of 1968, RF 658 has stopped opposite Glentrammon Road at Green Street Green a short distance from the terminus of short journeys run during the evening peak from Orpington Station. It has running number DG21 which indicates that it worked into Orpington on the 431 as a positioning journey for this 471 duty. The driver is Joe Edmonds, Dunton Green's snooker champion, and the bus is fitted with a Setright machine, one of a number made spare from Green Line reductions on the 704/705. The timing clock was used by conductors off the 51/51A. The stop displays an E Plate for the Orpington Rural Transport service to Biggin Hill which was taken over after London Transport's failed attempt to run the 479 in 1963. (Capital Transport)

The 1967 Transport Bill placed the main responsibility for the funding and planning of bus routes onto Local Authorities, and the particular issue of London and the suburbs led to the view that these operations should be planned, financed and run by the GLC (Greater London Council). Negotiations between the Minister of Transport and the GLC led therefore, at the end of 1967, to an agreement whereby the GLC would assume control of London Transport and all its assets. Geographically however, the GLC's influence extended only within its own area, and therefore all operations outside this – which comprised the great majority of the Country Bus area – could not be part of the agreement. The Government were also looking at the wider aspects of bus operations across the whole country, and the subsequent 1968 Transport Act provided that all the large territorial companies – the majority of which were either part of the Tilling or B.E.T. Groups – would be brought under the control of one publicly owned group to be known as the National Bus Company. This new group therefore provided the means whereby London Transport's Country Bus department could be removed from the agreement with the GLC and be transferred to become part of the new NBC.

The 1960s had been a decade of unremitting decline and the table below illustrates the reduction in the scheduled fleet.

	1st January 1960			31st December 1969		
	Mon-Fri	Sat	Sun	Mon-Fri	Sat	Sun
Double deck buses	743	665	363	558	379	102
Single deck buses	222	211	106	334	262	98
Double deck coaches	82	64	99	83	77	55
Single deck coaches	234	228	245	135	138	127
Overall Totals	1281	1168	811	1122	856	382

The figures speak for themselves, and the reductions in scheduled Green Line coaches illustrate just how many successive cuts had been made after the peak years at the end of the 1950s. On weekdays, one third of all Green Line coaches had been cut by the end of 1969, and on Sundays almost half. On Sundays, six out of every ten buses had been cut over the same period, the Sunday allocation being only just over 20% of the Monday to Friday total compared to just under 50% in 1960. Almost 30% of the Saturday bus allocation had been cut, significantly less than the 6% on Monday to Friday, although this small reduction disguises a far larger drop during off-peak and evenings. Amersham and Hertford, which had a higher proportion of rural mileage, and smaller garages like Dorking, Tring and East Grinstead with a higher proportion of Green Line work, had suffered proportionately greater reductions than the average.

Attempts were made to attract additional passengers to Green Line routes. Cheap day returns to Boxhill on Sundays and Bank Holidays were introduced, but timetables had been reduced to an hourly service and were no longer attractive when visitors could take their car. Worsening traffic congestion also made shopping trips to London less attractive, so that these initiatives met with little success. (Capital Transport collection)

SHOP IN TOWN BY GREEN LINE

Many shops in Oxford Street and Kensington High Street now remain open ALL DAY every Saturday.

Relax in comfort, chauffeur-driven.

Forget parking worries, go by Green Line.

£69/166G/1,500

Waterlow London

SUNDAY BARGAINS

to the SURREY HILLS

From March 23 every Sunday throughout the year (also Good Friday and Bank Holidays) on Green Line Coaches 712, 713 and 714

These Special Cheap Day Returns, now available on every Sunday, will take you swiftly and cheaply out of town to Box Hill, Dorking and miles of glorious walking along the North Downs.

There are no time restrictions—go and come home what time you like. Ask any driver on these routes for details.

MAKE A GREEN LINE FOR THE SURREY HILLS

MBS 293 was another of the batch sent to Hemel Hempstead for conversions of town services to omo standee buses. It is leaving the bus station on a journey to Long Chaulden on a route which had been run jointly with Bream Coaches until 1968. (Capital Transport)

The increasing imbalance between Monday to Friday peak period, off peak, Saturday and Sunday also meant greater inefficiency in crew rosters with many more split shifts, overtime and rest day working in order to roster the maximum number of crews for peak times. Although the proportion of Green Line cuts was much the same across all garages, the bus allocations for the five 'New Town' garages had avoided the worst of the decline.

	1st January 1960			31st December 1969		
	Mon-Fri	Sat	Sun	Mon-Fri	Sat	Sun
Crawley	28	26	16	38	25	6
Epping/Harlow	28	29	19	35	29	8
Hatfield	28	24	12	29	19	1
Hemel Hempstead	46	39	16	51	40	14
Stevenage	19	19	10	32	22	6
Totals	149	136	73	175	135	35

The 1960 total excludes GS allocations at Crawley, Hemel Hempstead and Stevenage

The increase in Monday to Friday totals reflect the population growth and new industrial areas. The Saturday totals remained unchanged in stark contrast to the reduction of a quarter across the total network, and which was actually a third if the New Towns' totals are excluded from the network as a whole. Only the drop in Sunday totals was almost in the same proportion to the whole network. Although these five garages still had largely profitable operations, the total buses they required for service at the end of 1969 still nowhere near represented the increase in the population of the New Towns which had been more than 50% during the decade, and who were some of the greatest contributors to the extra traffic congestion outside central London.

The ever-declining numbers of passengers had also been made worse by staff who had consistently been unwilling to accept or adapt to the consequences of the social changes since the War. It was true that wages had not always competed with manufacturing, but the Union had proved intransigent over many issues. Particularly damaging had been their unwillingness to accept the over-riding need for efficiencies and the extension of one-man operation during the 1960s without demands for an ever greater proportion of the savings which would accrue and which – in the end – were an absolute necessity for the survival of the Country Bus network. Staff shortages, overtime bans and a number of 'lightning strikes' at some garages in protest at new schedules simply disrupted services and drove passengers away, many of whom found other means of travel and never returned.

Frequent reference has been made to reducing passenger numbers and losses, and so it is worth summarising the 15 years leading up to the end of London Transport's operation of its Country Bus and Coach services. The table below comes from London Transport's own Annual Budgets and Financial Reports contained in the TfL archives, although the figures for 1959, 1960 and 1961 are missing. Nevertheless, they provide a fascinating commentary on the financial decline.

COUNTRY BUS AND COACH ANNUAL FINANCIAL SUMMARIES															
		YEAR													
		1954	1955	1956	1957	1958	1962	1963	1964	1965	1966	1967	1968	1969
Passengers (Millions)	BUSES	296.7	287.0	284.1	281.0	217.7	237.8	231.5	220.7	210.0	200.2	194.6	190.6	177.4
	COACHES	32.7	34.5	33.6	36.8	29.7	32.1	29.9	27.6	26.0	25.0	24.0	22.9	20.5
Miles Run (Millions)	BUSES	47.9	47.0	46.0	44.6	38.6	43.8	42.6	42.8	40.6	40.0	39.1	38.5	37.5
	COACHES	23.8	24.2	24.5	25.1	21.6	24.4	23.3	23.6	22.2	21.4	21.2	19.1	16.6
Traffic Receipts (£ millions)	BUSES	5.10	5.30	5.66	5.82	4.89	6.74	6.82	7.04	7.03	7.23	7.09	7.32	7.57
	COACHES	2.61	2.84	2.88	3.17	2.62	3.30	3.32	3.27	3.13	3.14	3.03	2.93	2.61
Net Operating Surplus (£ 000's)	BUSES	(34)	(48)	(145)	(192)	(467)	166	108	(116)	(471)	(690)	(824)	(763)	(622)
	COACHES	696	741	591	663	(371)	416	412	163	(140)	(267)	(457)	(301)	(9)
Overall surplus/ (deficit)		662	693	446	471	(838)	582	520	47	(611)	(957)	(1281)	(1064)	(631)

London Transport calculated Net Operating Surplus (or Loss) after deducting the costs of crew wages, traffic and engineering staff, fuel, central repairs (which was a contribution to Aldenham works), spares and depreciation.

The figures again speak for themselves and starkly illustrate the steep decline in both passengers and profit. The number of passengers carried on bus routes in 1969 was 40% below that in 1955, the drop in Green Line passengers being only fractionally less. The bus routes had briefly produced a surplus in 1962 and 1963 following service cuts and fare increases, but after that, the whole network spiralled into increasing heavy losses.

In 1969 the decline in passenger numbers had increased again to 6.9% on bus routes compared with 1968. Combined with a fall in miles run of only 2.4%, once again each bus was carrying fewer passengers. The fall in Green Line passengers was a staggering 10.5%, but at least the widening of headways on almost every route had cut miles run by 13%. The length of journeys on Green Line had fallen sharply by 12%, no doubt a reflection of traffic congestion and longer journeys into London being made more conveniently by train. It is notable that despite greatly increasing fares, the gross receipts in 1969 on Green Line routes were the same as 15 years earlier, illustrating the shorter average journey and reduction in passengers. The 1969 annual report refers to the fact that an overall operating surplus of £5.5 million in 1965 (which included Central Buses and the Underground) had turned in only three years to a deficit of £2.4 million in 1968. The deficit from Green Line, Central and Country Buses and was much greater however, and mitigated only by a surplus from the Underground. The Country Bus Department had lost almost £1.7 million in the two years 1968 and 1969, and just over £4.5 million during the five years from 1965 to 1969. The round of fare increases late in 1969 was estimated to provide an additional £50,000 per annum net to Country Bus operations but even this proved woefully inadequate. A small but significant

FARES COUNTY BUSES

New scales for London Transport fares will apply from Sunday, September 7 as follows:—

SINGLE FARES		
MILES	PRESENT FARES s. d.	NEW FARES s. d.
1	5	6
2	9	9
3	1 0	1 0
4	1 3	1 3
5	1 6	1 6
6	1 9	2 0
7	2 0	2 0
8	2 3	2 6
9	2 6	2 6
10	2 9	3 0
11	3 0	3 0
12	3 3	3 6
Fares for longer distances will be increased by a maximum of 6d.		

Fares on autofare routes will not be altered.

CHILDREN'S FARES will be half the adult fare with fractions of 3d. charged as 3d.

WEEKLY (6 return journey) TICKETS (Northern Area): The rates for these tickets will be increased proportionately (with a minimum of 17/-).

These increases have been authorized by the Minister of Transport under section 27(2) of the Transport (London) Act 1969 and by the Traffic Commissioners.

769/2688H/3,000 PANEL C   Waterlow London

London Transport's last fare increases on Country Buses were at the end of 1969. The longer distance fares for 6, 8, 10, and 12 mile journeys were effectively withdrawn and increased to the fare for the longer distance. (Capital Transport collection)

sentence in the 1969 report in paragraph 52 on fares also notes *The additional revenue from the fare increases on 7th September 1969 would be insufficient to meet the future financial requirements in respect of Country Bus and Coach operations which were to be transferred to London Country Bus Services on 1st January 1970.* A further fare increase was approved for 30th November of between 20% and 33% inside the LT Special Area, and the same increase was applied outside the area from 28th December, three days before London Country took over. During 1969, the NBC had highlighted the financial plight of the Country Bus department which they were to take over, but nothing was done in the way of assistance.

As part of the transfers to the NBC and the GLC, the Ministry of Transport had agreed to write off the whole of London Transport's capital debt, including that carried forward in January 1963 from the then London Transport Board. This alone amounted to £162 million, and between 1963 and 1969, further loans of £98 million had been made to pay for the Victoria Line, fleet replacements, and to subsidise the day to day operations. A further sum of just under £10 million had been loaned in 1969, so that a total debt of almost £270 million was written off before the final vesting day of 1st January 1970. Despite this huge sum no allowance for depreciation, or cash reserves for vehicle replacement or maintenance of premises was carried over, so that London Country would start with nothing – its only income being from daily fare revenues.

The last scheduling changes came just before the end when three of East Grinstead's XFs were repainted in a striking blue and silver livery and sent to Stevenage to start the new 'Blue Arrow' service linking housing estates east of the town to the Industrial area. The XFs were replaced at East Grinstead by three XA Atlanteans from the Central area, which in turn were exchanged for three Country area RMLs. The 'Blue Arrow' routes proved an instant success forming the basis of what would become the Stevenage 'Superbus' network, and there is an irony in that this new service was exactly the sort of innovation from which the network could have benefited much earlier had it not been for London Transport's moribund approach to change.

And so it was that on New Year's Eve 1969, London Transport operated its Country Buses and Green Line coaches for the last time. The next day, it handed over 28 garages, 5,463 staff, and a fleet of 1,268 buses and coaches running an unprofitable route network with far too high a proportion of crew operation. Almost three quarters of the fleet was already beyond the maximum service life which the National Bus Company had by then specified. London Country issued its first Traffic Circular on 31st December. On the front page was a message from Geoffrey Fernyhough the General Manager, the last sentence of which stated *'I wish you all the very best of luck and happiness with our new company in 1970'.*

In its last two years – once the decision had been made to hive off the Country Bus Area to the NBC – London Transport did nothing to critically review the loss making route network. This was perhaps understandable, but it was their apparent inability during the previous 15 years to look critically at its network and the over-provision of operating bases that was a major cause of the parlous financial state that the Country Bus department found itself in at the end of 1969. The optimism of Geoffrey Fernyhough's statement would soon become clear, and the disastrous situation in which London Country soon found itself was inevitable, came perilously close to being terminal, and would hound them for another decade. A few years after that, the Country Bus area as it had been since 1933 would cease to exist.

BIBLIOGRAPHY

My own recollections, records and large collection of timetables have provided much of the background for this book. I have also used many other sources, but should anyone read this and see something of their own which l have not acknowledged below, then please accept my apologies for the omission.

The following have all provided information :-

- 'Buses Illustrated' and later 'Buses' magazines from the late 1950s to 1969
- 'The London Bus Magazine' especially the series of '25 years ago...' articles by Ken Glazier; Les Stitson, Hugh Taylor, Peter Nichols, and Nicholas King which detailed changes in routes and vehicles.
- London Transport (Country Buses and Coaches) Allocation of Scheduled Buses and Coaches from 1950 to 1969.
- London Transport Annual Reports 1959, 1961, 1962, 1965–1969.
- London Transport (Country Buses and Coaches): Alterations to OMO services Ref D.30/A.1 (Alan Charman collection)
- London Transport (Country Buses and Coaches): Routes worked by omo 26 seater Guy Buses immediately prior to the introduction of RF type 39 seater OMO buses. May 1955 (Alan Charman collection)
- Various minutes, reports, letters and memos from the London Transport archives at TfL
- London Transport press release dated 25th July 1958
- Fleet history LT 12. GS, RC, RF, RFW Classes. PSV Circle 1995
- Several L.O.T.S. Publications but particularly:-
  SUP 14   Bus & Coach Operations 1962 by Les Stitson
  SUP 19   RT Demise by Les Stitson
  The London RLH by P. Gascoine 1976
- Reshaping London's Bus Services – London Transport 1966
- RT: The story of a London bus – Ken Blacker, Capital Transport Publishing 1979
- RF – Ken Glazier, Capital Transport Publishing, 1991
- Routemaster. Volume One. Ken Blacker. Capital Transport Publishing 1992
- The Motorbus in London Country – Kenneth Warren, Ian Allan 1984
- London Buses in the 1960s – Ken Glazier, Capital Transport Publishing 1998
- London Transport Garages – Ken Glazier, Capital Transport Publishing 2006
- RT Family Garage Allocations volume 2 – Stuart Robbs Publishing 2002
- Single Deck Garage Allocations (1951–1981) – Stuart Robbs Publishing 2016
- Tillingbourne – George Burnett & Laurie James, Middleton Press 1990
- London Transport Connections 1945–1985 – Philip Wallis, Capital Transport Publishing 2003
- Green Line 1930–1980 – D.W.K. Jones & B.J.Davis, London Country Bus Services 1980
- Terminal Points of London Transport Country Buses 1948–1969. Revised Edition. Barry Kosky 1981
- London's Local Railways. Alan A Jackson. Capital Transport Publishing – 2nd Edition 1999.
- Ministry of Labour Committee of Inquiry Report on the differences between the two sides of the National Council for the Omnibus Industry – HMSO May 1965
- Ministry of Labour Court of Inquiry Report into a dispute between Employers and Trade Union represented by National Council for the Omnibus Industry – HMSO March 1954.